IN PURSUIT

OF

EXCELLENCE

*Published on the Occasion
of the 50th Anniversary of
Greenebaum Doll & McDonald PLLC*

Published by:
The Sulgrave Press
2005 Longest Avenue
Louisville, KY 40204

in association with
William Butler
Butler Book Publishing Services, Inc.
P.O. Box 7311
Louisville, KY 40207

CONTENTS

THE ORIGINS OF THE FIRM

If Samuel L. Greenebaum were to enter the front doors of the law firm that still bears his name today, what would he see? A roster of 180 attorneys, many of them women; a modern Practice Group structure featuring a dozen major practice areas, some of which did not exist when he practiced law; offices in Kentucky (four of them), Ohio, Tennessee, and the District of Columbia; a worldwide legal presence in 87 countries through the Terralex alliance; and a digital information system of hardware and software that would rival anything he could have imagined at NASA.

And a different firm name. He might recognize the addition of the Lexington lawyer Angus McDonald's name over the door, joining his own and Bob Doll's, and wonder how that had happened.

But much of the physical surroundings would be familiar to him—after all, he had briefly worked in these same offices in the National City Bank building (then called the First National Tower) prior to becoming ill in 1973—but certainly the size and scope of the firm would exceed his wildest imagination. Indeed, by December 1973, when death separated him from the firm he founded, there were only 26 lawyers on the premises, and many of them had joined the firm only two years earlier. Louisville was the only location, and the thought of regional expansion was still many years away.

He would find the new tools of the law astonishing. The personal productivity devices that are a part of every modern lawyer's day would amaze him. Virtually none of the technological, digital and communications resources that are routine for attorneys today were even on the drawing board at the time of his death.

And the international reach of the firm would both please and astound him. Although Mr. Greenebaum was an experienced man of the world, who hunted every year in Scotland, the thought of practicing law on a global basis was a long-term dream that he couldn't have imagined would reach this scale so quickly.

Beyond the new furniture, the portrait of himself in the conference room that he never got to see, and the fancy electronic devices, Greenebaum might spot a few things here and there that would remind him of the old days—the conference rooms full of clients and lawyers with their sleeves rolled up working earnestly on important cases; the lights on well into the night while the rest of downtown Louisville was asleep; the young associates toiling away elbow-to-elbow in the law library, which is still in use every day. Perhaps he would think that things had not changed so much after all. Perhaps he would sense within these people the same commitment, character, and competitive fire that had powered the firm's growth from its inception in 1952 to its status today as a regional legal powerhouse.

How different it was from his beginnings in the legal profession in the 1930s, and indeed, how different the whole world was from the time of his youth, when America was in World War I and he was going to Male High School in Louisville, Kentucky, where he was valedictorian of his graduating class in 1919.

In 1902, when Mr. Greenebaum was born, Louisville, Kentucky had a population that exceeded 200,000 people and was one of the nation's twenty largest cities, twice as large as Los Angeles and Atlanta. But historians believe the socio-political fallout from the assassination of Governor Goebel in 1900 impeded the movement for progressive politics and economic advancement in the state, and events of the next several decades seem to validate that assumption. By the late 1920s, Louisville had neither grown nor receded, but on the whole represented a fairly typical American pattern of modest prosperity. Charles Lindberg piloted the Spirit of St. Louis to the newly opened Bowman Field. The University of Louisville, which Sam Greenebaum later represented as an attorney, moved to its new Belknap campus. The J.B. Speed Art Museum became one of the first such institutions in the south.

Young Sam Greenebaum came home to Louisville in 1927 after his graduation from the University of Michigan and Harvard Law School, and married Doni Selligman, daughter of the legendary Alfred Selligman, a monumental lawyer in Louisville history, who practiced with his younger brother, Joseph Selligman, as Selligman and Selligman. Greenebaum aligned himself with the Selligman firm, naturally, but did not go to work for his father-in-law immediately. Instead he clerked for L.D. Green in the late 1920s, then became Assistant County Attorney for a short while. He went to work for the Selligmans full-time in the early 1930s, and by 1935 he was a partner in the firm. After his father-in-law Alfred Selligman died in 1933, the firm had taken on others to become Selligman, Goldsmith, Everhart & Greenebaum, and clients of the firm included blue chip Louisville concerns such as American Standard, the Courier-Journal Job Printing Company, American

7

Radiator, the Seelbach Hotel, and Kaufman-Strauss.

After five years or so, things changed again. Goldsmith left the firm in the late 1930s, and by 1941 the firm's name had changed to Selligman, Everhart & Greenebaum. Then, when Joseph Everhart died in 1946, the firm became Selligman and Greenebaum. The last of the Selligmans, Joe, died in December 1948, leaving Sam Greenebaum, at age 46, the lone living member of the forty-year-old firm.

It was just as well. After 20 years in the practice of law Sam Greenebaum had become his own man, rivaling the considerable legal and civic accomplishments of both Selligmans. He was acknowledged as a consummate legal technician and writer, as befitted a lawyer whose training pre-dated the days when legal drafts could be revised on word processors. He had risen through the Dickensian days of legal practice, when correspondence and drafts were dictated to secretaries, and changes were laborious and time-consuming. It was said he could dictate perfect briefs the first time, immaculate and precise in wording and citation of law. (It always peeved him, even decades later, when the writing skills of the firm's lawyers did not meet this gold standard.)

He was a handsome man, beautifully dressed, erect, even noble, in bearing, athletic, and carried himself, as the older legal giants did, with an elan made more powerful by humility and magnanimity toward his fellow men and women. His son, John Greenebaum, writes of him, "My father was prototypically perfect. He never understood crass promotion, nor was it necessary for him to do so. He wrote perfect documents. He dressed immaculately, was a golf champion, and shot grouse in Scotland. He had an unpretentious, pleasant, ironic sense of humor, and a strong but unmoralistic standard of propriety. Clients and other attorneys sought him. He was their image of a perfect alter ego."

With his momentum not deterred by his last partner's death, and his confidence rising by the day, in April 1949, a mere four months after the death of Joe Selligman, Greenebaum engineered the merger of his firm with former U.S. Attorney Eli Brown III's firm, Brown & Eldred, to create a new partnership called Brown, Greenebaum & Eldred. Marshall Eldred and Dorsey W. Brown were the other partners in the new firm, with Henry T. Merritt, Charles B. Tachau, and later Tom Carroll joining the firm as associates.

Their offices would remain at 614 Kentucky Home Life Building, one of the buildings of choice in Louisville where many law firms had space, and where Sam Greenebaum had practiced law from his beginning with the Selligmans (and, incidentally, where he would stay until the move to the First National Tower in 1973).

In the same building, a few floors up, working for Judge Charles I. Dawson at the firm of Bullitt, Dawson & Tarrant, was a sharp young tax attorney named Bernard H. Barnett. He had come to Louisville in 1940 from Vanderbilt Law School, and had practiced in the city for a few years, specializing in tax law before joining the Navy in 1942 for the duration of the war. In 1946 he had returned to Louisville and was snapped up immediately by Judge Dawson's previous firm, Woodard, Dawson, Hobson & Fulton; quite a feat and compliment for those days. In the 1940s few Louisville law firms had more than a handful of attorneys, and the hundreds of returning GIs who wanted law careers were having a hard time catching on anywhere. (Many, including attorneys who figure in this history, had no choice but to disperse around the country, returning five or six years later when Louisville law firms were growing and the economy was booming.)

But this was not Barney Barnett's situation. Judge Dawson, a former federal district judge and, at age 66, a powerful legal lion in town, had made Barnett his protégé, and his future in Louisville law circles seemed bright and secure. There was plenty of tax work at the time, with new IRS rulings coming out of Washington at a regular clip, and Barnett was soon recognized, along with attorney Russell Smith, as the top tax man in Louisville.

In 1949, Judge Dawson took Barnett with him to the new firm of Bullitt, Dawson & Tarrant, which boasted nine lawyers and a client list that was the envy of town.

Here the paths of Sam Greenebaum and Barney Barnett crossed. Greenebaum was then working very closely with William Marshall Bullitt, the senior partner of the Bullitt-Dawson firm, on several matters. Although fourteen years younger than Greenebaum, Barnett would have known Greenebaum from seeing him in the Bullitt offices, and from eating lunch in the basement of the Kentucky Home Life Building. It was a regular fraternity at lunchtime, and Sam Greenebaum rarely missed a day. It was there, from time to time, that Barnett first hinted to Sam Greenebaum of his desire to join Greenebaum, either in the Brown, Greenebaum firm, or in a new one they would form. A Louisville lawyer of the era recalls Greenebaum saying that by 1952 Barney's communication to Greenebaum had passed the hint stage and was more like a full-blown courtship. It is speculated that the origins of Barnett's restlessness at the Dawson firm lay in a personality conflict with John Tarrant, an aggressive, hard-nosed Tennessean, perhaps along with a newfound feeling of kinship with Greenebaum, a fellow Standard Country Club member. Once Barnett decided he wanted to make the move, his legendary powers of persuasiveness took over, and Sam Greenebaum over time moved from a position of wariness about the man to the feeling that perhaps this Barnett fellow was a breath of fresh air.

Barnett may have sensed that his timing was right. By 1952 the Brown, Greenebaum & Eldred family had become a less happy one, with the partners not always seeing eye-to-eye in matters of profit distribution. In March, 1952, Greenebaum announced that he and Barney Barnett were joining forces as of April 1. His interest in Barnett was more than social. He must have reasoned, as others did, that the combination of their talents — Sam as the keen, precise practitioner of law and Barney as the rain-maker par excellence — would make a formidable team, plus the fact that the combined client list that each would take from their previous firms would give them a solid base and a fast start. The firm, to be called Greenebaum and Barnett, was seen by outsiders as a true partnership, and it was...almost. Records show that Greenebaum owned 55% of the new company, and Barnett 45%.

This firm lasted 20 days in that configuration. Greenebaum and Barnett quickly realized that they needed a trial lawyer in the firm, since Grenebaum didn't want to do it, and Barnett, according to one associate, "had never seen the inside of a courtroom." So on April 21, 1952, they added a young Shepherdsville, Kentucky lawyer, Thomas C. Carroll, who had been a fresh-out-of-law-school associate for the Brown, Greenebaum & Eldred firm in 1949, and had a few years of trial experience. The firm's name was changed to Greenebaum, Barnett & Carroll, although Carroll was a name partner, not a capital one, for the first two years.

Though they knew Carroll, and needed him, he seemed like an odd choice. Carroll was the son of Judge Tad Carroll, County Judge Chief Executive of Bullitt County, and an active Democrat with strong ties to the Democratic power structure of Earle Clements and Lawrence Wetherby. Greenebaum and Barnett were died-in-the-wool Republicans who would work tirelessly for Republican senators Thruston Morton and John Sherman Cooper. It was a philosophical division that, though never overt, may have provided some background for the split that came later. Carroll brought some bank business with him from Shepherdsville and around the state, but the power in the firm resided squarely with Greenebaum and Barnett, whose clients included J. Graham Brown, one of the richest men in Kentucky, whom Barnett had craftily purloined from his mentor, Judge Dawson.

Sam Greenebaum was 50 years old at this time, and had

For nearly twenty years the firm was headquartered in the Kentucky Home Life Building on the 6th floor, where Sam Greenebaum had worked since the 1930s. It was here that Sam Greenebaum and Barney Barnett agreed to start the original Greenebaum firm—Greenebaum, Barnett and Carroll—in 1952.

already had a robust career in law. He had been the president and a board member of the Community Chest and its agency, the Visiting Nurses Association. He had been the president of the Standard Country Club. He was a director of the Courier-Journal Job Printing Company and Levy Brothers. He had been through rough and tumble political campaigns on behalf of the Republican party. And yet here, in the spring of 1952, his life work was really just getting started, and his true legacy was ahead of him. He seemed ready for it. He was at the height of his powers, a man of respect and gravitas, in a town that revered him. The future of the law firm that calls him its patriarch stretched all the way to the horizon and beyond.

S.L. Greenebaum

THE GREENEBAUM ERA
1952-1968

For a man whose lawyerly appearance was right out of central casting—the strong jaw, the beautiful suit, the wise mien—Sam Greenebaum had an ill-fitting nickname: Bud. Not many people called him that. Bob Doll recalls that he always called Mr. Greenebaum "Mr. Greenebaum," even when both men had known each other for decades. But a few did, and Greenebaum often signed "Bud" on his hand-written notes to family and friends.

This nickname may have been the only incongruity in Sam Greenebaum's life, because in every other way he was exactly the man he presented himself to be. He was affable and social, but not overly so. Many thought him to be a shy man. He was proud of his new law firm, but was not a promoter of it, in the modern sense. "He didn't give a damn about getting any more clients," a partner recalls. He worked hard, and put in his share of weekend work, because everybody did in the early 1950s, but he basically worked 9 to 5, five days a week. His hobbies—bird shooting and golf principally—were lifestyle hobbies, and he traveled a lot for both of them and was as nattily attired for them as he was for work.

What Samuel L. Greenebaum seemed to be most about was practicing law excellently. He was a generalist, as were most of the great lawyers of the pre- and post-war years, but he was also a perfectionist. His practice was weighted toward real estate, leasing, estate planning, and a bit of litigation. In these matters he was a master technician, a student of the statutes and a writer whose phrasemaking was as precise as his preparation was diligent. His objective was simply to do good work, and if the client liked it, fine. If he didn't like it, that was fine too, as long as Greenebaum was satisfied with himself. His clients seemed to be more than happy with his work; most of them stayed with Greenebaum all the way to the end, and admired his every word and deed.

As the senior name partner Greenebaum also managed the firm, with Barney Barnett's nearly equal input in the early years. He was not a taskmaster, but was clearly the man who called the shots, and to whom responsibility fell for the overall quality of the firm. As has been noted he was not a "people person" in the Barnett style, and disliked confrontation, but he did not avoid it, either. He was firm in correcting some aspects of the firm's performance. Some of it was mild; his constant review of written documents prompted repeated urgings to the associates to use better grammar and vocabulary. His famous 1963 memorandum noting firm deficiencies and his expectations for all for members is a sample of his management style—he was annoyed, but he expressed his displeasure in writing, with restraint. His skill was such that he made his point, and it was a linguistic masterpiece.

Greenebaum also was the firm's King Solomon regarding compensation and other financial matters. He and Barnett (when he was in town) were judge and jury on money issues, setting salary levels and awarding bonuses with the scratch of a pen at the firm's annual meeting. Greenebaum was not a penny pincher, any more than any other CEO was in the 1950s and '60s. But he did let people know, subtly, if an expense offended his sense of proportion. Ivan Diamond relates the story of his annual dinners with Bill Ballard, of Humana fame, at the five-star Maisonette in Cincinnati, where the tab for four could easily reach four figures. After one such visit that included a sumptuous feast and lots of wine, Diamond dutifully turned in his expense report. A few days later Greenebaum called Diamond and said, "I see you and Bill Ballard had dinner at the Maisonette…I have eaten there for less." And hung up.

It is a measure of the respect people have for the legend of Sam Greenebaum that even his most competitive rivals still say of him today, "He was a gentleman and a scholar and a very fine lawyer."

꒰

Barney Barnett, though…they may not say the same things about him. The charismatic Barnett was the lightning rod of the firm, attracting brickbats as often as kudos all his professional life. In truth, most of the disparaging remarks that ever came his way were from rivals whose business had been pulled out from under them by Barnett, an occurrence that was frequent, lifelong, and to his business competitors, "infuriating." The praise—in volumes—came from his partners, his associates, his clients, and his small army of friends, whose number reads like a Who's Who of industry, politics, sports, and philanthropy.

Barnett was a man who lived for the deal, and in that way was Sam Greenebaum's polar opposite. "Maybe that's why they got together in the first place," speculates Bob Doll, "and why they were as successful as they were right from the beginning." Greenebaum was the "inside" man; Barnett was the quintessential "outside" man, always on the hunt for new clients and new opportunities. "Barney would try to figure out what you wanted," Doll says, "and then he'd give you plenty of it." He was smart, charming, and had the kind of magnetic personality that drew people to him—clients, opposing counsel, even opposing clients. It was not unusual for Barnett to wind up representing people and companies who had just faced off against him in negotiations.

But, as any of his clients would attest, Barnett was not just a charmer. For most of his professional life he was considered the best tax attorney in Louisville; maybe in the U.S. His business, in fact, came from all over—Texas, Washington, New York, California. And despite his reputation for partying with clients until all hours, he was a hard worker. Doll, who considers Barnett a mentor and worked closely with him for years, reveals a Barnett secret: he was a workhorse. "He'd go out and schmooze the clients, but then he'd come back to the office late at night. There was many a night that we worked all night on IRS protests and appeals."

Barnett's combination of intelligence, effort, and charisma was enough to make him a noteworthy success, but he added one more characteristic that made him a true force of nature— fearlessness. He had no hesitation, no fear, and no remorse about taking clients away from anyone, at any time. Judge Dawson discovered that when Barnett walked off with his biggest client, J. Graham Brown, in 1952.

His take-no-prisoners, aggressive style annoyed some of the blue-stocking firms in town who, to be sure, also stole clients but did so with less panache. "He was just a guy driving around town in a Cadillac he hadn't paid for yet," growled the head of one of Louisville's old-line law firms.

The Barnett style may have been irksome to many at the time but, in retrospect, it is clear that he ushered in modernism to the Louisville law scene. He had the first "fancy" office space in

Louisville, covering his walls in mahogany and decorating it with the kind of nice furniture and antiques that are *de rigeur* for law offices today. For 1952 though, "it was a shocker for the Louisville Bar," as one lawyer put it. Another is more gracious about it: "He was steps ahead of everyone in town in terms of a modern office. It was only when the new office buildings were built downtown in the 1970s that everyone else caught up."

Barnett was, in short, an upstart in the eyes of the hidebound legal establishment, and that was fine with him. It was fine with the firm, too. The long shadow of the upstart image has clung to the firm ever since the Barnett years. When the firm was in its first go-go stage in the late 1960s, and was the largest law firm in the state, the terms "aggressive" and "risk taking" were what people said about it. Those characteristics and traditions derive from the Barnett branch of the family tree, not Sam Greenebaum's.

⌐

Also in the office in 1952 was a very important cog in the Greenebaum machinery: Alice Spahn. She was Barnett's secretary, and was a stabilizing, orderly presence in the office, as well as an absolutely essential unifying force between the three principals for years.

⌐

Tom Carroll was the youngster in the firm, despite being 31 years old in 1952. He was a 1942 Harvard graduate with a law degree from the University of Kentucky in 1948. He was the designated trial lawyer of the group and did a wide variety of other work, too, from helping Mr. Greenebaum with his commercial practice through helping Barnett's client, J. Graham Brown, with different kinds of non-tax matters. It was said that if someone fell down the stairs in one of Mr. Brown's properties, Tommy Carroll would be there with an affidavit saying it was their own damn fault before they reached the bottom step.

This three-man firm—Greenebaum, Barnett and Carroll—along with Alice Spahn to keep them all straight, was the germinal firm from which the modern firm of Greenebaum, Doll & McDonald was born.

⌒⌒

The Firm Gets Started

The new firm of Greenebaum, Doll & Carroll was nicely positioned in 1952 to become a success. The two senior partners were both comfortably established in Louisville; they complemented each other's skills very well; and each had a long list of loyal clients already in the fold. Old-line Louisville establishments like Courier-Journal Lithographing, the Seelbach Hotel, Stein Brothers and Boyce, American Radiator, Kaufman Strauss, the Bernheim Foundation, and Wood Mosaic had been clients of Greenebaum for years, and to these Barnett had added J. Graham Brown's companies, Ralph E. Mills' companies and Sid Anderson's companies, among others. The general feeling among the partners was that they were doing very well. The firm's first tax return, dated March 31, 1953, showed total liabilities and net worth of $34,786. They had paid roughly $11,000 in taxes.

Sam Greenebaum, the senior man in age, was acknowledged by all as the head of the firm, and in most respects he was. But a strong case can be made that it was Barney Barnett whose activities were the most influential during this era. Barnett was ambitious, able, and aggressive, a volatile admixture of Irish and Jewish blood, who had personality and loads of charm. His dynamism in client acquisition was legendary. It was said he could not go on vacation without coming back with new clients. It was Barnett who expanded the firm quickly, acquiring tax clients primarily, both in Kentucky and around the country.

J. Graham Brown was a Barnett acquisition and the heavyweight client in the firm, visible from every direction. Besides hotels and office buildings Brown was heavily involved in timber and wood production in the South and had a charitable foundation that was courted by every civic and charitable constituency in Louisville. Between his work and the others it became apparent that three people couldn't handle it all. Help was needed.

⤍

A. Robert Doll Arrives

A year earlier, while Sam Greenebaum and Barney Barnett were finalizing their plans for a new firm, a young man from Tampa, Florida named Bob Doll was completing his law school work at William and Mary. He had graduated from William and Mary three years earlier, and while an undergraduate had been a part of the most dominant college tennis team of the era.

He had gone to William and Mary on a full tennis scholarship, and in addition to athletics and his school work had secured a highly lucrative side business—the dry cleaning concession for the whole school. Between the scholarship and his business income he was doing quite well for a young man in college. But as graduation neared, he was undecided about his future. Law school was a possibility—he had taken an interest in economics and tax law from an undergraduate class. A business career was possible, too, and Doll interviewed with several prominent national firms. The decision to pursue a law degree was made when he discovered that the starting salaries of most businesses were less than what he was already making in his dry cleaning enterprise.

So Doll went on to law school and graduated in February,

1951. At that time he became a member of the Virginia Bar and then went to Washington in the office of the Chief Counsel of the Internal Revenue Service. He worked, primarily, reviewing briefs prepared by IRS attorneys in the field, to be filed in the tax court. He reviewed them to make sure that they conformed with policy that was both published and unpublished. It was a valuable experience, and Doll stayed in Washington until January 1953, at which time the IRS had a reorganization, creating more district offices around the country. Doll had planned on returning to Tampa after leaving the IRS, but one of the district offices which did trial work, he was told, was to be in Louisville, Kentucky. This was 20 minutes from the family home of his wife, Mary Stanton, in Shelbyville, Kentucky. A relocation to Louisville so that she could be near her family, and he could gain trial experience, was too good an offer to refuse, and the Dolls headed to Louisville.

ᴝ

In 1953 the caseload of tax files in Louisville was heavy. The standard procedure was to settle 90% of the cases, just to get through them all. But amid this blur of work, one of Doll's cases stood out. It was with tax attorney Barney Barnett. Doll cannot remember the name of the case or even what the issues were, but he became great friends with Barnett during the negotiations. In the summer of 1953 Barnett started courting Doll to come to work for him, and the young IRS man went over to meet Sam Greenebaum and see the offices. But Doll still thought his ultimate destination was a law firm in Tampa, and with only six months of trial work, decided to decline Barnett's offer to join the firm. Barnett was not to be put off. He would invite Doll to his parties and call him on the phone, and by the end of 1953 Doll had decided to go with the Greenebaum firm. Money was the clincher. Barnett asked Doll what he was making at the IRS, and Doll told him

$4,300 per year. Barnett said, "Well I'll tell you what I'll do. If you'll come, I'll double it. $8,600." Doll could not believe that kind of money. He went home and talked to his wife, then called Barnett back the next day and said, "You've got a deal."

Even though Doll had had very little experience with trial law, he was the perfect addition to the young firm. Sam Greenebaum and Tom Carroll were handling their own clients and needed only sporadic help. It was the tax side that needed him, particularly Barnett, who was desperate for an alter ego to do the paperwork, client minding, and client grinding while he flew high in search of new plum accounts. Bob Doll was that alter ego. Doll not only had the vigor to handle the Barnett workload, he also brought a high level of new tax expertise to the firm. So much so that the firm soon garnered a reputation as the best tax outfit in town, a reputation that grew over the decades and has stood ever since.

Doll revered Barnett, with whom he worked for 14 years. "I must say that Barney was a delight for any young lawyer to work with. He had no pride in authorship. Once the client was in the door, he didn't care if he ever saw him again. So, as a result, all these cases were turned over to me, and the client would never see Barney again unless he wanted to. And I guess I kept them more or less satisfied, because they were happy."

Doll describes his participation with Barnett in the early days as carrying his briefcase, but Barnett clearly gave Doll a lot of responsibility, and used Doll to good advantage. When they would go to the federal courthouse at Sixth and Broadway to negotiate a tax case, Barnett would tell Doll, "If at any time I stop talking, I'm thinking. You take over and start talking until I start up again."

Given this level of responsibility early, it was natural that self-sufficiency and leadership would evolve in Doll, whose self-confidence and competitive nature had never diminished from his college athletics days. He was one of the heavy lifters throughout the Greenebaum era, but more than that, he made himself a trusted right hand man to both senior partners, and so became the logical person onto whom a lot of the daily burdens and decisions of the firm fell during the growth years of the late 1960's.

By the time the leadership torch truly and officially passed to Doll in the early 1970s, he had already been the *de facto* leader of the firm for many years, thanks, of course, to his own diligence, but also because Sam Greenebaum was content to let Doll run the daily show, and Barney Barnett continued to do his own thing, which was demonstrably not management.

⌢

Two New Lawyers, Gray and Greenebaum

By 1955, with Bob Doll acquiring new clients as well as Barnett, the client list had expanded to include more local blue-chip companies — Byck Brothers, Levy Brothers, Builders Supply, Martin Adams and Sons, the Cornwell Company, United Artists Theatre Circuit, and others. Two new lawyers were needed to handle the new business, and Charles Speed Gray and Sam Greenebaum's son, John, were soon brought on board.

Charles Speed Gray, 33 at the time he came with the firm, had been a trial lawyer in the office of the chief counsel of the IRS in Detroit and in Cincinnati, whom Bob Doll had met during his IRS years. Gray was a University of Kentucky graduate for both his bachelor's and law degrees. His addition is notable only for the manner of his departure one year later in 1956, when he joined Tom Carroll in a palace coup that failed.

Also joining the firm in 1955, fresh out of law school, was John Greenebaum, Sam Greenebaum's son and an Amherst graduate who, like his father, had graduated from Harvard Law School with academic distinction. The younger Greenebaum had felt destined to pursue a career in law, to return to Louisville to live, and to work for his father's firm, but he was not exactly a chip off the old block. Besides law he was interested in philosophy and physics, and felt more a part of the boisterous, post-war generation than perhaps a corporate lawyer in Louisville Kentucky ought to feel in 1955.

He was determined to set himself apart from his father's legal tradition, so John Greenebaum expressed his forward thinking by choosing to concentrate his career on a specialty — labor law. It was, he says, "a dynamic legal area far removed from my father's world of verbs and participles." The elder Greenebaum did not insist on a more traditional practice for his son. Good thing it was, too, because John's labor practice thrived for years. By carving out a proprietary area in the firm for himself, John probably kept the generational friction to a minimum, which was beneficial for both firm and family. "While my father and I liked and respected each other," he says, "a fair amount of professional separation made our relation if less intense, more durable." John Greenebaum was made a partner in 1963.

$$\approx$$

Greenebaum, Barnett and Wood

In 1956 Bob Doll was asked by Tom Carroll and Speed Gray to join them in confronting Sam Greenebaum and Barney Barnett about what they perceived to be pay inequities in the firm. At that time salaries and bonuses were decided by senior partner *fiat* — meaning that Greenebaum and Barnett decided what to pay Carroll, Gray and Doll, and they then split the rest. This seemed unfair to Carroll, who two years earlier had become a capital partner with a 15% interest in the firm. Both Gray and Carroll wound up leaving the firm after Doll declined to join the rebellion.

Their departure left the firm without a trial lawyer. Mr.

Greenebaum had had trial experience but had no interest in it; Barnett and Doll were not qualified to handle anything other than tax cases. The search was on to find a new partner with litigation experience.

⌒

Charles F. Wood, 1956

Charlie Wood had been an Assistant U.S. Attorney from 1952 to 1953 and U.S. Attorney in 1953. Like Charles Gray before him, Wood had been an acquaintance of Bob Doll, and Doll had brought his name up to Greenebaum and Barnett for approval for the open slot. They approved. Wood was the sixth attorney in the firm. He was 39 years old, about Barnett's age, and seemed to be the kind of senior trial man who would make a perfect replacement for Tom Carroll. Considering his experience, the firm rewarded him with a partnership immediately. The name of the firm was changed to Greenebaum, Barnett and Wood.

Although he was a name partner for eleven years (leaving in 1967) Wood was never a real factor in the management of the firm, and probably never expected or wanted to be. During the late 1950s and early 1960s the firm was run entirely, if informally, by the Greenebaum-Barnett duo, whose complementary personalities left no room for a third voice. Wood was content to work with an aging J. Graham Brown, whose reliance on Wood increased greatly after Barnett's health problems and subsequent lack of client attention in 1965. (With Barnett virtually on the sidelines, it was Doll to whom Mr. Greenebaum turned in the late 1960s for advice and co-management, not Wood, whom Greenebaum perceived as fixated on one client, not the firm as a whole.)

Shelly Weber, 1957

In 1957 the firm added 27-year-old Shelton R. (Shelly) Weber to the firm. He was a Louisville man, educated at Indiana University and the University of Louisville law school. Prior to joining the firm Weber had spent three years in the Judge Advocate General's department of the U.S. Air Force.

⁀

Greenebaum, Barnett, Wood and Doll

In 1958, Bob Doll's stature in the firm rose to partner level as a result of his work with The Colony, Inc., of Lexington, Kentucky, a real estate firm whose tax case had risen to the U.S. Supreme Court. The case involved a technical interpretation of tax assessment, and was nationally important because it hoped to settle a tax question that had been in litigation in lower federal courts for many years.

In its brief the Government stated that 180 similar cases and claims involving over $8 million were being held up pending the Court's decision on the Colony case, so there was more at stake than just The Colony, Inc.'s interests. In April 1958 Doll, age 30, pled the case personally before the Court, and won. The decision was 7-2, with Chief Justice Warren and Hugo Black dissenting.

The June 18, 1958 *Courier-Journal* played Doll's victory as a major local news item, putting it on the cover of Section 2. The headline emphasized Doll's youth, exclaiming, "Like No-Hitter for Rookie!" In the article Barney Barnett grabbed the first quote, opining that, "We didn't think we had a chance in this case." Doll said his experience before the court was "awe-inspiring."

The win was also reported in the *Lexington Herald*, the *Tampa Tribune*, the *Shelby News & Sentinel* (on the front page, under the headline, "Husband of Local Girl, Mary S. Willis"), and even the William and Mary Alumni newsletter. Congratulatory calls and letters poured in from friends, legal associates, the Dean of the law school at William and Mary, and clients from around the country.

Later that year, Doll wrote in correspondence to an Alabama friend, Bill Mahoney, "It was a real thrill appearing before the Court, and I was, of course, delighted with the way the case turned out. Your 'native son', Justice Black, really worked me over. I am glad that Chief Justice Warren was the only one that went along with him." (To which Mahoney wrote back, "The dissent of Hugo Black and Earl Warren is the highest compliment you could have been paid.")

The local and national publicity over the Supreme Court victory had a predictable effect on the firm's still-young associate. Barney Barnett initiated steps to make Doll a partner, and in November, 1958, the name of the firm was changed to Greenebaum, Barnett, Wood and Doll.

The news had other effects too, on the profile of the firm. Always known for tax expertise, the firm was now being talked about in national tax circles, and in corporate boardrooms across the U.S. The tax work not only increased in volume, but it increased in complexity as IRS rules became more dense and sophisticated. Soon the firm needed not just another tax man, but a great tax man, and into this door of opportunity strode Laramie L. Leatherman.

Laramie L. Leatherman, 1959

27-year-old Larry Leatherman joined the firm in 1959. Precocious in ability, Leatherman had graduated in 1953 from the University of Kentucky Law School when he had just turned 21. He had been a tax attorney for three years before becoming Attorney Adviser to Judge J. Gregory Bruce of the Tax Court of the United States in 1956.

In March of 1958 Leatherman had written Barnett asking

for an interview, because he "wanted to specialize in tax law."

Judge Bruce made contact with Barnett about Leatherman, and in late 1958 Bob Doll met with Leatherman in Louisville, interviewed him, and hired him right away. Doll by this time was traveling away from Louisville for weeks at a time, and needed someone to share the tax workload so he could resume something of a normal family life. Leatherman was that man.

He immediately started handling local tax cases that either Barnett or Doll had originated but could not work on personally. Doll counted on Leatherman the way Barnett had counted on him five years earlier. But Leatherman became Barnett's direct man, too, in connection with two significant clients. The first was Texas Gas Transmission, a Barnett client for whom Doll had done some initial work but had turned over to Leatherman. Leatherman became great friends with Bill Elmer, the CEO of Texas Gas, and both his good work and his friendship with Elmer cemented a client relationship that lasted well past Barnett's departure, up until Texas Gas was sold in 1967. The second client was Ashland Oil, another Barnett coup for whom the firm became tax counsel in the early 1960s. Barnett and Ashland's CEO Orrin Atkins had a very close relationship, and Leatherman was chosen to work with Ashland tax counsel, Jim Marcum. Again, Leatherman's work and his close connections within Ashland kept the tax work with the Greenebaum firm long after Barnett left, until Ashland took their tax counsel in-house.

⌒

Larry Leatherman and his Work Ethic

The relentless work habits that became legendary in Leatherman's years with the firm were plainly in place from the beginning. Leatherman's motor was in overdrive for most of his life. The torrid pace started at 4 a.m., as was his habit every day of the week, including weekends and holidays. It was a style and a behavior that fit in well with the Greenebaum crowd, no slouches themselves when it came to working around the clock and setting preposterously high goals and achieving them. Later, during the years he was managing partner, the man called "Triple" would raise the bar to even higher heights, creating for himself an aura that was admired, respected, and sometimes feared.

But here in these early years, Leatherman's ferocity was channeled into tax work, which the firm was bringing in in buckets. Leatherman was made a partner in 1963.

≋

Larry Pedley, 1960

In 1960 the firm hired a new lawyer, Lawrence L. Pedley. Pedley was a Hopkinsville, Kentucky native who had gone to The Citadel, and had received his law degree from Yale in 1959.

≋

Edwin H. Perry, 1964

By 1964 the firm had six partners, with the elevation of John Greenebaum and Larry Leatherman to that status. Larry Pedley was still an associate as he had been since 1960; Ken Kusch had come and gone, and Allan Solomon, a tax attorney out of Boston College law school and the NYU tax program, had lasted three years with the firm before going to work for National Industries. (Members from that era still remember Solomon as someone who had never been west of the Hudson River before moving to Louisville, a transition he considered perilous. After only four or five months in Louisville he had to go on business to Perry County, in the eastern mountains of Kentucky, deemed Indian country even to Kentuckians. To Solomon it was like going to Tasmania. It is purported that on his return he was visibly shaken, saying "You just won't believe what I saw down there. I mean, it's a whole different world!" It is further reported that a few days later the firm's Perry County client called to say, "We've never seen a man like Allan Solomon before in our lives.")

Into this mix in June of 1964 came Edwin H. Perry. He had been a 1959 graduate of the University of Louisville School of Law, and had worked for Russell Smith at Smith and Smith until the summer of 1963, at which time he went to New York University to get his masters in tax law. The decision to return to Louisville after that was not automatic, but was helped along by the fact that his wife still called Louisville home, and wanted to return with their two small children.

So in December of 1963, during the holiday break from NYU, Perry came home to interview with all the major firms, including the Greenebaum firm, one of whose partners, Bob Doll, had lived down the hall from the Perrys in the Green Hill Apartments some years earlier. The chances for a tax specialty, Perry recalls, were not good at some of the firms. "I asked Louis Seelbach, 'Who handles your tax cases?' and he said, 'What do you mean who handles them? Whoever represents the client. A tax case is like any other case.' And I thought, that really wasn't the place for me."

Greenebaum was the more logical place for Perry, but when he interviewed with Doll in December 1963 Doll told him they were looking for a securities lawyer, not a tax man. So, on this return to NYU for his final semester, Perry had one elective, and decided to take it in securities law. Eventually that course did not affect his hireability with Greenebaum, thank goodness, because, "I hated it," Perry says, "and I didn't understand any of it."

Fortunately, by the time he returned to Louisville in the summer of 1964, the firm had just hired their securities man, Irv Eisinger, so the prospects were more favorable for a tax hire.

31

The firm had a still-growing tax specialty, an increase in the sophistication and money significance of tax cases, and a general need for more hands. Actually, there was more need for hands them there was office space; Perry's first office was a side table in the hall.

The addition of Perry further solidified the firm's reputation as a premier tax firm, and did not diminish when Allan Solomon left two weeks after Perry arrived. For a moment, Perry was thrilled when Solomon left, because he inherited his office. But the office came with a price. "I walked into his office," Perry says, "and there was a stack of files a foot and a half tall. So I got off to a running start."

Shortly after joining the firm, Perry's wife, Anita, and three-year-old daughter, Beth, came to visit the office. Beth had often heard her parents talking about Greenebaum, Wood and Doll, and as she peered around the lobby Anita said, "What are you looking for, Beth?" She said, "Where's the wooden doll?"

Perry's pickup of the tax load fortuitously coincided with the diminishment in Barney Barnett's daily activities in handling tax cases. He was still a genius at bringing in clients, but the lucrative work he brought in required a high level of civil tax expertise that he himself was becoming unable, or unwilling, to provide. That's where Perry's advanced and recent tax degree became important to the firm.

In addition to tax work Perry also inherited the employee benefit work that had been Allan Solomon's bailiwick. Perry had had some training in this area at NYU, and because of that was the lawyer in the firm who knew most about it. Without really asking for it, for the next 10 years he was the employee benefits guru not only in the firm, but also in the state. It was not until the early

1980s that Perry's practice could be deemed primarily corporate instead of in the benefits specialty.

But, during this era, and for his first six years with the firm, Perry's primary work would be in the tax area, joining Barnett, Doll, and Leatherman as the A-team of local and regional tax cases.

∽

Irv Eisinger, 1964

Irv Eisinger was a Harvard-educated New Yorker who had been an attorney with the Division of Corporation Finance of the Securities and Exchange Commission since 1961. In 1964 he came to the attention of Bob Doll, who was beginning to feel the need for a securities lawyer in the firm because of the changing nature of the deals in which the firm was getting involved. Doll's January 2, 1964 memo to Sam Greenebaum about Eisinger recommended a close look: "I definitely think it would be worthwhile to check Eisinger out carefully since he does have the SEC background..."

The Greenebaum firm lured Eisinger to Louisville in the spring of 1964, hired him, and became the first firm in Kentucky with an SEC specialist. From that moment on the firm did lots of securities work, or at least as much as Eisinger could handle by himself until Frank Quickert and Ivan Diamond arrived to bolster the securities department. Eisinger is remembered as a skilled practitioner, slow and tedious by Greenebaum speed standards, but a serious worker once the work was in-house.

∽

Securities work represented another important diversification for the firm, and perhaps a harbinger of the explosive growth in specialties throughout the law for the next 20 years. This, combined with Perry's employee benefits practice, certainly signaled the beginning of the firm's serious expansion into specialties beyond civil taxation.

⌒

By 1965 the nine-lawyer firm had acquired a reputation for hard work and superior results, pushed along by the risk-taking Barney Barnett, who always promised his clients anything they wanted to hear. Barnett never told anybody no. No matter how difficult the case or how short the deadline, he always told his clients, "We can handle that." And he was right. The worker bees would somehow get the work done. In making Barnett look like a god to his clients, the younger lawyers learned how to take sleep deprivation to the ragged edge. But in so doing they were also earning a mystique for superhuman effort that in many ways carries over to the modern era. What they said about the Greenebaum firm then—highly-driven, result-oriented, hard-charging—they still say about it today.

The firm also gained a reputation for getting the highest fees in town, a reputation that was probably true, according to Bob Doll. But, Doll says, "We really weren't motivated by fees. We got high fees but it was based on solid principles. If you give quality service, do the work promptly, and get a good result, then you are entitled to a premium fee."

The firm charged a premium and clients paid it. In the 1960s that was foreign thinking in Louisville, with most law firms still billing at decades-old rates. But the Greenebaum firm pushed the fee bar higher, and other firms followed suit after seeing that Greenebaum clients were not only paying, they were happy to pay for good results.

Sam Greenebaum, then in his early 60s, obviously was not one of the go-getters, but he never had been. Neither was he invisible. His calming hand was always on the management tiller, and he was still indisputably the leader of the firm.

It was in 1963, in fact, that he wrote the internal memo that now has become Holy Writ in the firm, admonishing the firm's lawyers for careless work habits and other transgressions. The memo survives as both an artful exposition and a timeless statement about legal doctrine and behavior. Conveniently, no one remembers exactly who or what circumstances elicited this masterpiece; but everyone took it to heart:

Memorandum to Messrs. Wood, Doll, John Greenebaum, Leatherman, Pedley, Solomon and Kusch

I have from time to time indicated to each of you very substantial dissatisfaction with the work we produce and the methods we employ. I have prepared this memorandum so that there can be no misunderstanding concerning my feelings.

1.   I believe that I have the right to expect from you some degree of original thinking and imagination concerning the practical aspects of problems you have for solution. I find that you are far too prone to follow forms regardless of their applicability to particular situations. The forms which are available, whether they be found in texts or are those we have produced in this office, in addition to lacking universal applicability are in many instances incorrect or outmoded. You should employ them only to the extent that they are useful in helping you express legal concepts whose validity you have learned by experience or individual research.

2.   I believe that I have the right to expect from you, and I must insist that I receive, documents which demonstrate your knowledge of basic English and which are so

organized as to make their content easily digestible. This is true especially in the case of briefs, many of which I find dull, unpersuasive, slipshod, unorganized, and a chore to read and assimilate. If I, as a partisan reader, have this problem it must be obvious that a judge, without like motivation, will find the job of understanding what we are trying to say even more difficult than do I. Do not take up my time with material you have not proofread and corrected. I am not here to correct your grammar or stenographic misspelling.

3. I believe that I am entitled to expect that before you begin a contract, brief, or other document, you will have completed, with energy and intelligence, the obviously necessary prior independent legal research. I know from personal experience that acquiring maturity in legal thinking is a slow process but I must emphasize that there are no shortcuts. I am repeatedly amazed and disturbed, not by your lack of a full knowledge of the law applicable to a particular problem, but often by your unawareness of the existence of the problem itself. This points only to a lack of knowledge of fundamental legal principles. Do not bring your legal questions to me until you have completed your research.

4. I know from long experience that scheduling work is imperative. While I realize that there are emergency situations, I have no patience with the habit, which I find all too prevalent, of postponing completion of projects until deadlines are perilously close. I have determined that in the future, except in cases of genuine emergency, I will not be available to assist you in last minute attempts to conclude projects, the completion date of which you have known long in advance, or should have known in ample time.

5. Within the limits of your office commitments your time

is your own. There is no reason why each of you should not arrange your engagements so that you have ample time for vacations, recreation, and outside interests. If you leave the office for any purpose, you must advise the switchboard operator where you are going and can be reached if you are leaving on business, or if not, that you are taking time off, cannot be reached, and will not return that day. I have no desire to know about, nor have I any interest in, your personal or private affairs except insofar as they affect the office and its work. If you find yourself with free time and wish to take an afternoon or a day off, there is no reason you should not do so, but I am aware that at times some of you leave the office without information concerning where you will be or when or if you will return.

I am not concerned with discipline but I am determined that those of you who are associated with this office conduct yourselves like persons who are attempting to achieve ability, success, maturity and advancement in the practice of law.

If any of you have questions concerning this memorandum, or its applicability to you, please confer with me.

S. L. Greenebaum
July 2, 1963

Greenebaum also showed his displeasure in the matter of uncollected fees. He always reviewed the delinquent account lists usually prepared by Doll, and wrote notes to those attorneys who were responsible for collecting them. One such memo in May of

1964 was to Barnett, whose client National Industries was not only behind in retainer payments but also straining the firm in other ways. Greenebaum notes that the company owes the firm a lot of money, and that the time spent on its work is "way over the retainer." He also complains about the "complete absorption of Allan Solomon's time" which has "crippled our general tax work badly."

National Industries, and Barney Barnett's interest in it, would soon play a crucial role in the next important phase of the firm's evolution.

New Lawyers

New lawyers—Michael Shaikun, Tom Brown, and Ivan Diamond— arrived in the mid-1960s. All are still with the firm, and their presence in the firm has lasted nearly forty years.

Michael Shaikun, 1966

Michael Shaikun came to the firm in 1966 after receiving degrees from the Wharton School at the University of Pennsylvania and Harvard Law School. He immediately embarked on a career in real estate law and finance, and as of this writing is still involved in major real estate transactions.

Bob Doll recounts Shaikun as a key player in the firm's administrative structure by the mid-1970s. But his partners know him also as a great thinker who is always available to strategize on a transaction. He is today the firm's chief ethics and risk management guru, guiding the firm as it grows in size and complexity.

Tom Brown, 1966

Tom Brown joined the firm in September 1966 and was

the 13th lawyer in the firm. He came from the chief counsel's office of the IRS in Atlanta, and had spent a year doing criminal tax work and three years doing tax court litigation. A native Louisvillian with three kids and twins on the way, he felt he wanted to come back to Louisville after his four years with the IRS were up. Brown's father worked at Citizens Fidelity Bank, knew Sam Greenebaum, and called him to arrange an interview for his son with Bob Doll and Larry Leatherman. When Brown came to Louisville, Doll hired him on the spot on a Saturday. Brown noticed that practically everybody was in their offices, and later found it was common practice in those days to work on Saturdays until about 2:00. "It was just something that was expected," Brown says. "On Friday afternoons Bob Doll would interrupt our conversations and say to me, "We'll talk about that tomorrow morning. So you had the idea that you should be there."

Even Barney Barnett was there on Saturdays. He was a ghost to Brown, hardly ever in the office. But on Saturdays he would invariably be in his corner office with lots of people around, having what seemed to be important meetings. "Mr. Barnett didn't know me at all," says Brown. "The first year we were in Louisville my wife Brenda was pregnant with our twins, and she was fairly big. It was Christmas time, and the firm's holiday party was to be at Barney Barnett's house in Cherokee Park. I had been introduced to Barney, but he didn't remember me, particularly. At that time I had an old car with a bad muffler. On the day of the party, we parked halfway up the hill above Millvale, because I didn't want anyone to see my car. We walked up to the front door, rang the doorbell, and Barney came to the door and said, 'Can I help you?' He obviously thought we were lost or something. I said, 'Mr. Barnett, I'm Tom Brown, one of the new associates, and this is my wife, Brenda.' He says, 'Oh, yes, come on in.' He might have been a little embarrassed about not recognizing me, but I don't think he forgot me after that."

When Brown came to the firm Bob Doll, Larry Leatherman and Ed Perry were doing all the tax work. Brown immediately started doing federal tax work, and later started doing state tax work in 1973. Doll had numerous clients, all of whom were being audited by the IRS, and were in various stages of the audit—protest, Tax Court, or U.S. District Court—and Brown went to work primarily for these clients and did so for three solid years. "I did most of the analysis," Brown says, "but Bob is a very accomplished tax lawyer who knew everyone over at Sixth and Broadway. He was the one who did the most to change my attitude from being a government lawyer to a taxpayer's lawyer."

Ivan Diamond, 1967

Ivan Diamond had been at the Securities and Exchange Commission in Washington D.C., working for a man who became fairly well-known in legal, financial, judicial, and CIA circles named Stanley Sporkin, who was then the branch chief in the division of enforcement. The phone rang in Diamond's office one day in 1967—it was Irv Eisenger. "He asks me to come down to Louisville," says Diamond. "It happens I was reviewing a registration statement for a company called National Industries, a Louisville conglomerate at that time. Eisenger was the lawyer for National Industries. And he got me to come to Louisville. I arrived in Louisville in November 1967 in my 1957 Chevrolet." The idea was for Diamond to work with Eisinger on securities deals, and to build the securities department. "There never was an overwhelming amount of securities work here in Louisville," Diamond says, "but between Eisenger and me we soon built the reputation as the firm to come to in this part of the country for securities work." While perhaps not numerous, the majority of Diamond's deals, mostly transacted from the 1970s to the 1990s, involve the biggest players in modern Louisville business history—Humana, Kentucky Fried Chicken, Rally's, Chi-Chi's, Vencor, and Papa John's.

Today Diamond is the Chair of the Corporate and Securities Practice Group.

⁀

In 1965 Barney Barnett , the engine that had powered the Greenebaum vehicle for 13 years, suffered a heart attack, which by modern standards was probably not that serious. But to Barnett it was not only frightening, it was a first intimation of mortality. After a period of recovery he was still visibly affected and his demeanor, his associates noted, was demonstrably different. This change in personal attitude created a shift in his professional goals that had profound effect on the Greenebaum firm. Barnett no longer showed the zest for the finder game that had characterized his professional life and, even worse, he seemed to take little interest in the cases of the clients he had already brought to the firm. He began to concentrate on personal matters such as his newfound interest in the United Jewish Appeal and the state of Israel, and in his personal relationships with certain people, such as Orrin Atkins of Ashland Oil and Stanley Yarmuth of National Industries. He began to travel extensively, to Israel and to Iran, for months at time, leaving others to take care of his clients, who began to wonder where he was.

In retrospect, the heart attack marked the end of an era. Barnett continued to be a name partner in the firm for four more years, but his presence in the office rapidly diminished.

By 1967 Barnett's all-consuming involvement with Stanley Yarmuth and the business of National Industries had reached the point that he moved out of the Greenebaum firm and established offices at National Industries. Alice Spahn, his secretary, moved with him. Barnett, in effect, had left the Greenebaum firm and the practice of law. He converted to Of-Counsel status with the firm.

The firm suffered in two ways. First, the steady stream of new clients that Barnett always brought slowed. Second, his clients that were already with the firm were growing restless, and in some cases outright annoyed at Barnett's absence.

J. Graham Brown, in particular, despite his advanced age, was aware of Barnett's disappearance. Bob Doll recalls that "Mr. Brown wanted to know where Barney was, and we would track him down in Israel. Barnett would say, 'Tell Mr. Brown I'll be back in two weeks,' but he wouldn't show." Into this vacuum stepped Charlie Wood, who for 1967 did almost nothing but work for Mr. Brown. By 1968 Brown had had enough and—probably encouraged by Charlie Wood—left the firm. Wood went with him.

The loss of this client was a blow to the firm, and there was no love lost with Charlie Wood for abetting Brown's leave-taking. But at bottom this was a Barnett default, and the firm could do no more than to be fatalistic about its ability to restore Barnett's luster and recreate the glory days.

⤝

Brown wasn't the only client who faded away. Friedman, Koven, the Chicago law firm for whom Barnett did tax work, got their own in-house tax counsel. Billionaire J. Howard Marshall, a Barnett favorite, disappeared from the scene. And Kingwood Oil was bought by National Industries.

The only thing to do was to replace Barnett with a new business generator, and to think ahead to the day when Barnett's equity in the firm could be reduced in proportion to his involvement. That day would come in 1969.

⤝

With the withdrawal of Barney Barnett, Sam Greenebaum

became the sole managing partner, a situation that had happened to him only once before, in 1948 when Joe Selligman had died. Greenebaum's restraint and essential gentility were hallmarks of his personality, but in the context of the late 1960s and the aggressive nature of the new firm, they perhaps were not the appropriate leadership qualities for the times. The other senior man, Charlie Wood, had just left, and never was a factor in management anyway. So at this time Bob Doll naturally became, at the very least, an indispensable adviser to Mr. Greenebaum, and at the most a co-manager of the firm.

Greenebaum was 67 years old when Barnett moved to National Industries, and was slowing physically. At 40 years old, Doll was the next-highest ranking partner in age and experience, and was the logical person to become the sounding board and confidant of Greenebaum. But he was wise enough, and respectful enough, to stay in the second position, even though he gradually began to make many of the firm's management decisions on his own, including the compensation for all the lawyers in the firm.

In a few months, once Mr. Greenebaum was comfortable that Doll was taking care of the management side of things, he decided to take a step back and enter semi-retirement. He did not wish to worry about work as much, nor about the amount of money he would make each year. So he and Doll worked out a flat compensation arrangement of $100,000 per year. This done, for all practical purposes Bob Doll became the head of the firm.

Bob Matthews, 1968

The first order of business for Doll was the replacement of the lost Barnett revenue. For this he turned to Robert F. Matthews, a Kentucky Democrat who had just lost the lieutenant governorship of Kentucky to Wendell Ford by a few votes.

Bob Matthews was the final "name" partner added in the Sam Greenebaum era. His arrival was in direct response to the loss of J. Graham Brown and the lawyer who served Brown in the firm, Charlie Wood. The Brown loss was made possible, as discussed, by the inattention of Barney Barnett to Brown's interests. To shore up the revenue hole Brown's departure created, the firm took advantage of the availability of Matthews, whose high-visibility, statewide political profile promised a windfall of new business.

Bob Doll knew of Matthews through his wife's family connection to Shelby County (the Matthews family had been in Shelby County for several generations), but also from Matthews' public life, as Commissioner of Finance, Commissioner of Revenue, and in 1964, Attorney General under Gov. Edward T. (Ned) Breathitt.

Matthews had litigation experience as well as social and political connections, and was a good fit for the firm, which deemed his arrival important enough to make him a partner. The firm was renamed Greenebaum, Barnett, Doll, and Matthews.

There was only one of minor problem, and that was Matthews' high profile in the state Democratic Party, which placed him at political odds with, if not the firm itself, then with Republicans Greenebaum, Barnett, and Doll. It was a slightly ticklish subject for both Matthews and Doll when they met to negotiate Matthews' partnership agreement. Doll expressed the fact that the firm was characterized by some as a Republican firm, but that was not necessarily the case, he said. Doll asserted that he did not want the firm to be labeled politically at all, preferring to be called simply, "a professional firm," with no political agenda. Matthews's name in the firm, Doll noted, would help dispel the Republican tag.

Michael Fleishman, 1969

In 1969 Mike Fleishman was added to the firm, and was

the last associate brought on board in what we are calling the Greenebaum era. He had been recruited by the firm at Tulane, where he received his law degree in 1969. He had come to Louisville and had been interviewed by John Greenebaum, who offered him a job on the spot. As was the custom upon hiring, Fleishman was then escorted into Sam Greenebaum's office for the handshake and official blessing. As Fleishman remembers, "Mr. Greenebaum says, 'Mr. Fleishman, you seem like a perfect candidate. Too bad we don't have a spot for you!" Once that got straightened out, Fleishman started working and became Mr. Greenebaum's primary associate in real estate matters, corporate work, and other projects of particular interest to Greenebaum. He worked as counsel during the process of converting the University of Louisville from a city university into a state-supported school, and was involved in city of Louisville work with Republican mayor Kenneth Schmied, who was a Greenebaum friend. Fleishman later became involved in real estate development, food and restaurant ventures, and other start-up businesses during the first heyday of Greenebaum entrepreneurism, the 1970s and 1980s. But here on the eve of the Jones-Cherry merger, Fleishman had the privilege of working closely with Sam Greenebaum, and perhaps was the last member to do so before Greenebaum slowed into semi-retirement in the early 1970s.

Today Fleishman is the Chair of the Business and Commercial Practice Department.

The Jones-Cherry Merger

In early 1969 Bob Doll and an investment partner of his named H. L. (Dooley) Perrin entered into a real estate transaction with a Columbus, Ohio firm represented by a young Louisville attorney named J. David Grissom. The negotiations with Grissom,

as Doll remembers, were highlighted by heat and fireworks—
both Perrin and Grissom were outspoken fellows—but in the end
the deal closed and Doll was favorably impressed by Grissom.
(Perhaps Grissom made himself more memorable to Doll by
getting into a contretemps with Perrin during a snowstorm layover
at the Columbus airport. Perrin, then 60 years old, flew into a
rage at the 30-year-old Grissom, saying, "You s.o.b., I can do
anything better than you. I'll bet I can do more one-arm pushups
than you." And with that the two men got down on the concourse
floor and had a pushup contest. Doll forgets who won, but the
image has stayed with him for over 30 years.)

Grissom, together with David Jones and Wendell Cherry,
had left the Wyatt, Grafton and Sloss firm two years earlier to
create a new firm with William C. Boone, Marvin Hirn, William
Ballard, and others. In addition to being attorneys, Jones and Cherry
were businessmen and investors and had started a small nursing
home company called Extendicare. (Gordon Davidson, the
managing partner at the Wyatt firm, had reluctantly cited to them
a Wyatt rule that its attorneys could not have outside business
interests, which caused their departure.) Bill Boone and Marvin
Hirn had left Bullitt, Dawson and Tarrant to come with the new
firm, which was called Jones, Cherry, Grissom and Boone, with
offices in the Portland Federal building.

Perhaps Grissom reminded Doll in some ways of a
younger Barney Barnett. Grissom had already shown a Barnett-
like ability to attract blue-chip business, with Kentucky Fried
Chicken, Meidinger & Associates, Dixie Warehouse and Cartage,
Citizens Fidelity Bank, and, of course, Extendicare on his client
list.

By 1969 Extendicare was still a young company, but its
nursing home business was thriving, and there were ambitious plans
to start buying hospitals. Jones and Cherry decided to take the
company public. Lexington investor William T. Young and others

came along to guarantee financing for the company, and with that Jones and Cherry effectively ended their interest in being full-time lawyers.

Grissom and Bob Doll then approached each other to determine if a merger between Greenebaum and Jones-Cherry might be beneficial to both sides. For Doll, the answer was an immediate yes. To him the Jones-Cherry firm was a highly desirable target. Their high-profile clients included both old-line firms and the up-and-comers, and Grissom himself was the kind of lawyer/dealmaker that fit right into the Greenebaum mold. To Grissom, the Greenebaum firm represented a new breed of hard-charging lawyer, taking risks and making deals, and their numbers of client minders more than compensated for the loss of Jones and Cherry as daily work producers.

With both Doll and Grissom in agreement, the marriage was completed in August of 1969. The new firm was named Greenebaum, Grissom, Doll, Matthews and Boone. Grissom was made a name partner as was Bill Boone, who, although he was not involved in the merger negotiations, was a well regarded trial lawyer at the time. David Jones and Wendell Cherry became of-counsel.

Significantly, Barney Barnett's name was not included in the new firm name. Sam Greenebaum, who was still the titular head of the firm, and Bob Doll had discussed the thorny matter of Barnett, which must have caused the older man some unease. Despite being a founder, Barnett had not contributed to the firm in nearly three years, and clearly was not going to return. Worse, he was still being paid. In the end, Greenebaum had to go along with Doll's recommendation that Barnett's name be removed. But it made neither man happy. Greenebaum asked Doll, "Will you go over and talk to Barney?" Doll said he would.

The idea was to let Barnett down easily by offering him an annual salary to stay of-counsel. Doll held out some hope that

Barnett, preoccupied with National Industries, would be fine with the arrangement. But he was not. As Doll laid out the reality of the situation, Barnett became incensed. After using very strong language, he said, "I'm out! I don't need your damn charity. I'm out 100 percent!"

As resolute and firm as Doll had to be at that moment, he was also saddened. "That ended our relationship," he says. "That was quite a blow to me, because he had been not only my mentor but my idol. I went back and told Mr. Greenbaum what happened, and he simply said, 'Okay.'" That was it.

～

Barnett's view of his relationship to the Greenebaum firm was obviously much different than everyone else's. To him, the Greenebaum firm was just as much his as it was Sam Greenebaum's, and always would be. Perhaps understandably, he felt that his decades of rain-making had caused the flowering of the entire firm, and that contribution, no matter what he was doing at the moment, could never be devalued or diminished by time.

He let his old friend Sam Greenebaum know how he felt in a letter eight months later: "Last September when the original firm merged with the Jones-Cherry firm, I was chagrined at the attitude of the partners. Without prior consultation I was eliminated in the negotiations, and the subsequent offer [of a retainer] was ridiculous."

In a second letter the next day he said, "Frankly, I see no reason to carry this matter further, either in a personal discussion or in writing. It seems to me that the matter is terminated and it is simply a matter of settling our affairs. The separation is obviously complete, and I feel it is tragic that our relationship was affected by relatively small sums of money."

But he clearly misunderstood the nature of the firm's

problems with him. By vanishing from the firm he had played the major role in his own undoing. By being away for so long, the firm had accelerated away from him, and was having to clean up the cases he had left behind.

Even so, the imprint of Barney Barnett could not be erased completely, especially for Sam Greenebaum. He continued to try to reconcile with Barnett, at least on a personal basis. In June, 1970 Greenebaum sent Barnett a handwritten note on his birthday: "Dear Barney; Rita and I send you congratulations on your birthday Monday, and the hope that the coming year and those that follow will be good ever for you. I'm sorry we won't be able to celebrate this year as we have done on other occasions. Sincerely, Bud."

Barnett did not reply.

CLIENT AND CASE HIGHLIGHTS
FROM THE GREENEBAUM ERA

While law firms over time may take on the personal characteristics of their most influential founders or producers, it is the firms' clients who contribute most to their reputations. A law firm and its clients nearly always become closely linked—by the intensity of joint effort; by sharing closely-held secrets; by winning and losing on the legal battlefield together; and by having common interests. Inevitably strong friendships develop, tying firm and client closer than a mere commercial relationship.

The Greenebaum firm has always been fortunate to have close friends among its clients. Sam Greenebaum's clients were nearly all personal friends, as were Barney Barnett's. In fact, Barnett's big house on the corner of Millvale and Park Boundary Road was constantly full of out-of-town luminaries in full social swing, unwinding from, or on the verge of, important meetings in town. In the Greenebaum/Barnett years those clients and friends represented as colorful a cast of characters as any law firm in Louisville has ever had.

J. Graham Brown was the firm's biggest client from the beginning; a more interesting and influential person in Louisville history would be difficult to find. Reportedly the richest man in Kentucky, Brown was a short, rotund, fedora-wearing character who lived in the Brown Hotel. His meetings with the firm were usually held in Brown's private offices on the second floor of the hotel. He was a lifelong bachelor who loved horse racing and owned an impressive number of stakes-winning thoroughbreds. Though best-known for his hotel and real estate holdings, Brown's main source of wealth came from his vast timber holdings and lumber businesses in Georgia, Alabama, and northern Florida.

The firm did virtually all of Brown's legal work from 1952 until 1968, when Brown left the firm and took Charlie Wood with him. Brown died a year later, at age 86.

Less well-known in Kentucky but perhaps even more wealthy than Brown was **J. Howard Marshall**, an oil and gas man who was an important Greenebaum client for ten years. Barnett had met Marshall somewhere along the way, and in true Barnett fashion had struck up a close friendship that had turned into a business relationship. Marshall's business in the early 1950s was Signal Oil and Gas, headquartered in Los Angeles. The firm was hired to do Signal's in-house tax work. When Signal merged with Union Texas Petroleum, the firm got involved at that company's Houston, Texas headquarters. And eventually when Marshall merged that company into Allied Chemical, the firm did their tax work in New York. The firm also handled Marshall's interest in Kingwood Oil in Oklahoma City, which included tax and securities work.

Ed Perry and Bob Doll were in the midst of nearly all Marshall's oil and gas tax work, and recall that one of the most unusual cases of their careers was a tax appeal for Union Texas Petroleum. It involved a meeting with IRS agents in Houston. In their experience, meetings with IRS people usually took place in their offices or, if the meeting was informal, at a coffee shop. Here in Houston the IRS agents said they wanted to meet over lunch at the Petroleum Club. This was highly unusual, but Perry and Doll went along. "So we get a room up there," Perry says, "and the waiter came over and asks if we'd like a drink before lunch. Before I can say no, the IRS guy says, 'I'd like to have a martini.'I look over at Doll, who is wondering what's going on, but we say, 'We'll have one, too.' Then the waiter comes back in a few minutes, and the man orders another one. We order another one, too. By this time I'm thinking we're not going to have any problems with these guys. We're eating and drinking away. After lunch they clean off the table, and we start our meeting, and these IRS guys turn into the toughest s.o.b.'s we've ever seen. I mean, they didn't give us anything. Turns out they weren't being nice guys at all; they just wanted a nice lunch and a couple of drinks. On us."

And finally, the firm prepared a will and did estate planning for Marshall in the early 1960s. This is significant only for the fact that Marshall, thirty years later at age 86, married a Playboy model named Anna Nicole Smith, whose claim to the Marshall fortune after his death a short while later caused an intra-family lawsuit which became worldwide news.

$$\approx$$

Howard Koven was a name partner in the large Chicago law firm Friedman, Koven. It happened that his negotiation adversary in a matter in the 1950s was Barney Barnett. After settling the case Koven and Barnett became great friends. One thing led to another and Koven chose Barnett and the Greenebaum firm to become his firm's surrogate tax department, since they did not do tax work at that time. Barnett agreed, and in short order the Greenebaum firm was handling tax cases for Howard Koven's and Bill Friedman's clients—**Conrad Hilton** of hotel fame; the **Revson** family and its company, Revlon; and **Jerry Wexler** who was the real estate mogul of Chicago, owning the Drake Hotel and many more commercial properties.

≈)

Max Fisher from Detroit was another notable client from this era. A friend of J. Howard Marshall's, he was a wealthy oil and gas tycoon who had a Louisville connection through his wife, a daughter of Ben Snyder of the department store of the same name. The firm did both tax and foundation work for Fisher for many years. This Fisher/Barnett friendship continued after Barnett's break with the firm, through their mutual interest in the United Jewish Appeal

≈)

Sam Snead became a longtime Greenebaum client after becoming friends with Barnett during one of Barnett's frequent stays at the Greenbrier. In the mid-1960s's Snead was still a professional golfer, but he was making more money in his golf cart rental business than in his tournament play. Bob Doll and Larry Leatherman were instrumental in setting up Snead's corporations for that business, and John Greenebaum became his estate planner and investment lawyer for the next twenty years.

Snead once attended a 10:00 a.m. gathering of all his attorneys and accountants in Barnett's office at the Kentucky Home Life Building. While the suits huddled over his affairs, Snead sat on the couch, fidgeting. He asked if he could order a hamburger and a beer. He could. Then he ordered another beer. By the time someone looked up to ask him a question, he was stretched out on the couch, asleep.

⋍

During the 1960s there was a conglomerate mentality in the corporate world, and many companies hurried to acquire and diversify their operations. Often this entailed tax rulings and advice. Barney Barnett had a relationship with an attorney named Eddie Ginsburg, who was in control of a company called Rusco, Inc. An effort was undertaken to obtain profitable companies that in each case required a tax ruling. Barnett and Bob Doll spent a great deal of time in Beverly Hills, where the Beverly Hilton was established as headquarters. Barney spent most of his efforts in negotiations for the target and Bob did the paperwork. In one case, **Jack Haley**, who had played the lovable Tin Man in "The Wizard of Oz", was the principal of the company to be acquired. Doll recalls that businessman Haley was not the Tin Man at all, but one of the most disagreeable people with whom he had ever negotiated a deal.

⋍

In the mid to late 1950s, Barney Barnett became involved with **Ed Merkel** and The Madison Fund, which was a closed-end investment company listed on the New York Stock Exchange. The Fund owned a major interest in a railroad, known as the "Katy Railroad," that had accumulated a big tax loss. Barney was given the job of obtaining profitable companies to merge into the railroad company so that its losses would be carried forward against the new company's profits. Bob Doll and Barnett spent a great deal of time in Dallas, Oklahoma City, New York and other places, and Bob eventually obtained a tax ruling from the IRS that the losses could be carried over, much to the success of the Railroad.

One of the early large tax cases acquired by Barnett and mostly handled by Bob Doll was the Ralph E. Mills Co., a contractor in Frankfort, Kentucky. Mills, along with Morrison-Knudson, J. R. Jones Construction Co. and several other companies had built North African air bases during the war. This was a worldwide business undertaking that included dams in India, Africa and Egypt. When the war was over, Congress adopted what was called the "excess profit tax" that had a complicated process of using various accounting formulas to compute normal profits, taking into consideration inflation, costs, etc. If the profit exceeded the computation there was a huge penalty tax, up to 80% of the excess.

The Morrison-Knudson law firm out of Boise, Idaho was large and presumably capable, but because Barnett had charmed James B. McClary, the CEO, the Greenebaum firm became the lead counsel even though Bob Doll, who handled the case, was a least twenty years younger than the other five lawyers. Ultimately the case was favorably settled.

The only downside was many months spent in Boise. After working all day and into the night, in a dry state with no bars, there wasn't much else to do but gather at the local Arthur Murray Dance Studio. Some of the lawyers became very good dancers.

≈)

The Ashland Oil Case

In the late 1960s the firm interviewed for and was subsequently engaged to protest and defend Ashland Oil, Inc., in a federal income tax audit. Prior to the engagement Ashland Oil had been represented in tax matters by New York law firms. In substantially all of Greenebaum's previous tax cases, the issues had generally involved tens of thousands of dollars, but in this new case, most issues were in the hundreds of thousands of dollars and the total tax involved was in the millions of dollars. Clearly this was the biggest tax case in which the firm had ever been involved. The lead attorney for the firm was Larry Leatherman and he was assisted by Tom Brown. There were literally dozens of issues, both foreign and domestic, involving areas of federal tax law with which they had only general knowledge. They spent many hours in the Tax Library studying the tax law and formulating defenses and positions. A couple of months was required to prepare and file the protest and many more months of negotiation with the IRS which ultimately ended in a significant settlement victory for Ashland Oil. As a result of this case, Ashland Oil, Inc., engaged the firm to work on all of its other federal tax audits for over two decades until the company switched tax Vice Presidents and decided to handle all of its federal audits in house.

The Ashland case was the beginning of the Big Tax Case era for the Tax Department. As a result of that case, the Tax Department established a reputation at the IRS for excellent tax analysis and hard negotiation. The quantity and quality of the work the Tax Department performed for Ashland Oil required the firm to hire more tax attorneys, and as a result the Tax Department personnel ultimately expanded to where it is today. Virtually every Tax Department attorney (and many others outside the Tax Department) from the late 1960s to the present has at one time or another worked on Ashland Oil tax issues.

One of the big tax issues for oil and gas companies in the 1960s involved foreign operations, and in Ashland's case it involved drilling operations in Venezuela. It required a particular expertise in U.S. taxation of foreign subsidiaries, and the firm, through Larry Leatherman, was on the leading edge of that knowledge. "Leatherman knew more about that than anyone at the IRS did," says Tom Brown. "On that subject we knew we could hold our own with any tax firm in the U.S."

⇁

Ed Perry's Shopping Trips

From 1968 to 1984 Ed Perry perhaps spent more time on the road than any other Greenebaum attorney. His acquisition sprees took him all over the country, first on behalf of Bill Matthews, and then for Bernard Meidinger.

Matthews, owner of the *Shelbyville News* (and brother of Bob Matthews, a Greenebaum partner) in 1968 organized eight county newspapers into one company, Newspapers, Inc., and set out on a multi-year growth strategy that sent Perry around the country acquiring newspapers. "We probably bought 25 newspapers over the years," Perry says.

In the early 1970s Perry started representing Meidinger & Associates, whose growth strategy involved the acquisition of employee benefit consulting firms. For thirteen years Perry traveled to nearly every major American city, closing 30 buy-outs for Meidinger. In 1982 Peggy Lyndrup, whom Perry had mentored at the firm, left to become Meidinger's Vice President and General Counsel and remained there until the company was sold to William M. Mercer in 1984, after which she returned to the firm after much courting by Perry.

⇁

The Metridata Computing Transactions

One of the first things Ivan Diamond did when he got to the firm in 1968 was to take a company public for General Dillman Rash and J. David Grissom. The company was Metridata, a computer time-sharing operation which had no earnings, no assets, and no customers. The company brought in a fellow named Ernie

Bianco, a time sharing guru whom they had hired away from General Electric, for the initial meetings. Diamond had read the prospectuses of several time-sharing companies and started asking questions. From the answers he got back, it dawned on him that this company did not have a business; they did not have any definitive idea of what the business should be; and were looking to Diamond to tell them what the prospectus should say and what business the company should be in. "I felt that was rather a heavy burden for such a young lawyer to start out on his first deal," Diamond said. But he took the company public, got it through the SEC, and the company's financial statements indeed showed it was a development stage company, meaning it had no assets or earnings. It had only dreams and stock, which shot up dramatically. ("In 1998 and 1999, when I saw the dot-com companies soar, I said to myself, 'I've seen all this before.'")

The new company grew a bit, then got to the point where the owners needed to sell out. At this point Sun Oil came along with its young MBAs, whose mission was to make acquisitions and diversify the oil company. Diamond flew to Sunoco headquarters near Radford, Pennsylvania to negotiate the sale. The sale price was two or three million dollars, a footnote on the balance sheet of Sunoco. "But I noticed immediately," said Diamond, "that Sun Oil's counsel seemed to treat the deal like it was General Motors buying Ford. The paperwork was unusually detailed. I flew up there many times."

The closing took almost a week, and Diamond claims it is still the record for the longest closing in the firm's history. "The Sun Oil lawyer was overly cautious, to say the least," Diamond says. The pre-closing was on a Monday morning in Louisville. Monday night they ate at Casa Grisanti, consuming a case of wine in a wonderful celebration. They were to close the next day. "We got there Tuesday," Diamond says, "and their lawyer says, 'We've got to have this, we've got to have that, we are not ready to close.'

Day turned to night. They came back the next day. They worked all day and all night. They came back Thursday and still weren't finished. Diamond says, "My partners were dropping by saying, 'Wasn't this deal supposed to close Tuesday? Is it blowing up? What are you doing?"

Diamond had ordered champagne and it had been held since the previous Tuesday at the Top of the Tower restaurant of the First National Tower. Finally it was Friday afternoon. As happens in negotiations, it is not one's mental capacity that wins but one's physical strength. They had been locked in rooms day and night for almost a week, and the Sunoco lawyers did not want to spend the weekend in Louisville. They wanted to go home. As 5:00 o'clock approached on Friday the Sunoco business people handed Diamond a check for the sale price. Diamond called the restaurant, and the champagne flowed. "At the party, I noticed their lawyer with a legal pad, writing. He still wanted something else, even after we had the check." They partied into the night, and had to send somebody out to bring in more champagne reinforcements. "But we earned it," Diamond says. A year later, the losses Sun Oil absorbed in their first year of operating the company almost exactly equaled the purchase price.

<hr/>

Leaving the Greenebaum Era

By every measure, the 1969 merger with the Jones-Cherry firm was a watershed event for the Greenebaum firm. The new firm—Greenebaum, Grissom, Doll, Matthews and Boone—had become the largest law firm in Kentucky, with 25 members. The many new clients that came with Grissom, especially Extendicare (later Humana), Kentucky Fried Chicken and Meidinger and Associates, were all on the verge of growth that would keep the Greenebaum firm busy for the next twenty years. The innovative specialties of the firm—tax, securities, employee benefits—flourished in the new, fast-paced entrepreneurial environment. The firm split into two locations, with some members, including Bob Doll, relocating to the Portland Federal Building, never to return to the Kentucky Home Life Building.

The firm had hit the big time. Everything had changed, for the better. The days of roll-top desks and secretarial dictation were long in the past, and the Greenebaum Era was over.

A. Robert Doll

THE DOLL ERA
1969—1986

In 1969 the law firm of Greenebaum, Grissom, Doll, Matthews and Boone was on a roll. It was the largest law firm in Kentucky and was enjoying a tremendous upswing in business and reputation. Sam Greenebaum was the *eminence grise* of the firm, still on top of the masthead, and still involved in the firm's affairs, but it was Bob Doll's show now, and everybody knew it. The momentum of the merger with Jones-Cherry, and in particular the addition of David Grissom, had put the firm in the company of people and corporations that were changing the face of downtown Louisville and making the business environment younger, newer, and more exciting.

For law firms generally, the 1970s were the golden age of growth and development. Taxation, real estate, finance, securities, mergers and acquisitions, antitrust, international contracts, estates and trusts, employment law, white collar crime, and many others were the new facets of law requiring competent and specialized legal services in a booming growth-driven economy.

≈)

David Grissom was significant in this new dynamic. He was the one who brought the firm Kentucky Fried Chicken, the Kentucky Colonels professional basketball team, Meidinger and Associates, Metridata Computing, WLKY- TV, and the growing nursing home giant, Extendicare. Grissom had come to the firm as a full partner, but many perceived that he was still uncertain about whether he wanted to be a lawyer or a businessman. The firm's arrangement with him was that he could work part-time with Extendicare and part-time with the firm. But the migration back and forth between the firm and Extendicare was not difficult, since Extendicare's office was one floor up from the firm's new offices in the Portland Federal building.

Though business would eventually become Grissom's predominant occupation, it would be incorrect to say that his interest in the firm, and law in general, was luke-warm at this time. In May of 1971, almost two years after joining, he circulated to all lawyers an article he had read in *Law Notes* called "Building an Outstanding Law Firm," and attached these encouraging words: "I am encouraged because I think we compare favorably with most of the points in the article. All of us recognize, I think, that the firm may be on the verge of an exciting growth period, and the opportunities for our firm to become the undisputed No.1 firm in Louisville and a dominant force in the affairs of our community have never been greater. We have the technical specialists that no one else in Louisville has, and we have youth and enthusiasm, which can be a great substitute for long years of experience."

The other lawyers from Jones-Cherry also had an immediate impact. Bill Boone brought a good stable of clients and was well regarded as a trial lawyer. One of his main clients was V.V Cooke. Boone had gone to Baylor University with V.V. Cooke, Jr., and brought with him to the firm all of the Cooke automobile businesses. Brooks Senn represented the Kentucky Bankers Association and was highly regarded as a banking attorney. Marvin Hirn was a well respected litigator. Bill Ballard, who had only been at Jones-Cherry a few months, had come from the tax division of the Department of Justice; and Ralston Steenrod was a young family law expert and a member of the State Crime Commission.

Ballard did not last long, leaving to become Extendicare's in-house counsel in 1970. But the firm added six more lawyers—James Boring, Ellen Pedley (Larry Pedley's wife), Maurice (Larry) Miller, John (Jack) Reisz, Dan Kemp, and Robert Van Young—and was still the state's largest firm in 1970. It began to look as if the firm wanted its size to be its strength. But that was not the case. Bob Doll says, "I didn't necessarily think we had to be the biggest firm in town. I thought we should have sufficient size to attract major clients, but quality was the more important thing." And quality for Doll came from following the work philosophy he had developed over the previous twenty years. His vision involved three tenets: First, hiring quality people who were people-oriented and goal-oriented; second, getting the work done promptly with no procrastination; and third, charging a premium fee. "If you get a good result and get it fast," Doll says, "you're entitled to a premium fee, and clients agree." At times he had more specific visions—to start a new specialty or beef up a specialty—but Doll simply wanted the firm to be a full service, commercial, regional law firm that worked hard for its clients.

⁌

The Cantor Report

In 1970 Sam Greenebaum and Bob Doll were still the alpha/omega of Greenebaum management. "We were completely unstructured at that time," Bob Doll says. "Compensation was still determined by Mr. Greenebaum and me. We had no committees. We decided what the compensation was, just as Sam and Barney had done from the very beginning." But the growing size of the firm began to demand a new style of organization. The firm brought in the Daniel L. Cantor Company of Philadelphia, the preeminent consultant to the legal profession, to advise the firm on ways it could improve management and performance. Cantor recommended that the firm adopt a number of new management tools:

1. An objective formula to determine compensation.
Each lawyer would receive points for origination, for client responsibility, and for work produced. Each area would be weighted, to come up with a total points value. Bob Doll installed this point system, but used it as a guide only, feeling there were other factors to take into account. Each attorney's activities during the preceding year were analyzed based on the attorneys own submissions, the observations of the newly developed department heads, and input from other lawyers. Among the matters affecting compensation were hours worked, fees participated in, civic activities, professional activities, firm activities, and teamwork with other attorneys.

Although each attorney was expected to devote his full-time and best efforts to the performance of quality legal services on a prompt, efficient basis, there was no minimum hourly quota set per year for each attorney, as Cantor had recommended. "We always felt that different attorneys can work at different paces in different lengths of time in order to perform the type of legal service required," said Doll.

2. Set up a junior partnership category.
Under this plan some associates were made junior partners. They had no capital invested in the firm and had no percentage of the profits, but the firm allocated a certain share of the profits as a pool and then divided it among the junior partners. This plan only lasted one year before it was abandoned.

3. Two committees to deal with the compensation formula. Two committees were created: first, a Business Credit Committee to sort out credits that were in question or were not clear; and second, a Compensation Committee which was the forerunner of the Executive Committee. The Compensation Committee met only once or twice a year. Doll would take his suggested percentages of compensation to the committee based on the points formula and other criteria. Generally his percentages would be adopted, but sometimes they were tweaked. "In the latter part of my tenure there was more tweaking than there was earlier," Doll admits.

4. Divide the firm into Sections.

The firm broke lawyers down into their specialties; a chairman, who was charged with coordinating work among that section and training younger associates in the section, was appointed. This allowed cells to concentrate on their specialty with their own leadership. The first sections were Tax, which Larry Leatherman chaired; Securities, which Irv Eisinger chaired; Corporate and Employee Benefits, which Ed Perry chaired; Labor, which John Greenebaum chaired; Real Estate, Banking and Finance, which Michael Shaikun chaired; and Litigation, which Bob Matthews chaired.

The chief executive of the firm, even after Cantor, was the Managing Partner, and the Managing Partner—on paper—was Sam Greenebaum until his death in 1973. But Bob Doll ran the firm. The duties of the Managing Partner were increasing with the size of the firm, but Doll continued to practice law on a full-time basis. In the early days Doll figured his management time at about ten percent of his day; toward the end it was thirty percent of his day. Doll guesses that Larry Leatherman's was more like 50/50. Dolls regime was easier than Leatherman's, he says, "because not many people argued with me. I pretty well made all the major decisions. That doesn't mean I wouldn't talk to people. Larry became my chief assistant, so to speak. I talked to others; in fact I would always talk to someone first before making a big decision about them. It wasn't a question of being isolated. I was the managing partner, succeeding Sam, and that's the way we operated." But, he admits, "Others may perceive my administration differently."

⁀

Van Young, 1970

Arriving in 1970 from the law school at the University of Louisville was R. Van Young. In his 32 years with the firm Young has worked in commercial litigation; administrative law; product liability; securities; and construction law. At first he was a protégé of Bill Boone in the litigation department, then went on to handle major asbestos cases where he obtained favorable judgments for his clients. He recalls the day when Sam Greenebaum circulated a memo in which he asked, in light of the many new lawyers in the firm, that full names, not initials, be added to the bottom of all memos. He signed it "SLG."

⁀

Growth in Litigation

By 1971 the growing importance of the litigation section was hard to miss. The "litigious society" was abloom, and the firm had six full-time litigators—Bob Matthews, Bill Boone, Don Balleisen, Marvin Hirn, Van Young, and Sam Manley. Up until this time litigation firms did insurance defense work mostly, but the Greenebaum firm had never done any. In fact, in twenty years no one had ever put the words "Greenebaum" and "litigator" together seriously. But the pendulum had started swinging, and wouldn't stop for the next thirty years. By the turn of the century, litigation would be the largest practice group in the firm.

Larry Banks, 1971

After graduation from Duke University Law School in 1967 Larry Banks went to work in California as a litigator for Kindel and Anderson, and stayed long enough to meet and marry his wife, Julie. He then moved back to his native North Carolina, passing the bar there in 1970. After six months he took a job with the U.S. Tax Court in Washington, D.C., and studied for his Masters in tax at Georgetown in the evenings. At about this time Larry Leatherman, who was an attorney and advisor to the Court, was looking for a new tax attorney for the Greenebaum firm. Leatherman contacted a staff person on the Court and asked for a recommendation; Banks' name surfaced, and in the spring he agreed to an interview with the firm in Louisville. He found it to be very much like his hometown of Greensboro, North Carolina, and in short order Banks joined the firm, just after receiving his LL.M. from Georgetown in 1971.

Banks, now retired from the firm, worked at Greenebaum for 30 years, primarily with Bob Doll and Larry Leatherman, and a bit with Ed Perry in employee benefits. "Larry and Bob were my mentors," he says. In his years with the firm he also did real estate acquisitions, dispositions, and deal work for small companies, as well as critically important liaison work in Lexington after the McDonald merger.

He feels his most important work, though, was in his capacity as the firm's recruiter. He says, "I'm very proud of all the great people I hired for the firm over the years, especially people like Peggy Lyndrup."

A Bullitt merger?

In 1972 the firm flirted with Bullitt, Dawson & Tarrant in a short-lived merger courtship. It went far enough that financial documents were exchanged, but there was never enough enthusiasm from either side to make it happen. It would have been an interesting marriage, though, considering the origins of both firms and the relationships among past and present attorneys. In the end neither firm saw an obvious advantage to be gained by merger, but in hindsight it perhaps looks more intriguing than ever to the principals involved.

John Greenebaum resigns

In the same year the firm added four more lawyers, but lost one associate and two of its partners. John Greenebaum was a surprise departure. "I resigned from the law firm," he said. "Its structure necessarily involved some disciplines such as billing by the hour, and in many instances I could do this. But I wanted to be part of the businesses with which I worked; I wanted to help them grow. In many instances this involved being an equity participant. I could sometimes take stock in lieu of a fee when opportunities became available. At that time, this approach was a no-no for highly regimented law firms. My father was not pleased by my departure, but expressed only encouragement."

The younger Greenebaum was on his own for a year before learning that Barney Barnett wanted to practice law again. National Industries was not doing so well, and Barnett's real estate investments had lost money. Barnett and Greenebaum started a new firm called Barnett, Greenebaum, Martin and McConnell. In addition to Barney Barnett and John Greenebaum the partners included future Chief Judge of the Court of Appeals Boyce Martin and future Senator Mitch McConnell. Their first associate was Charlie Owen. After Martin and McConnell left, their firm merged after three years to become Barnett, Alagia, Greenebaum, Miller and Senn, but after two years John Greenebaum left again to become a sole practitioner.

⤸

At about this time Frank Quickert (known as FXQ) left the firm as a partner to join another firm. It did not work out, and Quickert returned to the firm one year later as an associate. Ralston Steenrod also left the firm, which was not a surprise to many. He had been perceived to be unhappy with the merger in 1969, and left to join what became the Stites-Harbison firm.

⤸

The Move to First National Tower

In 1973 the firm moved into the new First National Tower, one of the new, modern office buildings to punctuate the Louisville skyline. The firm had considered moving into the other bank tower, Citizens, but at Ed Perry's urging had settled on First National. "We had represented the bank when they did the deal, after all," Perry said, "and we owed them another look." He adds, "And thank God we did, because when we came back they gave us a better deal."

Nothing symbolized the "new" Greenebaum firm more than this move. The firm needed the space for all its new people, and it was a practical decision, but it meant much more than that. The center of town had moved back to Main Street along the river, and the Greenebaum firm had moved to that part of town, too—the center of commerce, the center of the entrepreneurial milieu, the center of the new economy. It was time to move out of the darker halls of the previous generations' lair, the Kentucky Home Life Building, and into the light of the new generation's gleaming tower of glass and steel. This was the start of a whole new attitude—of excitement and importance to all the new possibilities in town.

David Grissom leaves

It was an excitement that eclipsed even the recent departure of David Grissom. Grissom had left to go with Extendicare full time. "I begged him to stay," said Bob Doll. "I said, 'Whatever you want, dollar-wise, we'll do it.' But he said his interests lay elsewhere." His interests, apparently, were not with Extendicare, either. By the end of 1973 he acceded to Maury Johnson's wishes and became president of Citizens Fidelity Bank, leapfrogging over a passel of longtime Citizens senior vice-presidents. With that he severed not only his practice with the Greenebaum firm, but also his general practice of law, as his colleagues David Jones and Wendell Cherry had done before him. Bob Doll, who still considered Grissom a friend, negotiated his employment contract with the bank. But in short order the firm dropped his name. The new firm was named Greenebaum, Doll, Matthews and Boone.

Sam Greenebaum Dies

In September of 1973 Sam Greenebaum left for Scotland on his annual grouse shooting vacation, in apparently stable health. Earlier in the summer he had experienced severe back pain, but by the fall he was somewhat ambulatory and he felt fine to travel. It would have taken more than some pain to keep him at home; he never missed this trip. But while there he had fallen ill, and he was returned to the States in a wheelchair. A bone scan revealed he had cancer. Doctors suspected it was in the spine, which would account for his back pain, but the exact location was never really determined. For three months he lay in Jewish Hospital in worsening condition, until he died in December.

His unexpected death was the final confirmation that the old days were truly over. At age 71 he had been a full generation older than Bob Doll, who was 46. To the partners it felt like the death of a parent. To Sam Greenebaum's peers in other law firms, his death was felt to be the end of the moderating influence that had kept the aggressive instincts of the younger Greenebaum lawyers in line.

Greenebaum's death jarred the firm emotionally, but not professionally. Just as families quickly adjust to a new line of authority after death, so the firm adjusted, too. Bob Doll was no longer the shadow executive-in-charge, but became the official Managing Partner.

⌐)

The Sam Greenebaum Portrait

In September, when Sam Greenebaum had returned and discovered his condition was dire, Bob Doll had initiated the painting of a portrait of Mr. Greenebaum, in hopes of having it completed in time for him to see it before his death. Ed Perry was put in charge of getting it done. "I went to New York," Perry says, "and looked at a whole bunch of stuff and ended up with an artist named C.J. Fox." C.J. Fox had done portraits of John Tarrant and William Marshall Bullitt to everyone in that firm's satisfaction, so Perry authorized Fox to begin. "Over the next few weeks I kept telling Fox that Mr. Greenebaum's health was deteriorating," Perry says, "and I wished he would hurry up. We wanted to present the portrait before it was too late." So Fox finished the portrait, but it arrived about five days after Mr. Greenebaum's death. Even so, Bob Doll and Ed Perry took it over to Rita Greenebaum and John Greenebaum, and both seemed very happy with it. "We got a really good painting," Perry says.

The epilog to the story is that five years later Perry was reading in *Time* magazine about a tax case, and was astonished to read that the taxpayer was one C.J. Fox. The tax issue was the deduction of the amounts he had paid to other artists to have paintings done for him. Fox in fact had done none of the portraits at all, but had subcontracted them to other artists, which fact detracted not one bit from everyone's high opinion of the Greenebaum portrait. It hangs today in the main conference room on the 33rd floor of the Greenebaum Louisville offices. But in 1980 when Angus McDonald died unexpectedly just two years after the merger with his firm, Bob Doll had said, "We've got to get a portrait done of Angus." Perry had said, "Okay, I'll look around." Doll said, "No, I'm going to call C.J. Fox." To which Perry said, "Godammit, we're not calling C.J. Fox!"

New Attorneys

1973 also saw the arrival of three new attorneys—Jerry Abramson, Walter Butt, and Buck Wiseman. This was the last class of new law school graduates to have known Sam Greenebaum personally to any great degree. Only Wiseman is still with the firm today. Butt (now Dr. Walter Butler) is a practicing psychiatrist, and Abramson in the fall of 2002 was re-elected Mayor of the newly merged Louisville-Jefferson County Metro after practicing law privately from 1998 to 2002.

Buck Wiseman, 1973

Buck Wiseman came to the firm from the University of Virginia Law School with no specialty in mind, and in the beginning was doing a little bit of everything—securities, tax, corporate, and litigation. He was cannon fodder for every lawyer who needed help with something. Wiseman relates what it was like to be a young associate at Greenebaum in those years. "Larry Leatherman was notorious for marching down the hall looking for some poor associate to tackle a project that was going to take all night. So if we happened to be in the library and heard him coming, we would scramble up on top of the bookshelves and hide until he corraled somebody else." But eventually Leatherman found everybody. Once Leatherman called Wiseman into a huge project at noon on a Thursday. "But Larry," Wiseman pleaded, "I'm leaving on vacation at noon tomorrow!" Leatherman looked at him and said, "Well, hell, you've got 24 hours!"

Wiseman today is the Chair of the Real Estate and Finance Practice group.

⌐)

Eric Ison, 1974

Eric Ison was a California-raised graduate of the University of the South, who clerked at the firm in 1973 after being provisionally hired by Sam Greenebaum during a recruiting stop at Vanderbilt Law School. He invited Ison to come to Louisville, meet the partners and see if he liked it before signing on. On arrival in Louisville Ison went to see Mr. Greenebaum, who asked, "How was the drive?" Ison told him that he had flown to Louisville. "And I could tell by his face that he was very disappointed in me," Ison recalls. He said, 'Why on earth didn't you drive? I make that drive all the time.' And I said, 'Mr. Greenebaum, I don't own a car.' So he forgave me." Armed with the best in American legal education, Ison's first job as a clerk was to shelve all the law books (along with John Stites) that were still in cartons from the move from the Kentucky Home Life Building to the First National Tower. After that summer with the firm he returned to get his law degree at Vanderbilt, and returned in the summer of 1974 to begin his Greenebaum career.

Soon after his arrival, Ison was told by Larry Leatherman that he was going to make him a tax lawyer, to which Ison reports he said, "There's no way." Leatherman said Ison was going to work half the year with him in corporate tax and half the year with Marty Weinberg in estates and trusts. Unlike others of the firm who had made their careers in taxation, Ison knew he wouldn't like it, and, in fact, didn't like it. "After six months," Ison says, "I was going to leave, because it wasn't for me." Bob Doll, in a moment of inspiration, switched Ison to litigation (which needed him), and the rest is history. Ison worked with Marvin Hirn, helping him with his mixed practice of litigation and commercial lending.

Ison was present for the growth and development of the litigation practice at Greenebaum practically from its inception. His explanation: "In good times and bad there is litigation to do. It grew little by little, until it got big. When lawsuits became more prevalent in the '80s, we got the work, and when you've got the work you add the bodies." Eventually Ison became the head of the litigation department, and his cases (to be discussed later) are among the most important jury trials in the firm's history.

Today Ison is Member-in-Charge of the Louisville Office and Chair of the Litigation and Dispute Resolution Practice.

John Stites, 1974

After an undergraduate degree from Yale and a law degree from the University of Kentucky, native Louisvillian John Stites joined the firm in 1974. His initial interest was in securities work, and for a year or so worked with Ivan Diamond until the recession slowed the department. His work then turned to a coal and energy specialty, which is still the largest part of his practice today.

John Cummins, 1975

In 1975 John Cummins, a graduate of Brown and Harvard

Law School, joined the firm, working initially with Don Balleisen in litigation, then moving to trust and estate work with Martin Weinberg, John Treitz and Eric Ison. Although the firm had grown much larger by 1975, Cummins recalls the firm feeling small and close knit. Maybe that was because of the proximity of Larry Leatherman. "He never used the phone system," Cummins says. "I just remember him yelling, 'Cummins!'"

Trusts and Estates has always been a strong department at the firm because of the tax component. Tax rules change annually, and when the firm strategizes the movement of large sums of money from one generation to the next, or from one entity to another, cutting-edge tax expertise is at a premium. Cummins has stayed in this legal area for over twenty years, but that is not unusual for estate lawyers. "It takes two or three years to get the basic mastery of this area," he says. "It's technical and tax-overlaid, so lawyers who work in wills and estates tend to stay there."

But, as Cummins discovered, there is more required than technical ability. There are always emotional and psychological factors at work in creating trusts and wills, and the family dynamics that can occur following a death can place the attorney/executor in the center of dramas that are constantly fascinating. Disputes and contested wills are all-too-familiar to Cummins. "They say if you want to get to know someone, share an inheritance with them," he says.

But Cummins also gets a lot of satisfaction from his work. It is highly personal and private, with lots of one-on-one sharing of thoughts and sensitive plans with many affluent people who invariably are accomplished and intriguing. "I spend a lot of time with interesting, bright people," he says, "and that makes my work one of the most interesting and rewarding practice groups in the firm."

Cummins was the editor-in-chief of the firm's *Law Letter* from 1985 to 1998, and is the current Chair of the Trusts and

Estates Practice Group.

Charles "Chuck" Fassler, 1976

In the proud tradition of tax specialists at the firm, Chuck Fassler, a law graduate of the University of Wisconsin and the NYU tax program, joined the Greenebaum ranks in 1976. He is regarded as among the most gifted of the tax attorneys who have ever resided at the firm, and that is strong praise indeed, considering the rare competence that Barnett, Doll, Perry, and Leatherman, among others, brought to the firm. In addition to taxation, Fassler practices in the areas of partnerships, limited liability companies, compensation matters, and real estate law.

The Altman-Weil Survey

By 1976 the Altman-Weil Survey of Law Firm Economics placed the Greenebaum firm in the top rank of law firms in Kentucky, which Bob Doll noted in a memo to all lawyers in May, 1976. His conclusions from reading the Survey were: "We gross more per lawyer because we work longer hours"; "Our expenses per lawyer are significantly less"; and "The conclusion, as I see it, is that we work harder and longer than most comparative firms, and our work expenses are lower." Doll liked that. He signed off with, "LET'S KEEP IT GOING!"

April Fools Day

Two lawyers, John Treitz and Walter Butt, left the firm in 1976. Buck Wiseman and Sam Manley would have exited that year, too, if Bob Doll and Marvin Hirn hadn't had a sense of humor. It was April 1, and Wiseman and Manly were in the mood for an

April Fool's joke. As they recall, they had just received one of Bob Doll's standard inter-office memos announcing the departure of another lawyer ("We've enjoyed working with Joe, and we wish him the best in his future endeavors..."), but whatever the case, they were inspired to compose a tongue-in-cheek inter-office memo—this one announcing the resignation of Bob Doll so that he could run Bob Gable's gubernatorial campaign. They signed Marvin Hirn's name to it and sent it to Doll's office. Doll got a good laugh out of it and, not knowing that Hirn didn't really send it, decided to pay Hirn back by sending out a joke memo of his own. Doll's memo announced to the firm that Marvin Hirn was resigning immediately to pursue his woodworking hobby full time. Hirn, in his office and unaware of any of this, received the memo saying he was resigning, and all he could think of was that Bob Doll was trying to fire him. Wiseman, passing by Hirn's office and seeing the smoke coming out of Hirn's ears, quickly fessed up, and today swears that Hirn finally laughed about it...after a few days.

Charles Lavelle, 1976

Charles "Chaz" Lavelle clerked at the firm in the summer of 1976 while attending the University of Kentucky law school. "I knew I wanted to be a tax lawyer," he says, "and from what I could perceive of law firms, this was the place to be."

He worked with Larry Leatherman, who became a mentor and role model for Lavelle. "Larry Leatherman was my mentor, the guy who made me what I am. I always thought it was a privilege to get a job here, and I was going to do anything he asked me to do. He was extremely loyal. As long as you were out there trying to do your very best, he was behind you 100%."

He had only been clerking with the firm for six weeks

when Leatherman assigned him to the AMCA Resources case. It was Ed Weinberg's deal, but he needed help. AMCA wanted to acquire coal reserves and operating mines from the Badgett family. The deal was mostly done but not closed. Lavelle closed it, and returned to UK as the only third year law student who closed a $50 million deal on summer break.

Leatherman hired him full-time in the summer of 1977. "I believe I am the last lawyer hired when we were on one floor, in one city," he says. For the next fifteen years he and Leatherman worked on tax controversy cases, with an acquisition or two per year. Leatherman's work ethic rubbed off on him. "Larry didn't claim he was the brightest of everybody; he thought the way he was successful was by out-working everybody else. He was a clever and insightful guy, but that's how he thought about himself." Lavelle thinks it permeated the firm. "There is the thought here at Greenebaum that we're all blue-collar workers. We weren't born rich, very few of us grew up in country clubs. We got here by doing good work."

Today Lavelle is the Chair of the Tax and Employee Benefits Practice Group

⁐

Mark Ament, 1977

After Duke University Law School and an LL.M (taxation) from the University of Miami School of Law in 1977, Mark S. Ament joined the firm. He began as a corporate and real estate lawyer, and has developed a practice involving all aspects of law of concern to entrepreneurs, especially in the technology and health care sectors — venture funding, startup strategies, corporate structuring, and mergers and acquisitions. He is currently (2003) Co-Chair of the Emerging Technologies Group.

The McDonald Merger

By 1978 Doll and Leatherman embarked on a bold expansion campaign that would thrust the firm back into the headlines. They had talked before about expanding the geographical presence of the firm, and had agreed that Lexington was the logical place to plant the Greenebaum flag. They actively, if secretly, began appraising all the Lexington-area law firms, and by mid-February they had settled on a target—McDonald, Alford, Roszell and Scott, a six-man firm. The principals were Angus McDonald, W. Van Meter Alford, Calvert Roszell, Phillip Scott, Robert C. Stilz, and W. Van Meter Alford, Jr.

The McDonald firm was headed by Angus McDonald, with whom Doll had worked years before while negotiating the sale of the Edwards Sausage Company. Doll had liked McDonald immediately—"He was a prince of a guy"—so he naturally leaned his way as a merger candidate. But there were solid business reasons why the McDonald firm made merger sense. They were well connected in central Kentucky, and they had good clients who could use the sophisticated specialties the Greenebaum firm could provide, especially in the tax and securities area. Doll and Leatherman went to Lexington to talk to McDonald, and emphasized what the firm had to offer, not the least of which was the promise of enriched compensation for the partners. "We felt they could do a lot better with us than without us," Doll says.

And the Louisville firm could do better, too. Doll believed the McDonald firm could add many more clients if they just had more firepower, and thereby open a gateway to points east—or more specifically, northeast, where Ashland Oil was located.

Doll, of course, knew the Ashland/McDonald connection. In 1925 E.L. McDonald, Angus's father, was a Louisville-based title attorney, and had been approached by a man named Paul Blazer about doing some title work in eastern Kentucky for his start-up oil and gas exploration company, the Swiss Oil Company.

McDonald agreed, and moved his family to Lexington to be closer to his work. Blazer paid McDonald in stock rather than cash, and McDonald's 5% stake in Swiss Oil became a 5% stake in Ashland Oil some years later. Mr. McDonald remained close to the Blazer family for the remainder of his life, and served on the Ashland board of directors and as Secretary to the company. When his son, Angus, left the FBI in 1945 he, too, became an Ashland director and the Secretary to the company. Ashland had been the cornerstone client of the McDonald law firm since its inception.

Ashland was not a stranger to the Greenebaum firm either, of course; significant tax work had been done for Ashland for nearly twenty years. "But we had done nothing else at all," said Doll. "We figured we could do more if he [McDonald] had the horses."

It wasn't just the Ashland business Doll wanted. When W. Van Meter Alford had joined the McDonald firm in the 1950s, he had expanded its practice beyond oil and gas, and by the 1970s the firm had become a noted business law firm with a good cross-section of clients in Lexington and throughout the Bluegrass. Doll saw opportunity there, too, to build a base beyond the solid Lexington clients the firm already had, such as W.T. Young and John Y. Brown, Jr.

Angus McDonald looked on the merger favorably, not just for himself but for the younger men in the firm. Phil Scott, a Lexington native who had joined the firm eight years earlier as a trial attorney after a stint as a Marine lawyer, said McDonald pulled him aside before the deal was done and said, "You'd be crazy if you didn't embrace this. At your age this will be a wonderful opportunity."

Scott agreed. He also agreed with Doll that Kentucky was ready for a law firm that could serve the entire state. In only 75 days the merger was done. On April 1, 1978 the firm was renamed Greenebaum, Doll and McDonald, and once again became the largest law firm in Kentucky, with 38 lawyers. The Greenebaum firm was the first Louisville law firm to move outside the city in a significant way.

Mr. McDonald was 66 at the time, and Van Alford was 62, both patriarchal figures cut from the same cloth as Sam Greenebaum. They even looked like him—distinguished, with gray hair. The firm hadn't seen partners like that since 1973. "When we had the dinner to celebrate the merger," Ed Perry says, "I stood up and said that it was really nice to once again have senior partners that looked like they were senior partners."

Law firm mergers, since they do not involve one firm buying the other, are mostly about the joining of personnel. Both firms in this case seemed to want the same thing—one company, not two with the same name. For that to happen there had to be a mixing of people, and at first there were misconceptions on both sides. The Lexington people assumed that the Greenebaum lawyers were blue-collar (not a pejorative to most Greenebaum lawyers because that's what they said about themselves), but what they meant was...*nouveau*. Greenebaum was fast food and hospitals. The McDonald firm considered itself bourbon and thoroughbreds—venerable, genteel and well-brought-up. The Louisville firm, on the other hand, figured the Lexington crowd for hayseeds—slow and unsophisticated, an anachronism by modern legal standards. When the troops from both firms convened at the celebration dinner in June, it took only a few minutes to discover that all preconceptions had been wrong. Neither side was what the other expected, and everyone came away thinking the merger was a pretty good idea.

The new firm started attracting new business in central Kentucky immediately, and the partners noticed that the kind of business they were getting—taxation, securities, employee benefits—was the kind that used to go to New York or Atlanta firms. The plan was working, even though the Lexington office did not have a tax lawyer on the premises. In the Greenebaum tradition, the work was originated by one, but executed by others who were experts in the field. In the case of taxation, the work was done by lawyers in Louisville.

⬙

John V. Wharton, 1978

In 1978 John Wharton joined the Lexington office after receiving his law degree from the University of Kentucky. He had clerked for McDonald, Alford and Roszell from December 1976 until graduation from law school, the timing of which coincided with the McDonald firm's merger with Greenebaum. His practice has principally revolved around real estate law, but has included work in oil and gas, and in equine law. In those capacities he has played a major role in the firm's ongoing relationship with significant clients Ashland, Toyota, W.T. Young, Gainsborough Farm and Shadwell Farms. In February 1996 he moved to the Northern Kentucky/Greater Cincinnati office to help fulfill one of the firm's strategic objectives in establishing a stronger real estate/finance presence there. Today he is active in Cincinnati, Covington and Lexington in arts and cultural organizations, and is the current president of the Board of Trustees of the Japan America Society of Greater Cincinnati. In 2003 John joined Toyota Motor Manufacturing North America as its Manager of Corporate Affairs-Legal.

⬙

Integration of Lexington into the Firm

Shortly after the merger, Richard Holt, who had been in the firm's Louisville office but had left and moved to Lexington, re-joined the firm in its Lexington office.

In 1979 the firm was doing so well that it added 14 new lawyers, nine in Louisville and five in Lexington. The imposition of Louisville standards and procedures on the Lexington office had been mostly painless, but it was not quite performing as Bob Doll wanted. Larry Banks noticed it, too. "I wrote an 11-page memo to Doll," Banks says, "saying we need a liaison person in Lexington." Doll agreed, then asked, "Who's going to go?" The answer was Banks. "Bob told me the job was mine if I wanted it, so I went."

Banks's job was to spread the Greenebaum culture and demonstrate its ways of doing things—"with mixed results," Doll says. Ed Perry noticed the problem. "They were great lawyers in Lexington, but they were like Mr. Greenebaum—bright and capable, but generalists. They didn't have any special skills, and we wanted them to take advantage of our specialties and push for excellence in everything they did."

There was some sensitivity and resentment on the part of the Lexington lawyers to the thought of being balkanized by the Louisville firm, and epecially to being called a "branch office" by their Louisville counterparts. In a November 1979 response to a document he was asked to review, Phil Scott diplomatically makes that point: "There are several mentions of 'branch offices.' For the purposes of recruiting, it would appear more advantageous to the firm to indicate that we maintain offices in Louisville and Lexington, with neither being designated as the 'main office' or 'branch.'" Point taken.

June King, 1979

After graduation from the University of Kentucky Law School, where she was an editor of the Law Journal, June Nalley King joined the firm in 1979 as a corporate lawyer with concentrations in securities, banking, and health care. In the latter arena King left the firm and distinguished herself as Assistant

General Counsel at the health care giant Vencor, Inc., a company with deep Greenebaum ties, where she had responsibilities in regard to public offerings and SEC reporting, tender offers, Board and stockholder meetings, administration of stock plans and transfer issues, and shareholder communications. King re-joined the firm in 1996. Today she is a director of the Louisville Orchestra and a member of the National Association of Stock Plan Professionals.

Expansion

The firm expanded its physical space in Louisville in 1979, moving people into one-half of the 32nd floor of the First National Tower from the crowded 33rd floor. There were now 53 lawyers in the firm and, amazingly, 14 of them were full-time litigators. This marked a significant change for the firm.

The firm also embarked on two adventures, getting into the municipal bond business with Henry (Hank) Reed, and bankruptcy law in the Lexington office. These were minor excursions that did not last, but were indicative of the experimental, risk-taking mood in the firm. You never knew when a new specialty would take root.

A Health Problem in the Firm

Bob Doll, a national-caliber tennis player in college, and Louisville's Falls City Champion of 1955, had put his racket away from 1956 until 1968, simply because there had been no time to play. The travel demands of the firm had made it impossible. But here in 1978, at age 51, Doll was playing again, against good competition. In a match at the Louisville Boat Club in February, Doll squared off against Charles Will, a former junior champion whose playing style many Louisvillians remember as dropshot/ lob, dropshot/lob. Doll was running all over the court, up and back, when suddenly he felt chest pain. He stopped playing, but did nothing more about it. But over the weekend the pain persisted. "I remember sitting out by the pool," Doll said, "and the pain was enough to make me know I'd better go to the doctor." An angiogram revealed significant arterial blockage. "It was not a heart attack, technically," Doll says, "it was angina." Doll underwent succesful bypass surgery in the spring.

While frightening, the episode did not have serious consequences for the firm, as Barney Barnett's had in 1965. After a period of convalescence in the spring, Doll was back in the office. But Doll had had time to contemplate the practical consequences to the firm of his incapacitation, and it revived his internal debate about how the firm should be managed. By this time the firm had been organized into Sections, and there was an executive committee, but it was advisory only. In November of 1979 Doll sent a memo to all lawyers: "During my recuperation from surgery in the spring of 1979 I had an opportunity to reflect upon our firm, its growth, and the management thereof. I concluded that, in view of our growth, we needed more and better management. In particular, I came to the conclusion that we needed a 'diffusion' of management responsibilities…to bring some of the younger attorneys into the management so that they could gain experience, knowledge, and a sense of duty, with a view to being able to assume increased management responsibilities in the future."

Like a wise king, Doll was planning for his succession. The monarchy, it seemed, was hinting at a plebiscite, in the form of an Executive Committee that would have the force of law, and would be headed by a Chairman. What else could "diffusion" mean?

Not everyone agreed. Bob Matthews weighed in against it. "I believe that the diffusion of the management role will result in a weakened firm effort, and lead to more internal bickering. I frankly believe that a strong executive is the best form of government and management of law firms."

&

Peggy B. Lyndrup, 1979

A Canadian by birth, Peggy Lyndrup came to the Brandeis School of Law at the University of Louisville and won a summer associate position at the firm for both 1977 and 1978. After graduating as the valedictorian of her law school class, she could have gained employment in virtually any law firm in America, but chose to return to the Greenebaum firm in 1979 to work with Bob Doll and Ed Perry in the corporate department. "We were always thought of as a tax firm," she says, "but when I got here I helped Ed Perry build our corporate department. He had just been made chair of the corporate department and his goal was to grow it and develop it." For three years she worked in mergers and acquisitions, criss-crossing the country closing deals principally for Landmark Newspapers and Meidinger and Associates. In 1982 she left the firm briefly when Meidinger asked her to become their vice-president and general counsel. Lyndrup headed the legal department there until 1984, when Meidinger was sold to William M. Mercer, a subsidiary of Marsh and McLennan. Bob Doll and Ed Perry asked her to return to the firm in 1984, and she has been with Greenebaum ever since.

From the beginning Lyndrup was perfectly at home in the Greenebaum culture. Once during a massive snowstorm the office was empty except for two people—Larry Leatherman (of course) and Lyndrup. Leatherman had commandeered a four-wheel drive vehicle; Lyndrup walked in from her home in Belgravia Court. "I knew Larry would be there," she says, "and it sure didn't hurt in Larry's eyes that I was there." People who know Lyndrup say that she would have walked in even if Leatherman hadn't. She has always thrived on the long days and pressure of the Greenebaum office. "I never considered myself overworked," she says. "When I was working eighteen hours a day on an acquisition as a first-year lawyer, I considered myself fortunate to have that opportunity. The firm attracts the best and the brightest, and people like that don't leave at five o'clock. None of us left our law schools at that time, either."

Lyndrup was comfortable with the hours and the demands placed on young associates, and she was confident enough to give as well as she got. One Saturday in her first year she, Ed Perry, and a junior partner met with a client, after which the client left and she assumed the real work was about to begin. It was at this point that Perry looked at his watch and said he had to leave to play a two o'clock squash match. The junior partner said he had to leave to get to his tennis match. Peggy, looking stricken, said, "But guys, I have to take my kids to the dentist." Perry, taking pity, said, "OK, you go on, I'll do the…wait a minute! You don't have any kids!"

In addition to Meidinger, Lyndrup has accomplished acquisitions in manufacturing, mining, athletic goods, coal, chemical, coatings, communications, construction, distilled spirits, expositions, industrial gas, industrial equipment, investment advisors, investment management, milling, newspaper, retail, stone and gravel and steel fabrication. She has been especially devoted to Hillerich and Bradsby, the "Louisville Slugger" company which she has served as outside general counsel for 20 years. She counts the legal work done to facilitate H&B's move to their new headquarters/manufacturing plant/museum on Main Street as one of her proudest achievements.

In 1989 Lyndrup became the first Greenebaum partner to become the president of the Louisville Bar Association. Today she is the senior woman member of the firm, and is the Chair of the Corporate and Commercial Practice Group.

⬿

Abramson Goes to Frankfort

In January, 1980, John Y. Brown, Jr. took office as governor of Kentucky after a whirlwind campaign with his brand-new Miss America wife, Phyllis George. His candidacy had literally lasted only a few months, and after he was sworn in as governor he had not had enough time to put together a complete staff or to make all appointments. One of the vacant jobs was general counsel to the governor, a post that was critically important to the new governor's legislative agenda. To find the right person John Y. called his old friend, Bob Doll. The Greenebaum firm had done lots of work for John Y.—for his company, Kentucky Fried Chicken; his basketball team, the Kentucky Colonels; and his hamburger company, Ollie's Trolley. Brown told Doll that he needed a general counsel, and did he have any recommendations? Doll recalls saying, "John Y., we have a lot of good lawyers for you. Let me think about it." The lawyer who sprang to Doll's mind was Jerry Abramson, a sharp young lawyer who had come to the firm in 1973 and had made partner in 1978. Abramson was active in the local Democratic Party and had served two terms on the Louisville Board of Aldermen from 1975 to 1979, representing the 3rd Ward. It was understood that he had higher political ambitions.

Abramson was a bit surprised when he got the call from Brown. Abramson had supported Harvey Sloane, not Brown, in the crowded Democratic primary, and had not been a part of Brown's general election campaign. But he was excited to serve as in-house counsel to a governor, and relished the opportunity to meet and work with other Democrats, legislators, and business people state-wide. It would help his political profile down the road, and it was also a great way to get new clients and bring them back to the firm when the job was over.

By design, the job would be over in about a year. "Doll said I could go for a year," Abramson says, "and I stayed for a year and five months." Abramson left the general counsel's job in June, 1981, returning to Louisville and re-affiliating with the Greenebaum firm. The clients came, too, as planned, and Abramson enjoyed four more years with the firm until he ran for mayor of Louisville and won in the fall of 1985. In January of 1986 Abramson left the firm and spent the next thirteen years as Mayor of Louisville. As of this writing Abramson is Mayor again, this time of the new Louisville-Jefferson County Metro, which after city/county merger is the 16th largest city in the United States.

Rick Anderson, 1979

In December of 1979 a Cleveland law firm's loss was the Greenebaum firm's gain when Rick Anderson moved to town. A corporate finance/securities specialist, Anderson had been unhappy living in Cleveland, and in the fall of 1979 he and his wife visited friends in Louisville, liked it, and decided to look into it further. Anderson had really wanted to move back to his native Baltimore, but Louisville felt right, and his wife liked horses. Before he could change his mind Bob Doll offered him a job, Anderson accepted, and the firm had hired its future CEO.

It didn't hurt that he was a 1973 graduate of Bob Doll's law school alma mater, William and Mary, and that he, like Doll, was born in Florida.

Louisville was quite a transition for Anderson. "It was an enigma to me, not nearly as large as anywhere I had ever lived." But the firm felt big-city to him. "The firm had a really sophisticated practice. I felt you could take the firm and stick it in Cleveland, in

Chicago, or New York, and the quality of work would match any firm there." Anderson's experience with the large Cleveland firm he had joined out of law school enabled him to fit right in with the firm's tradition of hard work, long hours and devotion to client satisfaction. "I was used to handling deals all over the country and to long hours, traveling away from home for weeks. Greenebaum felt just like home to me."

Anderson, who had been a partner in his Cleveland firm, was hired as an associate, but became a partner a year later. He worked in corporate finance in the flourishing corporate department, along with mergers and acquisitions and securities work. He was elected to the Executive Committee, working closely with Bob Doll and Larry Leatherman on administrative and hiring issues. By 1994 he was head of the Louisville office, and after the death of Larry Leatherman was elected Chairman of the Executive Committee by the members, a position he still holds today. (More about Anderson's leadership role in The Anderson Era.)

McDonald Dies

The Greenebaum family lost a valuable member in April, 1980 when Angus McDonald died suddenly at age 68.

He had only been a part of the merged firm for two years, and had not had time to influence the Louisville office as much as he had the Lexington firm. He is remembered as a tall, imposing, athletic Scot, who played volleyball well into his 60s and whose sense of economy ruled his professional and personal life. It is said that he wore his dress shirts for ten years, until they became so threadbare that his secretary, Erna, had to go to Graves-Cox to buy him new ones. A Christmas gift from his wife of a cashmere overcoat was met with his disappointed comment: "Why did you buy it now? You know they'll be on sale after the holidays!"

His frugality aside, many people thought he was like Sam Greenebaum—old school, mannerly, a linguist who used precise wording, not volume, to make his points and carve up his opponents. He was an exemplary lawyer whose knowledge of oil and gas law was so renowned that he was once brought in to impartially review an oil and gas case in Judge Bradley's court in Fayette County. After hearing both counselors make their arguments, Judge Bradley is said to have asked, "Mr. McDonald, which side wins?" After McDonald gave his opinion, the judge said, "Well, that's how I'm going to rule." And neither attorney appealed the decision.

The professional work he performed in oil and gas, real estate, and corporate law was quite literally a labor of love. His holdings in Ashland Oil stock made him so wealthy that he did not need to work a single day. But the good Scotsman in him prevailed, and he was toiling away when a heart attack ended his life.

At his funeral it seemed as if all Lexington had come out to pay their respects. People filled Christ Church to capacity and spilled out into the street to honor the man acknowledged as the legal lion of Lexington.

In the aftermath of his death, Phil Scott soon became the Managing Partner of the Lexington office.

⮌

The Graftons, 1980

Innovation continued in the early 1980s. The well-regarded municipal bond lawyers Chip Grafton and his wife, Lillian Fleischer, were brought in to the firm in a bid to operate the new municipal bond department in a major way. Grafton stayed with the firm only a few years until his death at age 73 in 1982; Fleischer remained with the firm until her death.

John A. West, 1980

A 1967 graduate of the University of Cincinnati College of Law, John West went to work for a large Cincinnati law firm after graduation. After working for seven years there and becoming a partner, West felt the lure of returning to his Kentucky roots and moved to Lexington where he became the Assistant United States Attorney for three years. In 1979 Bob Doll and Larry Leatherman recruited West to come to Lexington where the firm badly needed additional litigation help, and West finally joined the firm there in 1980. In 1995 the death of his mother made it necessary for him to oversee the family farm in northern Kentucky. He and his wife decided to move back to the farm, where they still live today, and West practices out of the firm's Covington office.

Michael Ades, 1980

Following an economics degree from the Wharton School at Penn in 1962, and a law degree from Yale in 1965, Michael Ades returned to Lexington and joined the law firm of Stoll, Keenon & Park. His practice involved a range of commercial real estate and land use planning issues. After 15 years with that firm, the long arm of Greenebaum recruitment reached him, in the form of his brother-in-law, Mike Fleishman. Fleishman asked if Ades might be interested in joining the Lexington office of Greenebaum, to which Ades replied absolutely not: "After 15 years why would I want to do something like that?" Four months later in April, 1980 Ades was with the Greenebaum firm, and has been involved in land acquisitions and zoning work for a variety of firms including Toyota, whose relocation to Georgetown, Kentucky represents the most complex, fast-track work of Ades' career.

Henry C.T. (Tip) Richmond, 1981

After serving four years in the Army after graduation from Wake Forest University, Tip Richmond earned his law degree at the University of Louisville, then his L.L.M. at Miami University School of Law, then joined the firm after his graduation in 1981. Today he practices in the Trusts and Estates Practice Group in Lexington, providing estate planning and administration, business planning, and family business counsel. He is a member of both the Lexington and Bluegrass Estate Planning Council, and was a 2002 participant in Leadership Lexington.

⌒

Technology

The firm made a major commitment to computerization in 1980, buying a computer system to handle time sheets. It was a move toward efficiency but, as the firm discovered, the system did not override the need for all the lawyers to still turn in their time sheets promptly, which wasn't happening. Bob Doll's April memo tried to fix that: "It is still important and SOP for time to come in daily so that the computer and the oprators won't continually be under a crush."

It started a tradition of innovation that picked up momentum in the Leatherman Era and continues to this day. As will be discussed in more detail in The Anderson Era, Greenebaum has always been on the edge of technological innovation, both in the area of office productivity and communications. It has always been a function of client service to have Greenebaum lawyers connected to their clients. A willingness to use the latest technology and communications tools is simply an acknowledgment by the firm that clients' problems occur at noon on Sunday, too, and they should be able to reach their lawyers at that time.

The Hard Work Culture

In 1981 the firm added an amazing 21 lawyers to its ranks; now there were 66 in all. The onrush of new, young lawyers during this period meant that they all had to make an adjustment into the hard-working Greenebaum culture without benefit of the one-on-one tutoring that had occurred when the firm was much smaller. Some took to it, some did not, and for the first time the turnover at the associate level was noticeable. "We've been called a sweatshop in the past," Doll says. "But we expected hard work. I spent six or seven days a week here for many years, so did Ed Perry, so did Larry Leatherman and others. It was not unique. It was part of the culture."

Indeed, that culture began to be committed to paper, in a standard handout to new associates. It stated, among other things: "There are two major standards which have contributed to the growth and success of the Firm: a dedication to excellent legal work, and a commitment to hard work. There is no substitute for hard work. The best prepared lawyer, in any matter, has the greatest opportunity for success. It is recognized that people are different and some have a greater capacity for work without burnout than others. A commitment to this type of work is difficult for many young lawyers, but it is necessary for those who work for the Firm. Often the demands of the Firm will interfere with a lawyer's personal life, but in all but the most rare of events the lawyer must recognize that 'the law is a jealous mistress.'"

Too jealous for some. Some were bright enough but didn't fit in. Some didn't want to work so hard. Some were not smart enough. And some just didn't like the place. But that was OK with Doll. "Sam Greenebaum's philosophy, and mine, was that if you didn't fit in or couldn't cut it, you ought to leave." But Doll doesn't remember ever having to fire anyone. "If we thought they were redeemable we would work with them. If we thought they were not redeemable, we would tell them that, tell them why, and then we would try to get them a job at another firm. At one time we even had an outplacement service for that purpose."

Still, Doll did recognize that a bit of extra care with new people would be good for them and good for the firm. His November memo recommended structural changes to assure even workloads among associates, adequate supervision of associates, and adequate training of associates. "The firm is in a growth period at this point," he wrote. "It is mandatory that we keep a tight handle on our operations and obtain the objectives. Keeping in mind the bottom line, it is essential that we assure that the new people…are fully utilized, not overwhelmed, properly supervised, and properly trained. We can be killed by runaway expenses and inefficiency if the above is not accomplished."

There was no deadwood at the Greenebaum firm. The work ethic may have caused some good lawyers to flee, but for those who could handle the work and stayed, a partnership was almost always their reward, which to Doll was a fair bargain.

Rich Cleary, 1981

For Washington & Lee University and Georgetown Law graduate Rich Cleary the Greenebaum firm offered a great ground-floor opportunity: labor law. After clerking in 1980 Cleary returned to the firm in 1981 with the idea to build the labor practice from just a couple of practitioners to national prominence. It had been active once before, under John Greenebaum's leadership in the 1960s and Ron Ray's in the 1970s, and Cleary felt it could be again. He believed the future was boundless. "That was part of the attraction of coming with Greenebaum," Cleary says.

To make a practice group grow there have to be clients, of course, but before that there has to be support from within, and Cleary found that in Larry Leatherman. "Larry gave me unqualified support to build a labor practice," he says. "He thought it was essential that the firm compete for that business at the very highest level." That meant competing not just in Kentucky but in New York, Chicago, Atlanta—wherever large employers existed and retained counsel.

In the 1980s the activity level for labor lawyers increased in two areas—employment discrimination law (age, sex, race) and labor relations law—and Cleary's group became larger to handle the work, and developed a regional and national reputation along the way. As the practice grew with the acquisition of Toyota, Commonwealth Aluminum, Honeywell, American Standard, and many others, Cleary was able to attract more gifted lawyers who were committed to helping their clients with labor issues. More than other practice groups, labor lawyers have to be ideologically suited to handle one side or the other, and Cleary has been careful to bring on people of like mind. "You have to have a comfort level with what you do in this field," Cleary says. "We are determined to help our clients achieve success with serious labor and employment problems. We are a cohesive, close-knit group, with members who are talented, ethical, and conduct themselves with professionalism and judgment."

Today Cleary, who has chaired the ABA Committee on the National Labor Relations Act, and served as a co-editor for the principal labor relations treatise, *The Developing Labor Law*, is the Chair of the Labor and Employment Practice Group.

⤳

Hiram Ely, 1981

Hiram Ely III joined the firm in 1981 as a litigator and business law specialist. His areas of concentration have included commercial and tort litigation, including product liability, antitrust, securities, business and personal torts, and tax court litigation. Significant cases have included a major Metropolitan Sewer

District case in which he obtained a favorable judgment for his client in a chemical dumping situation. He was also instrumental in Kentucky election reform, serving as Chairman of Kentucky Attorney General Fred Cowan's Special Task Force on Election Fraud.

⤵

Environmental Law—Lloyd Cress and Marc McGraw

In 1981 Lloyd Cress arrived at the firm, followed closely by Mark McGraw, and together they established an environmental specialty, a first for any law firm in Kentucky. Cress had been the environmental lawyer at Ashland Oil since 1969; McGraw came from the U.S. Department of the Interior. It was Larry Leatherman who first saw the coming need for environmental lawyers in Kentucky. Leatherman's crystal ball had said that coal liquifaction and gasification were going to be big in Kentucky—a part of the re-tooling of U.S. energy resources in response to the oil embargoes of the 1970s. He wanted the firm ready to represent coal clients who were abundant in Kentucky. At that time there were only three or four environmental lawyers in the state, and Cress and McGraw were the only two who practiced on a full-time basis.

Coal liquifaction and gasification never happened in a big way, but despite that the environmental practice flourished. It was built solidly around Ashland Oil and other manufacturing plants in Kentucky, which Cress handled, and coal and mineral work, which McGraw handled. But when Toyota decided to move to Kentucky, their work really escalated. Before the first spade of dirt was turned on the site, the firm was drawn into "life and death combat," as Cress puts it, to defeat the twelve or thirteen environmental challenges that were filed by labor unions, who were seeking leverage and accommodation on labor issues. As soon as those challenges were resolved, a second phase of lawsuits arose from adjacent landowners whose litany of complaints were perceived to be nuisances in search of a cash settlement. Over time the firm resolved all challenges to Toyota's construction, but it was siege warfare for many years, occupying the full time of Cress and McGraw.

The firm also represented the Kentucky Oil and Gas Producers in the mid-1980s when the state and federal energy bureaucracy tried to impose regulations over the disposal of salt effluent from drilling operations. Ultimately the firm was not able to stave off these regulatory requirements but did delay their onset, keeping the industry alive for five additional years.

Today there are fourteen lawyers primarily in the environmental practice, some of whom are litigators and others perform an advocacy role in the legislative arena.

⮑

Barbara Hartung, 1981

Barbara Reid Hartung, a *cum laude* graduate of the University of Louisville Law School, and editor in chief of the Law Review, joined the firm after graduation in 1981.

Hartung was a litigator, but became interested in insurance law, where she soon focused her practice. In 1987 she achieved Chartered Property and Casualty Underwriter status. She has assisted clients in resolving complex insurance issues, facilitating many transactions. She has also been a practitioner in the health law field, concentrating on managed care issues, legislation, regulation, healthcare and insurance reform, and Medicare-Medicaid issues.

⮑

Van Alford Dies

In 1981 Van Alford, another of the Lexington senior men,

died. Like Angus McDonald, he was a highly esteemed lawyer throughout Kentucky, and one whose experience, judgment, contacts, and legal skills barely had time to influence the broader Greenebaum firm since the merger in 1978. Once again the firm found itself without a true elder. There was no one left of the Sam Greenebaum vintage, and there never would be again.

⌒

Janet Jacubowicz, 1982

In 1982, University of Kentucky law school graduate Janet Jacubowicz checked out the Greenebaum letterhead and saw there were six women on it—more than any other firm in town. She felt it was a sign of a progressive attitude. Then she was hired into the firm by Rich "Mad Dog" Getty, a litigator in Marvin Hirn's department. She worked with Getty exclusively in her first years, giving her a unique perspective on law and life that was progressive in its own way. Getty was considered by all a "colorful" personality. He was an aggressive litigator, histrionic and voluble by nature, who had been known to throw things during depositions. It was not a style that endeared him in all quarters, but Jacubowicz has to admit it was a wild ride, and a different kind of education from law school. The Getty crewmembers, including Jacubowicz, were all short and were dubbed the "Pygmy SWAT team."

For twenty years (with no appreciable increase in height) Jacubowicz has been involved in successful defenses in commercial and business litigation, RICO litigation and arbitration, and securities litigation involving coal, banking, brokerages, manufacturing and retail.

As a woman in trial law, especially one at Greenebaum, Jacubowicz has been challenged to put in the long hours and do the work, and at the same time raise a family. The tug of war between home and career has been a struggle. But, she says, "The job is still fun and a tremendous challenge. I've been able to balance it all and I've enjoyed it." She acknowledges that some women lawyers have left the firm, preferring to start families without the Greenebaum pressure. But she thinks that's a bit of a red herring. "All the firm wants is to get the work done," she says. "Your hours are up to you. But the firm always hires Type A personalities, so we work all the time anyway."

Today there are more women than men in the litigation department, so the firm has clearly been good to women. "It's not a strategy for hiring," she asserts. "We just look for the best and the brightest and hire them."

⁀

Margaret E. Keane, 1982

Maggie Keane, after graduating *magna cum laude* from the University of Louisville's Brandeis School of Law in 1979, began her career with the firm in 1982 as a trial lawyer and commercial litigator. Her concentrations include employment law, product liability cases and family law. She is a frequent lecturer and instructor in many aspects of trial practice at the University of Louisville, as well as at Kentucky Bar Association and Louisville Bar Association workshops.

She is extraordinarily involved in leadership positions within the Louisville and Kentucky Bar, including the presidency of the Louisville Bar Association in 1997 (the second Greenebaum attorney to be elected to that office). Her volunteer and *pro bono* legal efforts in Louisville are legendary, and have led to being named "Volunteer Lawyer of the Year" by the Legal Aid Society in 1990, and the Louisville Bar Association's Public Service Award in 1996.

James A. Kegley, 1983

After 17 years of litigation and securities work for a small Lexington law firm, Jim Kegley was approached by Bob Doll and Phil Scott about coming to work for Greenebaum's Lexington office. The office needed a securities and transactional lawyer, and Kegley had come highly recommended (as had Jack Atchinson, Kegley's boss, who was also asked by Doll to come over). Atchinson declined, Kegley accepted, and Lexington had hired an attorney whose personality and skills would soon play a key role in the growth of the firm.

It happened one afternoon in 1985. "I was in the conference room," Kegley said, "closing some kind of deal when my secretary comes in looking all worried. She says, 'Bob Doll is here. He's downstairs and he wants to see you right now.' Well, I thought I had screwed something up really badly. So I went downstairs and there was Bob with two Japanese gentlemen." The Japanese gentlemen were with Toyota, it turns out, and their company had just decided to make the Greenebaum firm their lead counsel in Kentucky. "Bob winks at me and says, 'Jim, we've been asked to do some work for Toyota, and we're going to get started today. But right now I have to go back to Louisville, and I want you to take care of these gentlemen.' And he leaves me there."

Bob Doll had figured Kegley was the right man, with the right personality, to be the lead attorney for Toyota, and he was 100% correct. Kegley immediately began an immersion into Japanese customs, language, business protocols, and even food. His wife, Linda, also became very involved, entertaining the Japanese and acclimating them to American culture. For over ten years Kegley lived and breathed the Toyota account, which utilized as many as 50 Greenebaum lawyers concurrently at certain times. Kegley, now retired and living near Fort Myers, Florida, says "The Toyota project was a tremendous opportunity to meet many wonderful people, to experience another culture, and to do great work. I'll always be grateful to Bob Doll and the firm for that."

⤳

Bob Doll's Heart Attack

In July 1983 Bob Doll had a serious heart attack. As before, he was playing tennis at the Louisville Boat Club when he felt a sharp pain in his chest. But it was worse this time. "It was like a truck had hit me," he says. Doll fell to the ground as his opponent, Dave Steere, rushed around the net to help. Doll thought a cold shower might help, but it didn't, and Steere rushed Doll to Jewish Hospital in soaking wet tennis clothes. Doctors confirmed it was a bad heart attack, and Doll lay in intensive care for nine days before he was out of jeopardy.

This emergency took Doll out of the office for three months, during which time Larry Leatherman took over, functioning as Managing Partner. Doll was 56 at that time, too young for retirement, but the second heart attack underscored the need for contingency planning for the firm's leadership. Leatherman had taken on the role of confidant and co-manager with Doll just as Doll had done eighteen years earlier with Sam Greenebaum. "He was the guy I leaned on," Doll says, "even before the heart attack." It looked like a natural changing of the guard, eerily similar to Doll's assumption of power when Sam Greenebaum died. The difference was that Doll lived and returned to work—diminished slightly, perhaps, by his health—but back in charge by early 1984. (During his recovery at home, Doll and Leatherman had talked by phone nearly every day, so Doll was basically up to speed on all firm activities.) Leatherman would have to wait a few more years to take over.

⤳

Lunsford Joins the Firm, 1984

In 1984 when the John Y. Brown, Jr. administration came to an end, the inner circle of Brown advisors and supporters—Carroll and Tom Ladt, Bob Cobb, Larry Townsend, Ron Geary, Bruce Lunsford, and others—filtered back into the private sector to make their own fortunes. To a remarkable extent, they all did. Bruce Lunsford, a lawyer and the former Commerce Commisioner, made his first move by joining the Greenebaum law firm on an Of-Counsel basis. Bob Doll, who had many professional and personal connections to the Brown administration and who was an astute judge of talent, saw in Lunsford the combination lawyer/businessman that had always done well at the firm. "Bob came to me," Lunsford remembers, "and said he knew I wasn't going to be a working lawyer, but since I didn't know exactly what I was going to do, why didn't I join the firm? He said he'd give me an office, a stipend, and a percentage of the business I brought in. And he said he thought having my name associated with the firm would help them. So I said yes."

Since his home was in Lexington, Lunsford set up shop in the Lexington office and started bringing in business. He stayed until moving to Louisville in the summer of 1985, when he closed his first hospital acquisition and the wheels were put in motion to create the company that reached Fortune 500 status a few years later, Vencor.

Lunsford's similarity to Jones and Cherry could not have been more striking. The firm took Vencor public as it had Extendicare; the company principals were all attorneys associated with the Greenebaum firm; and after going public both corporations turned around and gave the Greenebaum firm their business, allowing the firm to earn millions of dollars in hard-earned fees. In Lunsford's case the firm was given work by Vencor and its two spinoff companies, Atria and Ventas.

Mark Riddle, 1984

Mark Riddle came to the firm in 1984 from another law firm and fit right into the decade's accelerating volume of litigation work. A still-green lawyer, he nonetheless took a case to jury trial within six months of arrival at the firm and won it. That confirmed something for Riddle: he liked courtroom work. "It's the most exciting part of the practice," he says. Trying a case properly, he says, takes years of experience. Eventually a trial lawyer learns four things, according to Riddle: "Calmness in public; the power of persuasion; seeing the issue from the client's perspective; and being aggressive only when necessary." It also takes a little self-knowledge, says Riddle. "Most litigation lawyers are competitive. They want to win. But it takes wisdom to know when to settle, and when to go all the way."

Riddle has been involved in the firm's most significant litigation victories. He obtained a jury verdict in favor of an engineering firm in connection with natural gas pipeline explosion; he obtained a dismissal of class action lawsuit filed against a major bank; he has successfully defended a wide variety of business disputes, breach of contract, construction and environmental litigation matters in federal and state courts in numerous jurisdictions.

Today there are 25 attorneys and paralegals in his practice group, with women litigators outnumbering men slightly. "Greenebaum is a great place to work," he says. "The firm has a commitment and dedication to excellence. It's a challenging and energetic environment in which to work. Every case involves something new — manufacturing, banking, baseball bats — and that's what keeps it fresh and interesting."

Today Riddle is the Chair of the Louisville Litigation and Dispute Resolution Practice Group.

The Maktoum Brothers

In 1984 the firm began a fascinating and unusual relationship with the Maktoum brothers, of the royal family of Dubai. It started with Phil Scott in a social situation in Lexington, and grew into a business relationship that has lasted almost twenty years.

You can throw a horseshoe in any direction in Lexington and hit somebody in the horse business. Phil Scott, the member in charge of the Lexington office, was literally surrounded with friends and associates who made their living in one way or another with thoroughbreds. Scott himself had developed a specialty in equine law with the help of his friend Robert Clay, scion of Three Chimneys Farm, one of the elite thoroughbred farms in the bluegrass. In January of 1984 at an impromptu dinner party at Three Chimneys, Scott and his wife Roni found themselves seated with an Englishman named Richard Dunn and a distinguished Arab gentleman. The Arab was the Chief of Staff of Crown Prince Sheik Maktoum of Dubai, and Dunn was one of the prince's lawyers. The Maktoums, it seemed, were interested in buying property and establishing a horse breeding and training facility in Lexington. Scott's discussion with them revealed his knowledge of equine matters, and a meeting was set for the next day in the Greenebaum offices. In short order Scott found out about the alacrity and tenaciousness with which Arab businessmen, especially ones with the financial resources of the Maktoums, tackle projects. In a few months Scott was immersed in real estate transactions on behalf of the Maktoums, acquiring land along U.S. 60 in huge tracts, assembling the land parcels that would eventually become Gainsborough Farm.

The Maktoums themselves were rarely in Lexington, and so it fell to Scott and the firm's lawyers to construct, literally, Gainsborough Farm—its barns, its houses, its fences, its ponds, and its roads. The Greenebaum firm operated, in essence, as the contractor, supervisor, and caretaker of Gainsborough Farm, and has continued to do so since 1984. In addition the firm has acted as advisor and business consultant to the Maktoums, overseeing their increasingly avid interest in Kentucky and the thoroughbred industry.

$$\approx$$

Patrick Welsh, 1984

Unlike most young lawyers who came to the firm in their 20's right after college and law school, Patrick Welsh had a life before law school. He was a helicopter pilot in Vietnam from 1968 to 1972, then became an air traffic controller while also flying for the Army Reserve. By 1977 he had also graduated from Bellarmine College, and by 1984 he had his J.D. from the University of Louisville.

Considering his background, he was interested in aviation law and was headed to Washington, D.C., but changed his mind while clerking at the firm in 1983. That summer, despite his lack of experience, Welsh was thrust into a lead role in David Jones's acquisition of Belknap Hardware. Because of work conflicts, other attorneys could not go to New York to close the deal; Welsh was sent instead. "I spent a week in New York doing that deal," Welsh says, "and I was also trying to study for final exams." He was closing a deal of great importance not only to David Jones but also the city of Louisville, and he was not yet out of law school. "When I thought about it," he says, "I said, 'This is the place for me!'"

With that experience, Welsh was eager to get started when he began working for the firm full-time in 1984. He was excited when Bob Doll summoned him to his office right away. Thinking that if the head man himself called him in, it must be something important, he hurried to Doll's office. "Pat," Doll said, "I've got this mickey mouse deal for you to work on…" "And I remember thinking," Welsh says, "So I'm the 'mickey mouse' lawyer?"

Apparently not. Welsh worked closely with Rick Anderson in many mergers and acquisitions, and has concentrated on that field ever since. He and Anderson were known for working hard and then playing hard after the full day's work was done. Anderson says, "It's a wonder we survived some of those deals."

The mid-1980s were ripe for leveraged buyouts, and Welsh's work right from the beginning was plentiful. But M&A work waxes and wanes with the economy and the overall atmosphere for deals. Welsh left the firm briefly in 1990 to become in-house counsel for one of his clients, but returned in 1992. Today he advises clients on acquisitions, and sees growth opportunities in Japan, Asia, and Europe.

⇊

Holland Nimmons McTyeire, V, 1984

Quint McTyeire joined the firm after graduation from Vanderbilt University School of Law in 1984. Since that time Quint has had a versatile practice, concentrating in administrative and public sector law along with antitrust and securities work. He has had an extensive practice before the Public Service Commission on behalf of telecommunications utilities in matters relating to the Telecommunications Act of 1996. He has represented public sector clients in civil rights and state law claims, and has advised clients on price and monopoly matters. Further, he has been a litigator in state and federal courts in complex class action shareholder cases.

Away from work, McTyeire is known as a national-caliber backgammon player.

⇊

Tandy C. Patrick, 1984

Tandy Patrick began her career with the firm in 1984, six years after earning a law degree from the University of Louisville and, interestingly, one year before earning an MBA from Bellarmine University. Her practice has been diverse within a business law framework, including finance issues in property acquisition, business reorganizations, and corporate finance and loan transactions; real estate and commercial development; retail, office and commercial leasing; intellectual property matters; and equine law. An avid runner/athlete, she is a member of many athletic clubs and is a certified USA Track and Field track official. Today she is a member in the firm's Finance and Development Practice Group.

The Orlando Merger

In 1985 the firm opened an office in Orlando, Florida and sent one of its lawyers, Barry Sobering, to attend to the affairs of several of Mike Fleishman's clients who had business interests in the area, such as J.D. Nichols, whose company, NTS, was doing development deals in Orlando, and Citizens Fidelity Bank. Fleishman, while in Orlando, got to know an attorney named Robert Fraley, an effervescent 32-year-old who had a significant and growing business as a sports agent. Fraley had been the back-up quarterback to Kenny "Snake" Stabler at the University of Alabama. His clients included golfer Payne Stewart, baseball pitcher Orel Hershiser, and professional football coaches George Allen, Bill Parcells, and Joe Gibbs. Fraley had a small firm, Fraley, Heekin, Hyde and Davis, and at some point expressed an interest to Fleishman in merging with Greenebaum so that he could do what he did best—bring in clients—while the Greenebaum lawyers handled all the legal work. Both sides were agreeable, and the firms merged on January 1, 1986, but did so in Orlando only. The firm name was Greenebaum, Doll, McDonald and Fraley.

In anticipation of doing securities work in entrepreneurial Orlando, Irv Eisinger, whose Louisville practice had slowed, moved to Florida and passed the Florida bar exam. Unfortunately, the arrangement with Fraley was flawed, and the new firm didn't last long. The Louisville firm's understanding was that Fraley's sports-agent business would be tied to his law practice, which Eisinger was going to run. In reality, Fraley's revenues were generally funneled into his agency business, with little flowing through to the law firm. In the entire duration of the Greenebaum-Fraley firm, Fraley brought not a single client to Eisinger. The highlight of the short-lived relationship was the firm's representation of Hershiser in his baseball salary arbitration case. Fraley and Rich Cleary won the case for the client, securing baseball's first million-dollar arbitration award.

The story has a sad ending. Fraley was on Payne Stewart's jet when it encountered cabin pressure problems and crashed in South Dakota after a 1500-mile pilotless flight, as worldwide media reported in detail in October, 1999.

⤎

Acquiring Toyota

Back in 1983 and 1984, when John Y. Brown, Jr. was running state government "like a business", there were communications links established with the global business community, in hopes of international trade and perhaps the location of foreign businesses in Kentucky. One of John Y.'s targets was Japan, and delegations were sent over to show Japanese businessmen and politicians just what Kentucky had to offer. Ultimately, those efforts, and the efforts of the next Kentucky governor, Martha Layne Collins, led Toyota to select Georgtown, Kentucky in 1985 as one of the finalists for its flagship manufacturing plant in America.

Pending Toyota's final site selection, the big law firms in Kentucky lined up to contend for the Toyota account. The process involved making presentations and undergoing thorough question-and-answer sessions with Toyota officials. The Greenebaum team was headed by Bob Doll, Larry Leatherman, Lloyd Cress and Phil Scott.

Doll had scored points for the firm during a dinner party Governor Collins had given for Toyota at the Governor's Mansion. "She had invited two lawyers," Doll says, "me and Wilson Wyatt. But Wilson didn't show up for some reason. I was the only lawyer there, and it helped." At Doll's table was a tall, dynamic Japanese man named Mr. Okuda, who spoke perfect English. Mr. Okuda, it turns out, had spent a lot of time in Texas, and thus was a formidable combination of Japanese strategist and hard-nosed Texas businessman. Okuda was Toyota's lead negotiator with the state, and later became Chairman and CEO of Toyota (and the first person outside the Toyoda family to run the company).

Still, the Greenebaum team had to win at the interview table. Toyota had developed a rating system for each firm, divided into ten categories. Phil Scott noticed during the interview sessions that governmental relations seemed to be an important criterion for Toyota, and this did not bode well, he thought, since the firm was not aligned strongly with the Democratic Party. In reality Toyota rated the Greenebaum firm highest in that category because they did *not* want a firm tied to party politics. Their perception—correct, it turns out—was that power shifts from party to party over time, and that an independent firm would not suffer one way or another with a change in the political weather.

The Greenebaum firm was selected by Toyota to be their lead firm in Kentucky. In a confidential memo on November 18,

1985, Larry Leatherman wrote his colleagues: "After considering five of the leading law firms in the state, Toyota Motor Corporation has selected our law firm to represent it in the investigatory phases of possibly establishing a $600 million automobile plant in Kentucky. If Kentucky is selected [as a site] then Greenebaum will become regular Kentucky counsel." Toyota did, indeed, select Georgetown as its site, and Greenebaum was named its lead counsel. It represented business of huge proportions. "If ever there was a watershed event for the firm," Phil Scott said, "getting Toyota was it."

The firm began immediately doing Toyota's acquisitions, contracts, regulatory work, employment, and labor work, the latter handled by Rich Cleary and Pat Nepute. Japanese lawyers were moved into the Lexington office. Jim Kegley was the lead attorney chosen to work with Toyota, and he took to the work with such a flourish that he and his wife immersed themselves in Japanese culture and learned the language and customs needed to handle the client.

There was so much work that more lawyers were needed. Phil Scott arranged to merge another Lexington law firm into Greenebaum to bring in more troops. In addition to Toyota work, the firm began doing work for the many satellite automobile parts companies that located in Kentucky after the Toyota announcement.

It was such an increase in work volume that in 1986 the firm hired 40 new lawyers, bringing the total to 108 lawyers in all. There were so many new faces, and so much activity, that new work rules and new systems had to be imposed to manage it all. New associates were given important work right from the start, but the old Greenebaum impatience with non-performers was still in evidence. Sam Harris, Greenebaum's Director of Administration at that time, wrote in this August 1985 memo: "I would suggest that six months after a new associate comes on board, he/she be given an evaluation...The Executive Committee would then determine, based on the recommendations in the evaluations, whether to release or retain the associate." Bob Doll okayed this suggestion.

∽

Philip C. Eschels, 1985

Phil Eschels began with the firm in 1985 after graduation with honors from the Indiana University School of Law in 1984, and a year of legal practice in Indiana in 1984. As a member in the Labor and Employment Law Practice Group, Eschels' practice has involved a wide range of labor issues, including employment litigation, sexual harassment, smoking policies, disability issues, unions, employee discipline, EEO matters, and hiring/firing issues. He was a Contributing Editor for over a decade to the firm's monthly Kentucky Employment Law Letter, and was the chapter editor for the ABA's 2001 Cumulative Supplement for Employment Discrimination Law. In addition, Eschels is on the Board of Directors of Actors Theater of Louisville.

∽

Bob Doll Resigns as Managing Partner

In March of 1986 Bob Doll decided to resign as Managing Partner of the firm. His health was the main reason; he didn't feel that he had the energy or the strength to continue. But his attitude had changed, too. His patience, for some reason, had gone out the window. "I was getting hard to live with," he says.

And he had recognized that there had to be further changes in the way the firm was being run. "You don't run a 108-person firm the way you run one with three or four," he said. The structural changes that were coming were simply too bureaucratic for the man whose management tradition stemmed back to the benevolent despotism of Sam Greenebaum. "I was still in an entrepreneurial mode," Doll says, "and I didn't like all the committees that were being formed, and all the compromising that is necessary when everybody has a voice." For the first time in 32 years Doll would have to admit, "The firm was beginning not to fit me."

Plus, he started sensing some dissension in the firm, or at least some tension, about compensation matters. Some of the younger members were uncomfortable under the old rules and, for the first time Doll ever remembered, were grousing about them out loud. That was enough to make Doll leave active management. In March he announced his resignation as Managing Partner and as Chairman of the Executive Committee, effective July 1, 1986.

Doll continued as a law practitioner though, dealing with old friends like W.T. Young and others. In fact, he began to practice more law than he had done for years, relieved of other duties.

The changing of the guard was noticed and acknowleged by friends and clients. Tip Richmond, then Vice President of Trusts at Citizens Fidelity Bank, spoke for them all when he wrote to Doll: "Contrary to General MacArthur's statement that 'old soldiers never die, they just fade away,' your spirit, wisdom, and character will forever be as much a part of Greenebaum, Doll and McDonald as that of Sam Greenebaum."

Doll's resignation was the end of what can only be called the firm's "golden" era, when the firm was not just successful, but was also small enough to have a collegiality and a unity that simply was not possible with a large, diffused workforce. Ed Perry remembers the Doll era: "We had great spirit back in those days, the 1970s and '80s. We would meet in here [the conference room] and have a drink at the bar and talk…and then we'd all go back to work. But there was a lot of camaraderie, and there was the feeling that we were better, we could do better work, than the other firms in town."

CLIENT AND CASE HIGHLIGHTS
OF THE DOLL ERA

As the Doll Era began in 1969, the firm had become a player in big-time regional business because it represented many of the new movers and shakers in Kentucky. No one moved or shaked like the men—inside and outside the firm—who kicked off the Doll Era in grand style—John Y. Brown, Jr., David Jones, Wendell Cherry, Bill Ballard, David Grissom, and W.T. Young.

David Jones and Wendell Cherry

David Jones and Wendell Cherry are the Hewlett and Packard of Louisville's business history—two men, humble beginnings, a dream, hard work, and an idea whose time came in a huge way.

In the early 1960s as Louisville's manufacturing base was being gobbled up by national concerns, two young attorneys built a nursing home on Bardstown Road, and in doing so set in motion not only the birth of one of Louisville's most important businesses, but also the beginning of a major economic shift in Louisville— from products to services. By 1965 the company was called Extendicare, and owned a handful of nursing homes. An aggressive program of expansion called for constant new investment, and many people in Louisville today still remember Jones and Cherry going practically house-to-house in the mid-1960s looking for capital. They were turned down by many, but those who invested in a significant way were rewarded over time with the kind of investment wealth that comes along once in a lifetime.

In 1969 Jones and Cherry became part of the Greenebaum family through merger, and the firm began assisting Extendicare in its growth strategy, soon taking the firm public. By 1972 the company had moved on to hospital acquisitions and owned 45 of them, with the Greenebaum firm becoming an important component of the Extendicare rise to prominence. In 1974 the company renamed itself Humana, and four years later became a nationally imposing and significant health care giant when it bought American Medicorp, Inc., effectively doubling its hospital holdings.

Although neither Jones nor Cherry were working lawyers after 1970 when the law firms merged, they were Of-Counsel with the firm for five years, were paid by the firm, and Bob Doll was only too glad to write their checks. As Doll always recognized, tying men like Jones and Cherry to the firm was like tying success itself to the firm. He would have preferred the two men to be working lawyers with the firm, but he would take them any way he could get them. In 1970 it may have been difficult to see over the horizon and know the full extent of Humana's glorious future, but Doll could see two winners in front of him, and he wanted Jones and Cherry aligned with the firm. If Humana had failed, he knew there would have been another business startup from those two.

Over the years the size and scope of Humana deals have sometimes inspired unusual moments of comedy. Ivan Diamond recalls a day in 1982 on Wall Street in New York when Humana received a check from Lehmann Brothers for $113 million. Bill Ballard, Humana counsel and CFO, who was accompanying Diamond, did not want to walk around New York with a check of that size in his pocket. So, at Diamond's suggestion, they walked into the nearest bank to deposit the money. "I figured," Diamond says, "that it was Wall Street. This would not be unusual." Ballard got in the teller line. When he got to the front and handed the teller the check, bells start going off and people started scurrying. Diamond says, "Apparently you can't do it that way. Even on Wall Street."

By 1982 Humana was feeling flush enough and confident enough to initiate an international architectural competition to design the firm's new headquarters at the southwest corner of 5th and Main. It made news all over the world. The winning architectural design was by Michael Graves, and his 27 story post-modern masterpiece, completed in 1985, became a signature building not only in Louisville's city center, but in the catalog of important architectural constructions around the world.

The world looked on again in 1985 as Humana, which had grown to some 90 hospitals in size, boldly took the lead in artificial heart research. It put its 1984 profits of some $200 million on the line and agreed to pay for 100 artificial heart operations using the innovative Jarvik-7 device. William Shroeder, the first patient, became a household name, as did Dr. William DeVries, as a result of a well-planned and well-financed public relations campaign that brought the story to every media outlet in the world.

David Jones did not flinch from criticism that the whole program was about publicity. "We hope to establish Humana as a brand name that stands for high-quality health care services at affordable prices," he said. "To the extent that this is helpful with that, it will be a plus for the company."

A stroke from a thrown blood clot caused Shroeder's medical case to end in question rather than in triumph, but the name Humana had been on the front pages of the world's newspapers and on television screens for months, and as a result it quite simply became, along with Ashland Oil, Hillerich & Bradsby and others, one of the firm's most recognized, marquee clients.

In 1985 Jones also launched a strategy that had implications for Humana that were huge but unseen at the time. The idea was to sell insurance as a means of funneling patients into Humana hospitals to improve its "utilization rate." It cost the company a lot of money at first, but it set the stage for the conversion of Humana from a hospital company into an insurance company a decade later. The narrowing margins of hospital ownership had observers wondering whether Humana would use its huge capital stockpile to plunge deeper into hospital ownership by buying Hospital Corporation of America, or tweak the insurance plan into something big. The answer would come during the Leatherman Era.

John Y. Brown, Jr.

Everyone knows about John Y. Brown, Jr. The archetypal entrepreneur, he made his first fortune by investing $7,000 in 1960 and taking over a small fried chicken operation called Kentucky Fried Chicken run by an older man named Harland Sanders, and turning it into the largest restaurant chain in the world (4,500 stores in 23 countries). Brown was all charm, all opportunity, all sales, all hustle, all charisma, all the time. And he was smart, too. A lawyer by training, he was guided by lawyers, including his father, called "Senior", and later by the lawyers of the Greenebaum firm. When KFC moved its headquarters back to Louisville from Nashville in the late1960s, the company was acquiring real estate and new franchisees at a tremendous clip, and the firm began handling all the closings and agreements.

Keeping up with Brown was a challenge for the firm. In one year alone he opened 862 stores. "We didn't know it couldn't be done," Brown said, "we just did it."

The firm was involved in the sale of KFC to Heublein, Inc. in 1971, which ended local ownership of the company. Brown then turned the firm's attention to his new food enterprise, Lum's, a regional restaurant chain that he bought in 1971.

The firm also was involved in Brown's ownership of professional basketball teams. Ed Perry handled the deal when Brown became sole owner of the ABA's Kentucky Colonels, buying out his partners, among them David Grissom and Bruce Miller, and installing his wife, Ellie, as the president of the team. Perry also was involved when Brown, refusing to pay what he considered an extortion to the NBA to join that league, folded the Colonels, then bought the Buffalo NBA franchise. His innovative idea was to bring that team to Louisville, but was unsuccessful in finding enough local investors to make it happen.

When Brown ran for governor and won in 1979, the firm helped his administration by supplying his general counsel, Jerry Abramson, who also became head of Brown's Justice Cabinet when Neil Welch resigned in 1982.

Bill Ballard

Humana's Bill Ballard, another Greenebaum alum, also was a big part of Humana's success, and a close friend of the firm's. Bob Doll remembers offering Ballard a job in 1968 when he wanted to return to Kentucky from his job with the Department of Justice. Ballard joined the firm of Jones, Grissom, and Boone instead. "Once spurned," said Doll. Then, after Ballard joined the firm anyway in 1969 through the merger of Greenebaum with Jones-Cherry, he decided to leave to become Extendicare's in-house counsel. "Twice spurned," said Doll. Twenty-two years later, richer and wiser, Ballard rejoined the firm of-counsel. "We welcomed him back with open arms," said Doll. "Joy finally returned to Mudville."

W.T. Young

Renowned businessman W.T. Young was a generation older than many of the "up-and-comers," but he could teach them all a thing or two about entrepreneurism. Throughout his business career he has had the Midas touch with enterprises as diverse as peanut butter, real estate, hospitals, storage, and thoroughbreds.

Mr. Young received a B.S. degree in mechanical engineering from the University of Kentucky in 1939. He was the founder of W.T. Young Foods, Inc., a company that became one of the nation's leading producers of peanut butter. He sold his business to Procter & Gamble in 1954, but continued to manage the peanut butter manufacturing operation, under the brand name Jif, until 1957. He then founded W.T. Young Storage, Inc., and in succeeding years made substantial investments in a variety of enterprises, including Extendicare/Humana in the 1960s.

He has been a major contributor and supporter of both the University of Kentucky and Transylvania University. His donation of $5 million in 1993 to the state-of-the-art William T. Young Library at the University of Kentucky was the largest cash gift ever given by an alumnus at that time. Mr. Young was inducted into the UK Hall of Distinguished Alumni in 1970. He is a former member of the UK Board of Trustees, and the Transylvania Board of Trustees.

Today he is well known throughout Kentucky as an outstanding citizen, philanthropist, businessman and thoroughbred owner, whose success includes wins in major stakes races, the Breeders' Cup, and the Kentucky Derby with Grindstone in 1996.

The Galbreaths

In the early 1970s Ed Perry was First National Bank's attorney during the leasing phase of the bank's new building at Fifth and Main. First National owned the land on which the building was situated, they were the major tenant, and they were one-third of the ownership with Equitable Life and John Galbreath. Galbreath informed Perry, Equitable Life's in-house counsel, and Galbreath's own law firm that they were going to close on February 28, 1971. Perry recalls, "And we all said, 'We can't do it. We just can't do it.

We're not going to do it. Can't do it.' They said, 'You're going to do it.'" So the lawyers went to work and stayed up nights and finally closed it in the morning on February 28. "After the closing we went to lunch at the dining room over in First National," Perry says, "in the old dining room. Dan Galbreath, before lunch was even over, got up and made a little speech about how happy he was to be in Louisville, what a great project it was, and said he'd love to stick around a little longer but he had a plane to catch. He was going bird hunting in Mexico. We beat our ass to the ground so we could time the close so that guy could go bird hunting in Mexico."

But it was a great lesson for Perry, who realized its value. "I have told any number of clients since then that when they say, 'How long is it going to take?' I say, "You tell me when you want to close, and we'll close.' I also say, 'If you give us all the time that we can take, we'll close in four months or six months or whatever. But if you tell us we're going to close next Tuesday, then we'll close next Tuesday.'"

⌒

"The Sting" Case

After Bob Matthews joined the firm as a name partner in 1968 one of his clients was the University of Louisville. In 1973 a university faculty member, Dr. David Maurer, brought suit against Universal Studios and director David Ward for stealing the essential details of one of his books, *The Big Con*, and making a movie out of it. Maurer's book was about the language and practices of confidence artists, and the movie that Maurer alleged was based on it was called *The Sting*. It starred Robert Redford and Paul Newman and was one of the most successful films of 1973. In pre-trial depositions Ward had admitted he had read the book; in fact it was on his bedside table. The trial was to be held in Louisville, in Judge Charles Allen's federal courtroom. The judge had ordered that the jurors see the film before the trial date. Matthews had put both Redford and Newman on the witness list, and Louisville celebrity watchers were looking forward to their arrival on the stand. Just before the fun was about to begin, however, the studio offered to settle. Matthews asked Maurer what he wanted to do, and the professor declined to take the lawsuit any further. He was in bad health, and was concerned that he would not survive a long trial. A money settlement was soon reached, which the studio and the producer could easily afford because *The Sting* went on to become one of the better grossing films in history.

⬉

Louisvillian Paul Hornung was a superstar football player, and was additionally gifted with the kind of good looks and bachelor lifestyle that was tailor-made for the press. He was football's Golden Boy for many years, but was tarnished once in a gambling fracas with NFL commissioner Pete Rozelle. Hornung and Alex Karras were disciplined by Rozelle for making a few bets and associating with gambling types—a slap on the wrist, really, but it came back to haunt him in 1985.

The cable television network WTBS wanted Hornung to be its color commentator for college football games. The network submitted his name to the NCAA as their contract required, but surprisingly the NCAA rejected Hornung on the grounds that the taint of his gambling "conviction" was not good for college football. Hornung called Bill Boone, and together they hauled the NCAA into Judge Ed Schroering's courtroom at Jefferson Circuit Court to fight the decision. Mark Riddle was part of the litigation team, and called sportscasters Lindsey Nelson and Chris Schenkel to take the stand to support Hornung, as well as Pete Rozelle, whose testimony disputed, not confirmed, the NCAA's claim that Hornung's association with gambling disqualified him from calling college games. When it was all over the jury found for Hornung and awarded him a judgment of $1.2 million. The NCAA appealed the case to the Kentucky Court of Appeals, and lost again. They appealed finally to the Kentucky Supreme Court, which reversed the decisions of the lower courts.

Despite that, Hornung went on to participate as an analyst on hundreds of college telecasts.

⁓

Jake and C.H. Butcher, alias "The Butcher Brothers"

When the recession hit in the early 1970s and the demand for securities law declined, Ivan Diamond was approached by Bill Isaacs of First National Bank, who had an idea that he thought might lead to some legal business for Diamond and some new loans for the bank. It had to do with the purchase of small correspondent banks around the state. It was an attractive investment for entrepreneurs who could get tax benefits by deducting the loan interest against the earnings of the bank, and First National would take bank stock as collateral for the loans. It was a good idea, and for five years or so the Greenebaum firm closed the loans for these bank acquisitions, which were plentiful in Kentucky because the state was one of the few that did not allow (at that time) multi-bank holding companies, which would have enabled the big banks to swallow up all the little ones, leaving all the entrepreneurs out of the game.

One day Isaac called Diamond to say that he wanted the firm to represent the bank on a very large loan to Messrs. Jake and C.H. Butcher, the Knoxville brothers who owned a number of small banks in Tennessee and wanted to expand their banking empire to Kentucky. The loan closing went smoothly, and Diamond discovered C.H. Butcher to be the businessman of the two, while Jake was more interested in politics. "C.H. was just a helluva nice guy," Diamond says. The feeling must have been mutual, because a week after the closing C.H. called Diamond and said, "Ivan, we want to keep expanding our banking network in Kentucky. We liked the work you did, and would you represent us in acquiring some banks in Kentucky?" To which Diamond replied, "Sure C.H., I'd love to." That was the start of a lovely relationship—for a while.

The Butchers went on a buying spree. Diamond did all the closings. "Some days C.H. would pick me up in his airplane at 7:00 a.m. and we would buy three banks that day." Their roll didn't last long. The Butchers were borrowing heavily to buy the banks; in fact, the empire was built completely on borrowed money. When the recession bit deeper, interest rates went to 18%, and the Butcher loans were floating on the prime. So their loan rate had nearly doubled, and at the same time their own banks were losing money on risky loans they had made. It was a double whammy that they could not overcome. There was not enough revenue to cover the loan payments.

But they tried to delay the inevitable. Working off tips regarding when the bank examiners were coming, the bad loans were moved from bank to bank just ahead of the examiners' arrival, so that each bank's balance sheet showed no problems to the authorities.

Diamond knew there was trouble when the state banking commissioner called him to ask that he attend a meeting one day in his office, in a matter involving the Butcher brothers. As Diamond walked in the next day, the Butchers were already there, along with representatives of the FDIC and the Federal Reserve of Cleveland. They told Diamond that they were on to the Butcher scheme, that all their banks were to be simultaneously audited, and they had every reason to believe that every Tennesssee bank would fail and their assets would be frozen. The Kentucky banks, though, were not in bad shape and they didn't want to close them, but they had to be sold to new owners as soon as possible. And for that, they needed Diamond's help. It was Wednesday; the banks—five of them— needed to be sold by Monday, or they would be closed.

An incredulous Diamond saw that all eyes were on him, realized what this meant, and his protest began:

Diamond: "How can the federal regulatory process possibly be shortened? It takes weeks, if not months, to approve a change of control of a bank! Just to fill out the papers alone for one bank in four days would be a huge task."

Federal Reserve: "Here's my home number. If you have questions, call me. You file 'em, we'll approve 'em."

FDIC: "Same here."

Diamond: "But there are loans on these banks. It's a mess!"

Everybody: "Ivan, we're counting on you."

Diamond: "I'm a lawyer. I'm not Houdini!"

Silence.

Diamond: "Can I use your phone?"

Diamond called the office and asked that no one leave. In short order teams of attorneys were working in several rooms at the firm, negotiating the sale of five banks simultaneously. The Butchers settled in, bringing Tennessee sipping whiskey. "The week was a blur," Diamond says. "I moved from room to room, approving this, signing that, talking on the phone. People were sleeping on couches. All the food was brought up. Three a.m. looked like noon around here."

By Monday morning the paperwork for the sale of five banks had been completed. Airplanes were chartered to take the documents to St. Louis, Memphis, Cleveland, and Washington. C.H. Butcher stood on the tarmac and shook hands with the departing attorneys, like Winston Churchill sending the Spitfires off to battle the Luftwaffe. Diamond went home to get some sleep.

By 4:00 p.m. all the change of control papers had been approved. Unlike Tennessee, not a single Kentucky bank closed.

The Butchers went to jail, and their $1 billion empire collapsed. At that time it was the largest bank failure in American history. But throughout the ordeal the regulators never lost their respect for the Greenebaum firm. Diamond was glad it was over. "In all my years of deals," he said, "that was the toughest." C.H. Butcher died in April, 2002.

Bruce Lunsford

As John Y. Brown's Secretary of Commerce from 1980 to 1983, Bruce Lunsford found himself surrounded by a Hall of Fame lineup of Kentucky entrepreneurs — John Y. himself; W.T. Young; Gene Smith; Frank Metts; George Fischer; Carroll Ladt; Ron Geary—everywhere you looked there were dollar-a-year guys filling cabinet posts and advisory slots. He could not have come out of that environment without big plans and an ambitious agenda. A lawyer and a CPA, he came to the Greenebaum firm in 1984 as a business producer while keeping his eye on the deal landscape. IPO specialist Ivan Diamond says, "I liked Bruce tremendously, and he told me he would one day have a company to take public. And he did."

Vencor was founded in 1985 when Lunsford purchased one hospital, and converted it into a specialty healthcare provider concentrating on ventilator-dependent patients. Diamond soon shepherded Vencor into a publicly-traded company in 1985, and watched with satisfaction as the company's stock rose during a period of growth that looked a lot like Humana's a decade earlier.

In the second half of the 1980s the firm worked for Vencor as the company began an aggressive growth campaign. Lunsford saw Vencor as a billion dollar company, and at the end of the Doll Era it certainly looked possible.

⁊

Leaving the Doll Era

By mid-1986 Larry Leatherman's time had come. As Bob Doll had done before him, Leatherman had made himself a trusted right hand to the firm's senior man, and had been heir apparent for many years. The firm he inherited was much like the one Doll had taken over in 1973—specialized and hard-working—but now it was a behemoth. The firm had gone from 38 lawyers to 108. There had been two mergers, in Lexington and Orlando. There had been a huge expansion in services and specialties, and there were many more clients, spending a lot more money.

Doll had given his successor a hand that was all trumps. But managing the cards was going to take a new and different set of skills and, as the firm was about to find out, Larry Leatherman was just the guy to do it.

A GREENEBAUM
FAMILY ALBUM

The firm's "name" partners are Samuel L. Greenebaum (left), A. Robert Doll (below), and Angus McDonald (below left).

Sam Greenebaum was an avid hunter and bird shooter.

The incomparable Barney Barnett.

Barney Barnett (right) with Israeli Prime Minister David Ben Gurion.

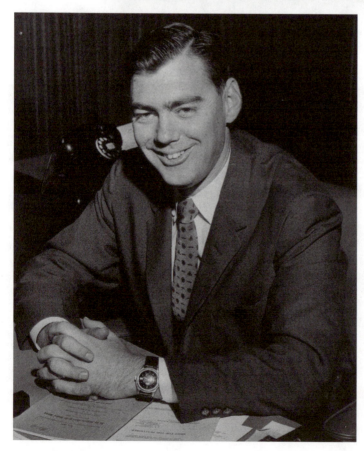

Bob Doll after his Supreme Court victory, 1958.

Mary Stanton and Bob Doll at Churchill Downs, 1959.

Accompanying Bob Doll at the dedication of his portrait are Lloyd Cress, Tom Brown, Rick Anderson, and Bill Robinson.

*Bob Doll in front of the
Sam Greenebaum portrait.*

*Ed Perry and Bob
Doll, circa 1970s.*

Mike Ades and Larry Banks.

Mike Shaikun and his wife, Phyllis, at the celebration of Mike's 30th anniversary with the firm.

Tom Brown and Ivan Diamond.

Larry Banks and Teri Barnett at a firm Summer Gala in the 1980s.

Tom Brown and John West at a partners black-tie dinner in the 1980s.

Bill Greeley, W.T. Young, Bud Greely and Darby Turner at Idle Hour Country Club, 1999.

"General" Bob Matthews and Lillian Fleisher at an '80s Summer Gala.

Larry Leatherman as Managing Partner (above) and as a new associate in 1959 (right). Both below, Leatherman with wife, Portia.

Ivan Diamond and Bruce Lunsford at the New York Stock Exchange listing of Vencor, 1992.
Right, above, and below: Mementoes of securities achievements.
Below right: Former Greenebaumer Charles "Chuck" Schnatter, VP and General Counsel of Papa John's.

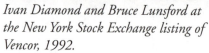

*Above, Eric Ison.
Right, Richard Holt and Tom
Fryman at a black-tie dinner.*

*Rick Anderson and Carmin Grandinetti, former Greenbaumer now Vice
President and General Counsel for Atria Communities, Inc., in the mid-1980s.*

Hall of Fame jockey Eddie Arcaro with Executive Vice President of General Tire, Tom Reese, guest of Peggy Lyndrup at the Derby in the 1990s.

Phil Scott and Larry Leatherman at a partners affair in the late 1980s.

Right, Phil Scott and Bruce Cryder at a black-tie dinner, early 1990s.

Mike Shaikun and Mike Ades, 1990s.

Right: Jim and Mary Eaves at a late-1980s firm gala.

Below: Hiram Ely and Buck Wiseman in the early 1990s.

John A. Hillerich III, Peggy Lyndrup, and William Becker at Becker's retirement party at 610 Magnolia.

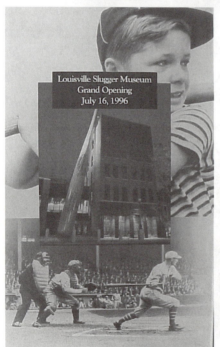

The invitation to Hillerich & Bradsby's Grand Opening.

Raising of the Louisville Slugger bat at Hillerich & Bradsby's new Louisville headquarters, 1995.

Peggy Lyndrup, Jerry Abramson, Jack Hillerich, Hubert Roberts, and the Slugger plant project team at the 1995 opening of Hillerich & Bradsby's Major League Baseball plant in downtown Louisville.

John A. Hillerich IV, Billy Williams, and Jack Hillerich at the Slugger Museum Opening Gala.

Graham Watson of Louisville Hockey, Mark Messier (then New York Rangers captain), and line-mate Rick Anderson at Hillerich & Bradsby celebration.

Larry Leatherman and Chaz Lavelle at winter dinner, late 1980s.

Right, Chaz Lavelle and John Cummins at the partners winter dinner, 1989.

Below, Chaz Lavelle and John Stites at a firm function in 1988.

Bob Doll's first and Jim Kegley's second trip to Japan. The man on the far left and woman on the far right were members of Toyota's public relations department. To Kegley's right is Isao Inoue, now retired, but at this time was Toyota's overseer of all legal work done in the U.S., and the man who recommended the hiring of the Greenebaum firm. To Doll's left is Kojiro "Koji" Tanaka of Toyota's legal department, who had oversight responsibilities for environmental matters at the Georgetown, Ky. plant.

Jim Kegley and Lloyd Cress in Nagoya, Japan, having dinner with three members of the Toyota legal staff—Norihiko "Nick" Shimada, Mr. Sakurai, and Kunihiko "Kent" Ogura.

Bill Robinson, Doug Jones, and Harry Rankin at the lease-signing for the firm's Northern Kentucky offices in the River Center in Covington, with developer Bill Butler and Covington Mayor Denny Bowman.

Bill Robinson, Harry Rankin, Doug Jones and guests have an office-warming party while the offices are being completed on the 18th floor in 1990.

Ed Perry and Patrick Welsh.

Left: Ed Perry and his wife, K. Shaver, at Ed's retirement dinner.

Below: Ed and Janet Jacubowicz.

Former Greenebaumers Pat Nepute (left), now General Counsel, Toyota Motor Manufacturing, North America, and Danny Reeves, now U.S. District Judge, Eastern District of Kentucky, at a firm function in the 1990s.

Below: Leatherman's legacy—Chaz Lavelle, Tom Brown, Chuck Fassler and Mark Sommer, circa 1998.

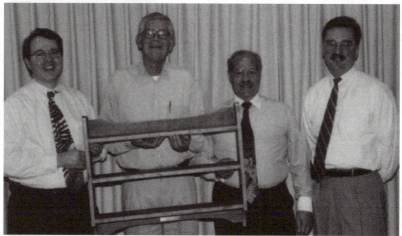

Sale of Porter Paint to Courthaulds PLC in 1987. Present are Pat Northam, Bob Niblock, Vice President of Porter Paint, Bob Champagne, President of Porter Paint, Ed Perry, Jim Davis, Chairman of Porter Paint, and Peggy Lyndrup.

Former Greenebaumer Laurel Garrett.

Barbara Hartung at a Partners winter dinner.

Carolyn Brown with son, Greg, at the firm picnic, 1989.

Marilyn and Rick Anderson.

John Wharton.

Tip Richmond.

Marc McGraw.

David Owen.

The 1990 firm picnic at Kentucky Kingdom, 1990.

Laramie L. Leatherman

THE LEATHERMAN ERA
1987—1994

Larry Leatherman had been the presumptive leader of the firm since Bob Doll's heart attack in the mid-1980s. If not for health problems, perhaps Doll could have continued his leadership of the firm, but as he himself has suggested, there were personal reasons to start leaving the job, and certain indications that it was time for him to step aside. The firm was evolving, and had reached the point, as all firms do, when it had to change to meet new realities. New leadership made the transition easier, but Doll was certainly not pushed. The decision to step down as managing partner was entirely his own.

Leatherman had been a close working associate of Bob Doll's for nearly 30 years, was the heir apparent, and that line of succession was clear to everyone, if not popular with everyone. He was the senior partner in age; he controlled a lot of firm business; and he was looked up to as the guy who would naturally lead the firm.

He had been a tax lawyer in the beginning, in true Greenebaum style. He was an excellent practitioner, but worked differently from Doll and Barnett, his mentors, who had an instinct and a flair for tax work. Leatherman's skill was all learned, the result of hard study. "Larry was more of a technician," Tom Brown says. "The Internal Revenue Code was only 3,000 or 4,000 pages long back then, but it was still complicated and Larry knew it from start to finish." Chaz Lavelle was once sent by Leatherman to the library to check a tax case. After half an hour he still had not found it. "Larry walks in, turns right to the page, and puts his finger on the case," Lavelle says. "That's how well he knew it."

"He was a good mentor," said Rick Anderson, "and trained all the people in the tax group. He was a tough cookie when it came to the practice stuff. I would not have wanted to be on the other side of the table from him in a tax matter."

But his impact on the firm was more than just practicing law. He was a force to be reckoned with, a driven individual whose inner metronome was always set on high. He awoke at an early hour and worked all day, every day, as if the loss of a productive hour were a personal failure. "Larry was a giant," says Rich Cleary, "with an incredible work ethic."

He applied that work ethic to himself, obviously, but as he took on positions of responsibility, he extended his total commitment to the firm. "He was such a mentor to so many people," says Cleary. "His commitment to the firm was unparalleled. He took great pride in the success of all the practice groups. It wasn't just a ballgame for him alone. He wanted to win for the whole firm. He loved to be associated with success at all levels, in all departments. He was a hands-on problem solver."

"He was a real driving force," says Chaz Lavelle, "and he set the standard. He didn't ask anybody to do anything he wouldn't do, or work harder than he was working. I remember one Saturday when six or seven of us were working on a huge tax case.

Leatherman was reviewing our stuff as we went along, and at one point he said to me, 'What else can I be doing for you?' And I looked around and said, 'Larry, I think the only thing we need right now is some lunch.' And with that he got a piece of paper and started taking sandwich orders. He was the head man, but he was willing to do that."

Peggy Lyndrup says that Leatherman's most lasting influences were his dedication to excellence and his insistence that all the firm's attorneys bring business to the firm. The latter represented a slight break from the past, when certain people were major business producers for the firm, and others did the work. "His greatest strength was his dedication and effectiveness in bringing business to the firm," says Lyndrup. "He challenged others to bring in business, too. I did not work with him in tax, but one thing he gave me was tremendous commitment to go out and get in front of business. He felt that you cannot sit in your office and hope the business comes to you. It's important to make sure people know your talents."

His fanaticism and dedication to the firm was such that it compelled him to press others not just to a high quality standard, but to a high work standard, and it was this imposition of pressure on others that caused some firm members to mildly dislike him, and others to actively avoid him. "Larry was hard-nosed," says Tom Brown, "and an excellent lawyer. He was great to work with, for me. But there were lots of people in the firm who were afraid of him. He was a real taskmaster. He was very particular about how things should be said and written. He was the final arbiter of all that. A lot of people perceive that he was hard to get along with. My feeling was that he was such a damn good lawyer that he intimidated people. We used to travel back and forth to Ashland together, and we clicked. Our values were the same. We got along great, but I knew there were people who hated to work with him. Just dreaded it."

"Larry was an old-fashioned, demanding guy," said Rick Anderson. "He told you what he wanted, and made it clear: he wanted you to produce." Anderson's first full year was in 1980, and even though Leatherman was not the managing partner then, Anderson recognized a general when he saw one. "When Larry called me to come to his office, I jumped down there in about two seconds," Anderson says. "I said 'Yes, sir Mr. Leatherman, what can I do for you, sir?' And if he said 'We're going to Ashland on Monday and I need a 30-page brief from you telling me what the applicable law is on the XYZ case,' then you just did it. You were here for the weekend. There was no 'Well, I can't do that because I've got something else to do.' There was never any question."

The Defection

In May of 1987, the firm caught wind of a plan that had Hirn and a handful of other lawyers in the firm leaving to start their own firm. Certainly departures had happened in the past. There were a number of former Greenebaum lawyers who had gone to work for other firms, or had joined companies as in-house counsel. But this departure was different because it was the first group to leave the firm. It was also the last.

It was happening all over the country — whole segments of law firms were leaving, rather than one at a time. It was a trend. And now it was happening in Louisville. The lawyers who decided to leave together were small in number — Marvin Hirn, John Reed, David Harper, Jim Cox, Scott Brinkman, and Gary Weitkamp.

The acquisition of Toyota in 1986 was such a work accelerator that the defection in 1987 had no appreciable effect on the momentum of the firm. Squabbles aside, the firm was on an uptick. There was work in abundance in all practice groups. Over the next few years the number of lawyers in the firm continued to grow.

❦

Jeff McKenzie, 1986

A University of Cincinnati Law School graduate, Jeff McKenzie came to the firm in 1986 and immediately established a broad and multi-faceted real estate, planning/zoning, construction and economic development practice. For his clients he has negotiated hundreds of millions of dollars worth of economic incentives; has guided the financing, re-zoning, acquisition and development of industrial, commercial, recreational and residential properties and air rights; and has provided expertise and counsel before planning commissions and other government agencies.

He is the co-author of the Real Estate Practice Handbook, has been the chairman of the business section of the Louisville Bar Association, and has earned many awards, including a Bingham Fellowship in Economic Development in 1998.

❦

David Owen, 1987

After Clemson University and a law degree from Northern Kentucky, David Owen came to the firm in 1987. He started as a general litigator in the Lexington office, but after two years moved into Lloyd Cress's new Environmental Practice Group where he handled litigation in both state and federal court. He is still involved in many environmental cases and issues with clients such as Marathon-Ashland Petroleum LLC, but he also is involved in construction law and eminent domain cases.

He has handled, with Jack Bender and others, many high-profile cases, such as the Jamestown (Ky.) pipeline case, the Gallatin Steel toxic tort claim, and work for Tomen Corporation, a Japanese holding company.

At the end of 2001, as Danny Reeves left the firm to become a federal judge for the Eastern District of Kentucky, David took over the management of the five-member Lexington Litigation Practice Group.

⌐)

Larry Leatherman and Technology

Larry Leatherman was leading the charge to a new level of client service. He himself was a dynamo of personal client contact, but his interest and fascination with the new computer and communications technologies planted the idea in his head that an even higher level of service was possible. He looked at the cutting-edge devices of the late 1980s—cell phones, fax machines, and portable personal computers—and saw the beginning of the 24/7/365 lawyer. "Larry loved technical innovations," said Rick Anderson. "He was a huge fan of PCs, and had a fax machine in his car. He got a big charge out of that stuff."

And he made it plain that all lawyers were going to use them, a policy which he must have known was going to be a struggle. There were still lawyers at the firm who remembered dictating letters to stenographers. But he was dogged on the issue. To him it was a new way to be more helpful and available to clients, and that was Leatherman's primary motivation. But there were other benefits to his technological thinking—productivity; speed; efficiency; cost savings. And ultimately, he believed, technology would allow lawyers to be lawyers for more hours in the day, freed from document production, research time, and communications delays.

In short, Larry Leatherman envisioned the modern wireless, digital law firm, and began to make it happen long before anyone else did. He was impatient with those who did not embrace his vision. "Larry got mad as hell at me one time," said Anderson. "PCs were just happening, and I was behind the curve. We were working on some sensitive document, and I was supposed to output it from my computer. I couldn't do it, and I made the mistake of giving it to his secretary." Uh-oh. "Larry yelled at me, 'I can't believe you did that! Why didn't you do it yourself?' I was embarrassed to admit I didn't know how." But he learned a lesson. "I was in my late 30s and Larry was in his late 50s, and he was way ahead of me." Four years later Anderson, as Chairman of the Executive Committee, would spearhead his own round of innovative changes based on technology, following the lead of Larry Leatherman.

⤳

The Humana Tax Case

In 1987, the firm played a central role in a landmark tax case that had national implications, and was the largest case, in terms of "dollar effect", in the history of the Greenebaum firm.

The issue involved captive insurance, with the firm representing one of its blue-chip clients, Humana. Humana had taken measures in the mid-1980s when its insurance coverage was cancelled to incorporate Health Care Indemnity, Inc. as a captive insurance company to provide insurance coverage for Humana and its other subsidiaries. In 1987 the IRS introduced a revenue ruling that essentially outlawed this form of "captive" insurance, and thereby put not only Humana but also dozens of Fortune 500 companies in the crosshairs for IRS scrutiny, back taxes and penalties. The IRS immediately took some companies to court on the issue, and had won every time. Humana was considering a settlement with the IRS, but the feds were eager to try the case and not in the mood to settle. The case was brought to trial and Humana lost. The firm and Humana both still felt there was merit in their case and asked the Tax Court to reconsider. On the second round Humana lost again, but there were some judges who dissented from the majority, including the trial judge.

In the post-mortem discussion on Round 2, Humana indicated a willingness to cut its losses and settle, but the firm—principally Larry Leatherman and Chaz Lavelle—believed there was still hope for a win, and offered to handle the appeal on a contingent basis. Humana agreed to let the firm try, and the firm pressed on with the appeal to the Sixth Circuit. In Round 3 in the summer of 1989, Humana won. It was the first captive insurance case in the nation won by the taxpayer. In 2001 the IRS presented another revenue ruling that said, in effect, that they would follow the Humana ruling in all cases. (More about this case in Client and Case Highlights of the Leatherman Era.)

It was a big win in every sense of the word—a precedent-setting decision, a triumph of perseverance, and a very nice fee.

And a feather in the cap of Larry Leatherman, who on July 30, 1989 could barely contain his excitement when he sent the following memo to all attorneys and paralegals in Louisville and Lexington:

"As you know, on July 28 we received the opinion of the United States Court of Appeals for the Sixth Circuit holding that Humana had prevailed to the extent of approximately 90% of the amount at issue in this case. The dollars at issue in this case and the subsequent dollar effect of such holding causes this case to be by far the largest dispute this law firm has ever handled. Furthermore, since the government has invented the "economic family" argument in 1977, this decision is the first one in the United States to decide the captive insurance issue in favor of the taxpayer. There have been several well known taxpayers, including Gulf Oil and Mobil that have been unsuccessful in defending their position when challenged by the IRS.

"All of us know that the final chapter in this story has not yet been written because of the potential for review by the United States Supreme Court. Nevertheless, in light of this unprecedented holding by a United States Court of Appeals, I believe it is now appropriate to recognize the team of Greenebaum and Humana professionals who have successfully carried the effort this far. Accordingly, we will host a cocktail party on July 31 to do so.

"P.S. If we are ultimately successful, I promise you we will have a truly memorable bash."

Having a "bash" wasn't a normal Leatherman reaction, but if there was anything that put Larry Leatherman in a party mood, it was a firm win of that magnitude.

~

Northern Kentucky and Wm. T. (Bill) Robinson III, 1990

Starting in 1986 Larry Leatherman, Bob Doll and others who had been involved in the successful merger with the McDonald firm in Lexington contemplated, with varying degrees of urgency, the creation of a Greenebaum office in the northern Kentucky/ Cincinnati area. It was plain to see that the economic growth curve in Cincinnati was far outstripping Louisville and Lexington in the mid-to-late 1980s, and the new international airport to be expanded in northern Kentucky was going to rev up the economy another notch. Leatherman, for one, was absolutely convinced that the firm needed to be there, and as early as 1988 said, "Our instincts told us that there should be opportunity for a quality law firm to have a successful operation in Northern Kentucky." But no steps were taken at that time.

In mid-1989 a series of exploratory conversations were held with "a small Cincinnati firm with a Northern Kentucky clientele" but, as Leatherman reported, "No further contact was made because there did not seem to be a strong economic potential."

But things changed in 1990. At the Kentucky Chamber of Commerce Annual Meeting in Louisville in May, 1990, Larry Leatherman ran into an acquaintance, a young, dynamic lawyer, Bill Robinson, from the Cincinnati/Northern Kentucky area, who told Leatherman that he was interested in discussing a possible merger with the Greenebaum firm.

Bill Robinson remembers it well: "I was at the Chamber meeting in Louisville at the Galt House. Larry Leatherman and I had served together on the board of the Kentucky Chamber of Commerce, and we had known each other from our work with the Alumni Association at the University of Kentucky law school. During a coffee break I said to Larry, 'I'm thinking about making a major move in my career. We've known each other a long time. You know I have tremendous respect for you and your firm, and I'd welcome some thoughts from you on how I ought to go about this.' Larry said, 'I've got an idea for you; let's meet for breakfast in the morning and we'll talk about it.'

Robinson had co-founded a boutique litigation firm in the late 1970s with Mark Arnzen, a close friend from the University of Kentucky law school, and together they had grown the firm to twenty lawyers. Though successful, Robinson did not feel the firm could grow fast enough to service the business opportunities that were developing in Northern Kentucky. As chairman of the Northern Kentucky Chamber of Commerce and one of the founders of the Tri-County Economic Development Corporation (TRI-ED), Robinson had a good feel for the business future of the region. "I had at that time pretty much made up my mind that I was going to affiliate with one of the big, state-wide law firms because I had come to the conclusion that Northern Kentucky in the 1990s was going to explode with corporate business development."

To Leatherman, Robinson looked like a Greenebaum lawyer. Robinson had spent the past 18 years developing many business contacts, and had been instrumental in forming a development corporation whose mission was to increase the viability of Northern Kentucky for new business and economic development. Through his efforts a number of companies had opened new businesses in Northern Kentucky, and Robinson was naturally interested in engaging these companies as corporate counsel. His firm had made the short list of many of them in the 1980s, only to be disqualified in the end because the firm did not have the kind of business law firepower a big corporation needed to bring to bear on its interests. This was a frustrating situation that Robinson wanted to rectify by aligning his firm with another law firm that had the resources to handle major tax, finance, securities, employee benefits and labor matters.

By the time Leatherman and Robinson met for breakfast in Louisville, Leatherman had already made some calls. "Larry had already appointed a committee," Robinson said, "and was prepared to have that committee meet with me later that afternoon, and basically said, 'You don't need to talk to anybody else. We're the firm you should be talking to. We've already made a business judgment that we're going to move into Northern Kentucky and Greater Cincinnati, and we'd like to talk to you.' And the rest is history." Leatherman communicated to Robinson at that time that he would forward Robinson's interest to members of the Executive Committee. He did so soon after, meeting with Peggy Lyndrup, Tom Brown and Eric Ison. The group agreed that the matter deserved to be discussed further, which was done at the firm's Executive Retreat. The Business Planning Committee at the retreat officially recognized the possibility and potential of a new office in Northern Kentucky.

In Covington, Robinson's partner made it official that he did not want to make the move to a big firm. "He wanted to stay with the original firm," Robinson said, "so we decided I would go my way and he would stay and keep whoever else wanted to stay. Harry Rankin, Doug Johnson, myself and three associates decided to merge with Greenebaum if the firm offered."

While negotiations went forward, Leatherman weighed in with his opinion on the day of the Members' merger vote, August 1, 1990. He had not waivered in his support for the merger and his belief in Bill Robinson. His memo to the Members said:

"<u>My Views Regarding Northern Kentucky</u>. I believe that Northern Kentucky is headed toward a high degree of economic growth in the next 10 years because of the airport expansion and the proximity to Cincinnati. This means that many new businesses will be established. It also means there will be a substantial need for more legal services. I believe that if the firm is to take advantage of this growth opportunity it must move promptly to establish an office in Northern Kentucky and place in that office leadership well positioned to capture a large share of such growth as well as attract existing business. Such leadership must also be of a quality, character and vision that will make the Northern Kentucky office a strong, harmonious player in the Greenebaum business plan. I believe that if the firm takes such action it is highly likely that it will prosper significantly more in the next 10 years than if it does not.

"I believe that Bill Robinson offers the firm by far the best overall opportunity to attain those objectives. He is not only a well regarded litigator he is also a highly energetic, effective rainmaker with the strong desire to join a firm and contribute to the firm's overall success by developing a much larger profitable practice in Kentucky. His joining our firm will strengthen our firm not only in Northern Kentucky but will permit us to attract business in many other areas throughout the state because of his high name recognition among business leaders."

But Leatherman was leaving the final decision to the

Members which, in the context of firm history, was a remarkable constitutional development. In the old days, Sam Greenebaum and Bob Doll would have decided. In 1990, a change of this importance was a voting matter. Like a good party chairman Leatherman instructed the Members on the issues:

"During the next ten days it is probable that the Executive Committee will present to you for your formal consideration an agreement which will provide for the inclusion in the Partnership of Bill Robinson, Doug Jones, and Harry Rankin. It is noteworthy that most of the provisions of the Agreement provide the methodology for determining the compensation and the other new partners. That is appropriate because it is critical to establish a method of compensation that is fair to my existing partners as well as those being admitted to the firm.

"In your consideration of the proposal of the Committee, I urge that you consider compensation as only one factor to be weighed. In my view the most important factors are: (1) Character of the proposed partners; (2) Potential for attracting new business either directly or indirectly as result of opening Northern Kentucky office; (3) Rainmaking ability of proposed partners; (3) Legal ability of proposed partners; (4) Ability to integrate Northern Kentucky office effectively into firm; and (5) Long-term impact on firm's competitiveness."

The Members did, in fact, vote in favor of the merger, and in doing so the firm put a large footprint on the largest metropolitan area in the Ohio Valley. In Bill Robinson the firm had a Member In Charge who was connected not only to Northern Kentucky but also to the power structure of Cincinnati and the robust corporate community there.

The firm started out on a lower floor of the River Center

building in Covington while the design and renovation of its offices on the 18th floor were being completed. They moved into their new space early in 1991, and today the firm occupies the entire 18th floor of the building.

~

The Northern Kentucky office of Greenebaum, Doll & McDonald was successful right away, but its composition of mainly litigators was very different from the firm's other offices. And everyone, including Bill Robinson, knew that had to change. "We started out with a litigation base," he said, "and a smattering of business clients, but we knew from the very first discussion about opening an office in Northern Kentucky that it could only be successful in the long run to the extent that we could recruit expert lawyers in the business and commercial areas of law practice." That became Robinson's determined goal, and over time the office has been successful in balancing the firm's complement of lawyers in litigation and business law.

~

Wm. T. (Bill) Robinson III

A graduate of Thomas More College (1967) and the University of Kentucky College of Law (1971), Robinson began doing trial work in the areas of personal injury, malpractice, and product liability. But he was not a typical litigator; he was and is the rare trial man who also is a rainmaker for the firm in all areas of business. He works hard at making personal and professional associations that put him at the center of the action. It's all there in his resume: a board member of the Cincinnati Institute of Fine Arts; board member of the Cincinnati/Northern Kentucky International Airport; board member of the Cincinnati Symphony

Orchestra; Northern Kentucky Division Chair of the Fine Arts Fund of Greater Cincinnati; board member of the Cincinnati Chamber of Commerce; chair of the Kentucky Chamber of Commerce; and founding board member of the Tri-County Economic Development Corporation to name just a few. Professionally he is currently a member of the American Bar Association Board of Governors, and Chairman of the ABA's Finance Committee, along with having served on many other committees of both the ABA and the Kentucky Bar Association. Robinson has been recognized with a number of prestigious awards in the legal profession and in the community at large, including, most recently, the Cincinnati Bar Association's highest award, the Themis Award, in 2003 (only the fourth recipient) for "Extraordinary service by an attorney to the Cincinnati Bar Association, the legal profession, and/or the general community, which displays a high level of commitment, dedication or courage."

Robinson is aware of his uniqueness as a litigator. "Historically, most litigators in larger law firms have not been significant developers of new business," he says. "My uniqueness may be a result of my varied involvement outside the practice of law in the civic and business life of the community. It's somewhat unusual for a trial attorney to hold leadership positions in various chambers of commerce, economic development initiatives, human relations programs, and the arts, coupled with fundraising for the United Way, the Fine Arts Fund, and a wide variety of other civic and professional causes over the years." Robinson notes that more lawyers throughout the firm, including younger lawyers, are accepting and fulfilling significant volunteer leadership roles in all of the communities in which the firm has offices. "Over the years this has become a signature characteristic of our firm," he says.

Litigation and dispute resolution are Robinson's focus in

the practice of law. "I like the competition and the intellectual debate," he says. "But the real privilege is in representing as an advocate the interests most valued by the persons and companies we are privileged to serve. The stress of litigation has different effects on people; for me it has been energizing. I have found every litigation experience, regardless of outcome, an opportunity for personal growth and additional learning. Litigation provides exposure to a wide variety of persons of talent and expertise throughout the business community, and it has been endlessly fascinating to make those acquaintances. Going through litigation is analagous to being at war. And when you're at war you get to know the other people in the foxhole with you pretty well."

The Death of Larry Leatherman

It was Monday, March 24, 1994. By 10:00 a.m. Larry Leatherman and Chaz Lavelle had already talked about a long list of tax cases, and Leatherman had said to Lavelle, "I was lobbying over the weekend." There had been a business tax bill moving through the state legislature, and Leatherman, as the chairman of the Louisville Chamber of Commerce, had driven to Frankfort to lobby against it. "Typical Larry," said Lavelle. They talked some more, and planned their timing for a tax court meeting after lunch.

After lunch they got in Leatherman's car for the drive to the Federal Building. They parked in the back parking lot, walked up 6th Street, and entered the building through the front doors on the east side. The elevator doors to their right opened, but instead of stepping in, Leatherman said to Lavelle, "We're not going to do this."

"What?" said Lavelle.

"We're not going up."

They walked back outside and down the steps to Broadway.

Lavelle, staring at Leatherman, said, "What's wrong?" Spotting a policeman nearby, Lavelle said, "There's a cop right there if you need one." Leatherman said no, there's nothing wrong. But as they walked back toward the car, Leatherman handed his keys to Lavelle, who was now worried. As they drove away, Leatherman said to Lavelle, "Take me to Audubon."

Lavelle protested, "Larry, there's a policeman right there."

"No," said Leatherman, "*you* take me to Audubon."

As they drove east on Broadway, Leatherman tilted his seat back, which Lavelle had never seen him do before. Lavelle crossed Third Street and said, "Larry, we're near a bunch of hospitals on our left," to which Leatherman responded with force, "Take me to Audubon!"

As they crossed under I-65, nearing Methodist Hospital on their left, Leatherman groaned audibly, and Lavelle had seen enough. He quickly pulled into the emergency entrance at Methodist, where doctors and attendants came right out. They took Leatherman out of the car, unconscious, and wheeled him directly into the emergency room. Lavelle filled out paperwork and called the office to relate what had happened. Immediately an effort began to find Portia Leatherman or other family members.

Not being family, Lavelle was not told the news by the doctors. Larry Leatherman was dead. He had died of a massive heart attack at age 62.

CLIENT AND CASE HIGHLIGHTS
OF THE LEATHERMAN ERA

Bruce Lunsford and Vencor

As an of-counsel lawyer with the firm from 1984 to 1989, Bruce Lunsford had looked out over the national commercial landscape in search of an entrepreneurial opportunity. He didn't know exactly what it would be, but knew it would be big, and told Ivan Diamond, only slightly in jest, to get ready to take him public. And just as Lunsford had predicted, his ship arrived, and what a ship it was. It was called Vencor, a hospital company offering specialty and long-term healthcare services, and to many local investors it was Humana all over again.

Ivan Diamond did indeed take Vencor public in 1985. The stock in the beginning was strong and steady, and "everyone was happy about it but Bruce," said Diamond. "Rally's went public about the same time as Vencor," he said, "and its stock zoomed through the roof while Vencor's stayed about the same. Bruce called me up and said, 'Ivan, how can this be? I've got a very nice healthcare company here and nothing's happening. My company has much better margins than Rally's, better profits—what's going on?'" (There was something going on, but that's another story. See below.)

Lunsford should not have worried. During the period that coincided with Larry Leatherman's leadership of the firm (1987 to 1994) Vencor grew at an astonishing rate, and was considered one of the high-flyers on the American economic scene. Large and frequent acquisitions were the Vencor way. They fueled the company's thrill ride to the Fortune 500 list and, like Humana, gave chairman Lunsford the confidence to announce plans to build a grand new addition to the city's skyline near the corner of 6th and Main, in perfect alignment with the Humana Building.

Lunsford himself was in his element. A legendary entrepreneur, he was rolling up and consolidating specialty hospitals at a fierce clip, keeping the firm busy with acquisition work.

By 1994, near the end of the Leatherman Era, Lunsford was considering the most audacious move of all—buying Hillhaven Corp., the second-biggest nursing home operator in the country, a company four times Vencor's size.

Bert Sugarman, Jim Patterson, and Rally's

The firm's connection to Rally's—a drive-through fast food restaurant—was and is Mike Fleishman, who represents owner Jim Patterson in many food enterprises, and who became a director of the company. Ivan Diamond also was involved with Rally's, specifically in its initial public offering of stock, which occurred after the firm helped roll up all the individual restaurants into one chain.

In addition to Patterson, who is well-known in Louisville and Palm Beach for his astute investments in food and real estate development, Rally's was part-owned by Hollywood businessman and entertainment investor Bert Sugarman, who was married to

Mary Hart of "Entertainment Tonight" fame.

It was well known that Patterson and Sugarman, who each owned about the same amount of stock, did not see eye-to-eye on management matters, and Sugarman set about maneuvering himself into position to take over the company. Unbeknownst to Diamond, Patterson, or Fleishman, Sugarman went into the market after the IPO and started buying every share of Rally's stock he could get. The stock went up accordingly. The SEC investigated, fined Sugarman, but in the end Sugarman gained control of the company. Jim Patterson decided to sell his stock to Sugarman, and settled on a number that was below what he thought it was worth. But Patterson got happier with the sale price later when Rally's faltered during expansion, lost a lot of value, and eventually merged out with Checkers.

Humana Keeps Growing

By the time Larry Leatherman's reign was well under way, Humana had become a giant in the health care industry. In 1988 its $2.8 billion in revenues stood out from the pack of other hospital companies like a diamond amid coals. After capital spending it had about $230 million left over, dwarfing its nearest rival, Hospital Corporation of America, which was scrambling to break even.

For the industry as a whole, government regulation and rising costs had reduced margins to low levels, and caused a rash of consolidation. But Humana was sporting some $300 million in cash and securities, $320 million in insurance investment premiums, and $500 million in receivables.

But experts who looked ahead a few years saw a bleaker picture for hospital companies. The combination of high debt loads, severe cost containment, shrinking margins, a brutal regulatory environment, and heavy economic pressures made some Humana executives think twice about re-investing in the hospital business. They started thinking about getting out of the hospital business altogether.

In the fall of 1991 Humana was called before the House Energy and Commerce Committee to explain its practice of "cost shifting," and in essence to defend itself from charges that it was gouging customers. Politicians like Rep. John Dingell jumped on the bandwagon, calling for wider probes, and it was clear that there were forces in play which opposed the very idea of "for profit" hospitals.

In this climate Humana made the decision in 1992 to spin off the hospital side of its business to Galen Healthcare and retain its insurance company as Humana. Galen, then under the leadership of Carl Pollard, a firm client, made the decision to merge the hospital company with Columbia Hospital Corp. Columbia, headed by Richard Scott, agreed to keep the hospital company headquartered in Louisville, but after buying Nashville-based Hospital Corporation of America for $5.7 billion in 1993, moved its corporate headquarters there.

"Papa John" Schnatter, Charles Schnatter and the Little Pizza Company in the Closet

Charles (Chuck) Schnatter was a corporate attorney with Greenebaum in the 1980s and '90s, and his brother John was a food entrepreneur who was experimenting with a Dominos-type pizza delivery model. Chuck, after long hours working with Peggy Lyndrup in the Corporate Department, worked on the franchising of the concept. The business grew, and John soon needed money to expand the business further. Peggy Lyndrup and Ivan Diamond, among others, suggested to Chuck that going public would be a good way to raise capital. "But Chuck said he didn't know if John wanted to do that—the public scrutiny, the SEC, and so forth," said Diamond. But soon their expansion plans demanded an influx of cash, and "Papa John" decided to go public. Diamond and others took the company public, and today it is the fourth-largest pizza chain in America, nipping at the heels of Pizza Hut which, ironically, is also headquartered in Louisville, Kentucky.

The firm also is involved with PJ America, a once-public company that emerged from Papa John's as a franchisee corporation led by Mike Fleishman, and which recently was returned to private ownership.

Chaz Lavelle's European Vacation

Many lawyers participated in the famous "multi-national, simultaneous" that Rick Anderson coordinated for his client, Abrasive Industries. No one's role was more interesting in that deal than Chaz Lavelle's.

It was an ambitious undertaking—closing interlocking acquisition deals in Louisville, Dallas, Toronto, Luxembourg, and Bonn, Germany at the same time, with a deadline. If one failed, they all failed. Nearing the deadline, Anderson became concerned that the Luxembourg piece would not fall into place. To bird dog the closing there, he sent Chaz Lavelle, who had done some acquisition work before and had the most important qualification— he had a passport.

The deal had to close by 2:00 p.m. on a Friday. Lavelle arrived a few days early, and was impressed that the Luxembourg lawyers could speak eight languages. But they were slow as hell. For a Greenebaum attorney it was excruciating. Late Thursday afternoon the female Luxembourg counsel said she wished they had a resolution for something. Lavelle asked what it would say. She told him. Lavelle called the office in Louisville and related the terms of the resolution. By 9 o'clock the next morning the resolution had been faxed and was waiting for him at the front desk. Lavelle says, "I handed it to her and asked, 'Is this what you wanted?' She couldn't believe it. She said, 'How did you do this?' You'd have thought I had handed her the Ten Commandments."

The closing was in Germany. Unknown to Lavelle, German

practice calls for all legal documents to be read aloud, *in toto*, by a notary before signing. As the papers were read, Lavelle nervously checked his watch. The deal had to be closed by 2:00 p.m. They weren't going to make it. At 1:45 the Canadians closed their piece. Next the Americans closed their piece. Anderson called Lavelle, asking what the problem was. The clock was ticking, and Lavelle had to stand up, interrupt the proceedings, and ask, "Is there anyone here who doesn't believe this thing is going to close, ultimately? Can this deal go ahead, and we'll do the reading and the signing later?" The money was then wired, in time, to preserve the deal structure.

But the reading went on for another two hours. Almost at the end, a bank lawyer said, "Oh my god, I've forgotten something. I wish we had an officer of the U.S. company here, because I need a signature to close the deal." Lavelle poked through his briefcase. "I pulled out a resolution we had drafted two weeks earlier making me an officer of the company. I signed, and it was over."

～

The Labor and Employment Law Practice
Expands Rapidly and Develops a National Reputation

It was during the Leatherman era that the labor practice grew in size and stature. From 1981 through Larry's passing in 1993, Rich Cleary was joined in rapid succession by Phil Eschels, Jeff Savarise, Tom Birchfield, Rob Hudson and Brent Baughman, who formed the nucleus of what is today a thriving practice. Good friend and colleague, Pat Nepute, left the group in 1991 to become Toyota's first employment counsel, later joined by Stephanie Prewitt, another alum of the group. Pat is now General Counsel for Toyota-North America. Jeff Savarise leads the firm's Toyota relationship, serving this important firm client nationally on employment litigation.

The success of the group was due in part to the fact that these attorneys recognized early that effective counseling and client training helped diminish the risk of employment disputes. When those disputes could be neither avoided nor resolved, the group represented its clients successfully in nationally important cases arising under the NLRA, ADA, FMLA, and the Federal and state civil rights acts.

The practice also developed a strong following of clients for its expertise in negotiating labor contracts in a multitude of industries including aluminum, tobacco, steel, transportation, auto parts assembly, grocery, chemical manufacturing, tire manufacturing, and retail and service. No longer content to be a player merely in Kentucky and the region, the reach of the practice is broad as the firm serves as national labor and employment counsel to many of its clients.

Leaving the Leatherman Era

In the aftermath of Larry Leatherman's death, the firm held steady. "We all knew we had to bind together," said Chaz Lavelle. "Nobody panicked." But after a period of mourning there would be a need to choose new leadership, and decide how the firm's governance would change.

One of the prevailing governance ideas was to structure the firm like a modern business. It had always been a business, of course, but its management style had been autocratic, personality-driven, arbitrary in some cases, and to a certain extent, secretive. Larry Leatherman had come from that era, but he must be given credit as the one who made the first steps toward modernization. It is ironic, perhaps, that the man whose personality was the most outsized in firm history would be the man in whose era the management power in the firm was decentralized.

His insistence on members' participation in the acquisition of new business, and his application of new technology to the practice of law were both harbingers of a new era, and precursors of the modern law office.

But if Larry Leatherman had a true legacy, it was his zealous, near fanatical, attitude about serving and protecting his clients. It is safe to say that there has never been a Greenebaum attorney, before or since, whose passion, sincerity, and commitment to serve clients equalled Larry Leatherman's. After his death, one client, Columbia HCA, was so grateful and so appreciative of his years of service that it took the unprecedented step of running a large ad in the *Courier-Journal* as a tribute to him. Above a picture of Larry was the headline:

"On the Values of Commitment, Hard Work and Decency—
A Tribute to Larry Leatherman."

The text of the ad is as fitting a tribute to the man as any client could ever give:

"Tenacious. Talented. To the great benefit of our community Larry Leatherman applied to his unbounded civic commitment the same skills that made him an outstanding counselor to our company and many others.

"Character. Concern. With all this drive, these qualities coupled with warmth and humor made him: a decent guy. The kind of friend we'd all like. We appreciate that friendship, and the benefits it bestowed on our community. We'll miss Larry.

"From those he touched at Columbia/HCA Healthcare Corporation."

Peggy Lyndrup speaks for all Greenebaum attorneys when she says, "I remember reading that ad in the paper and thinking that it would be my deepest hope that, if I were to die, my clients would think that much of me."

There could be no successor to match Leatherman, and the firm didn't try, because it was time to install a new type of leader—a chief executive officer, a long-range planner, a business analyst—who could run the Greenebaum ship on a full-time basis, and guarantee to the Members a manager who was watching the dollars and cents for everybody. That new leader was Rick Anderson, and shortly after Larry Leatherman's death, Anderson was elected by the Members to lead them into a modern era of unprecedented growth, reputation, and financial power.

Rick Anderson

THE ANDERSON ERA

The Creation of the Large, Modern Firm

By 1994 the firm had matured in its political and administrative development to the point that the old yardsticks for leadership in the firm — charter status, seniority, force of personality, or equity in the firm — were, if not unimportant, then less critical to the smooth and profitable running of the enterprise than they were in the previous four decades and three administrations. The Executive Committee — the "Board" — had assumed the real power in the firm, and the chairman of that board was the head of the firm, and had the same kind of power a CEO had — broad and generally unfettered, but checked on all doctrinal matters by a vote of the larger board, and in some cases by a vote of the whole membership. The firm had evolved, in short, into a modern business entity, using a system of corporate management not unlike the systems that governed the successful businesses to whom the firm provided legal counsel.

If less charming, the new corporate business structure was

emphatically the right way to run a law business in the middle 1990s, and the change felt especially timely to the Greenebaum lawyers who had been with the firm for many years, who sensed the end of a certain leadership style with the death of Larry Leatherman. The advent opportunity was to renew the firm, to modernize it, and to become as structurally savvy as possible.

This new corporate structure came to mean more than just a new way to wire the Greenebaum parts together—it was a new culture, one that put the emphasis on the firm rather than its patriarch or a few key lawyers. Gordon Davidson points out that the same thing was happening all over town: "In the old days," Davidson said, "someone would say, 'Arthur Grafton is my attorney,' or 'Wilson Wyatt is my attorney.' Today you'd say, 'Greenebaum is my attorney,' or 'Wyatt is my attorney.' It's the firm that matters, not the individuals."

Not every single Greenebaum lawyer embraced the new concepts at the time, but from the perspective of 2003, the new management tools installed in the 1990s have paid off handsomely, not just in revenues but also in better organization, communication, logistics, client service, hiring, marketing, long-range planning, and virtually all the performance criteria one could name.

In its 50th anniversary year the firm finds itself bigger, more versatile, more state-of-the-art, more comprehensive, more talented, and more robust than it has ever been, with a major role to play in the legal and economic life of the midwestern and southern United States.

⤸

But in 1994, in the wake of Larry Leatherman's death, the firm was just on the cusp of that fulfillment. Eric Ison, who was on the Executive Committee at that time, says, "As we all sat around and thought about it we collectively determined that we still needed a leader, and we still needed to be led out of Louisville. So who among us would it be?"

There had never been a formal line of accession in the firm—no Vice-Chairman who was automatically slated to take over at the death or retirement of the Chairman. So, amid real concern for the future of the firm, there was a lot of discussion and weighing of candidates. There were many senior people to consider—Ed Perry, Mike Fleishman, and several others in Louisville. There was Bill Robinson from the Northern Kentucky offices, who was president of the Kentucky Bar Association and very visible in leadership positions in the industry. There was Phil Scott in Lexington.

But the man everyone came back to was Rick Anderson. Anderson had been on the Executive Committee for a long time; had worked closely with both Bob Doll and Larry Leatherman on Committee matters; had been Member-in-Charge of the Louisville office; had a strong corporate law background; had worked with virtually everyone in the firm at one time or another; and was people-oriented. The Committee met often during this time, and there were side meetings among people who favored one candidate or another, but ultimately Anderson's name came to the top and stayed there.

But did he want the job? Luckily, yes. "At first it was a daunting task," Anderson says, "because of following Larry Leatherman and his longtime leadership. I hadn't thought about it before, because I thought Larry was going to go on forever. But after Larry's death, when I realized the firm's future was at stake, I felt I could do a good job and apply the skills I had learned over the years to lead the firm. I was 44 years old, but I was ready. And I was honored to be selected."

In the end, said Ison, "We were very lucky. We decided on Rick, we got behind him, and after nine years now he's done a fabulous job. He's a better Managing Partner today than he was nine years ago; he's just gotten better and better. And everyone has been very supportive of him."

And well they should have been — the job facing Anderson was huge.

The firm that Rick Anderson was elected to lead in 1994 was considered by all observers as one of the pre-eminent law firms in Kentucky and the Ohio Valley — one that could compete with any law firm anywhere. Its scope was broadly regional, but national from time to time and in certain specialties. Certainly the companies the firm represented were large and multinational in scope and had enough financial resources to hire the best lawyers available to handle their legal work. In terms of excellence of legal product, Greenebaum was right there with the best.

In terms of hard work, exceptional performance level, client service, diligence and commitment, Greenebaum maintained the rich tradition of its forebears. The firm has always operated with a healthy sense of urgency, and there was no fall-off with the new administration.

So all the traditional attributes were in place and ticking right along, but the firm began to differ from its earlier versions in one huge respect — management structure. Anderson felt strongly that in light of compelling changes in their clients' business behavior, and the changing relationship between attorneys and clients, that a comprehensive overhaul of the firm's infrastructure was necessary. Anderson explains: "By 1994 things had really changed. In the old days lawyers seemed to control the relationship with their clients, telling them what they needed to know. Over the years the clients became far more sophisticated and the relationship has turned around. The client is in firm control. They're smart and sophisticated, and a lot of that has to do with the information age. Suddenly the knowledge lawyers used to guard as priests is now available to everyone, on the internet and other places, and that has changed our business."

Clients began to insist that their lawyers operate at least as efficiently as they did, and in fact, adjust to their business practices. "We had gone through all the evolutionary stages that law firms go through, " Anderson says. "We were multi-office; we had bigger billings than ever; we had regional, national, and international clients. We had to start using modern business management techniques, without losing the things that had made us successful—the commitment and hard work of individual lawyers. The management system we wanted, therefore, had to be designed to maximize individual professionalism and client service."

The management system Anderson favored was an extension and expansion of an idea Larry Leatherman had floated in the early 1990s—that of organizing around Practice Groups. "It was necessary to continue what Larry had started," Anderson says, "personal productivity tools and the transformation of our business practices to match our clients'. So we started to change the way we behaved internally."

Practice Group management wasn't exactly new. It was a popular idea in the 1990s for all law firms that had grown past a certain level of billings. It was a borrowed idea from the general business world. Practice Groups—consisting of attorneys who concentrate their practice in common or related areas, or who serve a particular industry—were to be business units of the firm, much like corporate divisions. Each practice group would be headed by an attorney who functioned as the CEO, directing all the operations of the individual business unit, in addition to being a full-time practitioner. As in other businesses, the Practice Group CEO would report directly to the Board.

This was a major departure from the old system of department heads, which to Anderson's mind was a marked improvement. "In the past," he explains, "the lawyers with the biggest books of business usually became Department Heads. And that was fine for its day. But when a firm gets big life becomes more complicated. The problem was those Department Heads were great lawyers and great business-getters, but they weren't necessarily great administrators."

And leadership combined with management was what was needed in the new, modern firm. Larry Leatherman had recognized this as early as 1988. "One time [in the late 1980s]," Anderson recalls, "Larry got into Total Quality Management. He arranged a TQM session here, and afterward he asked me what I thought. Being a young smart-aleck I said, 'Larry, I think TQM is a great management idea. But don't you think we should have some actual management before we worry about its 'total quality?'" There was very little management level underneath him, no accountability, no express system of organization. The Department Chairs were great guys, great lawyers, and tremendously valuable people, but it wasn't the right way to manage the business."

But the firm spent two more years — from 1994 to 1996 — operating the same old way. They were good, profitable years for the firm, so there was no real sense of urgency to change. Rick Anderson thought things would never change unless he, himself, were to push for it. "Ultimately," he says, "in 1996, after two good years under the old system, I suggested we change to the model I had seen in the business world, which was a board of directors and a line of division presidents who were responsible to the board, and were compensated for what they did. If their line of business grows and was profitable, they get paid well. If it doesn't, they don't get paid so well — or get replaced."

So the Practice Group system was finally put in place. Not everybody was in favor. "There is always resistance to change," Anderson says, "but we tried to create a consensus by showing how this would improve on the system that had been fine for a certain size firm, but had been outgrown. We tried to show how it would mirror what our clients did, and how it would enable the lawyers to do a better job, attract more business, and make more money."

There being no point in trying to derail this locomotive of change, the members fell in line behind the Practice Group system, and when they did Anderson had succeeded in three ways: first, he had imposed the system he wanted; second, he had created a clear break from the past, shrugging off all vestiges of the old order, forcing everyone to look forward, not back; and third, he had demonstrated the kind of leadership the members had hoped he would exercise when they elected him.

Anderson gives the members the credit for making a smooth transition. "The members have been great at embracing new ideas. They'll occasionally disagree with me, saying 'No, you're off the deep end there,' but generally they are receptive. One of the good things about my management style is that I do listen to them. They're very smart people, very competent, very experienced, and I've got to listen."

Today the Practice Groups are the pillars of the firm. There are eleven of them—Corporate/Commercial Law headed by Peggy Lyndrup; Corporate/Securities Law headed by Ivan Diamond; Health Care and Insurance Law headed by Vickie Yates Brown; Finance and Development Law headed by Plumer (Buck) Wiseman; Tax and Employee Benefits Law headed by Charles (Chaz) Lavelle; Trusts and Estates Law headed by John Cummins; Environmental and Natural Resources Law headed by Carolyn Brown; Labor and Employment Law headed by Richard Cleary; and Litigation/Dispute Resolution in three locations, Cincinnati-Covington (Harry Rankin), Lexington-Frankfort (David Owens), and Louisville-Nashville (Mark Riddle), so divided to address jurisdictional differences and procedures.

The purpose of Practice Groups is not purely economic or internal. They are devised to facilitate client service. Practice Groups are designed to focus concentration in specific areas of law and specific industries, in order to maintain a high level of proficiency in the increasingly complex legal disciplines that affect business operations in the United States and abroad, and to speed the firm's response to every situation.

Under this system, no matter what kinds of legal services a client needs, the first point of contact is always their primary attorney, but in many cases the primary attorney guides his client to specialized services provided by other attorneys in the firm.

Practice groups are firm-wide, meaning that the sitting location of any lawyer is irrelevant—he or she serves all firm clients in matters in their legal discipline no matter where the client is located.

Harry Rankin

Following graduation with honors from Transylvania University in 1975, the University of Kentucky College of Law in 1978, and an internship and staff job with Senator Wendell Ford from 1975 to 1977, Harry Rankin began his career in law as a litigator in 1978. Immediately a player in the economic life of Northern Kentucky, he was president of the Chamber of Commerce's Leadership Northern Kentucky in 1981. In 1983 he became the Kenton County (Ky.) Commonwealth Attorney, as well as teaching Litigation Skills at the Salmon Chase College of Law from 1983 to 1990.

Today he is a versatile attorney in the Cincinnati/Covington office, concentrating on civil litigation, injury and malpractice law, white collar crime, and commercial and business law. He is also Chair of the Cincinnati/Northern Kentucky Litigation and Dispute Resolution Practice Group.

Vickie Yates Brown, 1994

Vickie Yates Brown, now head of the firm's Health and Insurance Practice Group, and one of the first attorneys to concentrate on health care law, joined the firm in 1994.

In 1979 she began working with the National Association of of Physicians, a relationship which was pivotal to the growth and development of her now-prestigious and nationally renowned health care law practice. After moving from Lexington in 1990 back to her parents' farm in Spencer County, Yates worked as Assistant Spencer County Public Defender and enjoyed working on the farm, but was soon courted by the Greenebaum firm. "I struggled about whether I really wanted to leave and come into town," she says. In 1994 she came to town, and made an immediate impact in the firm. Her expertise in health care matters vaulted the firm into the first ranks of health industry law firms in the nation. "She has brought tremendous health industry expertise and led our health practice group, which she chairs, to a point of excellence equal to anybody, and really exceeding most," says Rick Anderson. "She keeps us on the cutting edge."

She serves on the boards of many regional and national health-related organizations, and is on the NIH Advisory Council for Human Genome Research and is a council member of the American Bar Association's Health Law section, one of eleven attorneys in the nation who influence Congress on national health legislation.

⌐

New Offices, New Opportunities

By 1995 the firm already considered itself regional, with offices in Louisville, Lexington, and Northern Kentucky. But the competition for new business was increasing. There were more lawyers than ever before, more law firms, more *big* law firms (through mergers), and more sophisticated marketing throughout the legal community. In this climate Rick Anderson made growth a priority for the firm. "In the early days of my chairmanship," Anderson says, "we made a strategic decision to expand further because of economic realities. We wanted to increase our regional reach—not just to get new business, but to serve our clients nationally."

In addition, the strong growth of many Greenebaum clients in national and international scope and stature—Humana, Columbia, and Vencor, for example—plus perennial internationals Ashland and Toyota, thrust the firm into larger and larger legal arenas, and into increasingly sophisticated legal niches. The momentum to grow in numbers, in specialties, and in locations was undeniable.

The priority decision for Anderson and the Executive Committee related to new office locations. The firm did not want to push outward frantically; measured growth seemed the right way to go. But everyone knew that to be regional the firm had to expand out of Kentucky. "So we picked two expansion points," Anderson says. "The first was to be our southern axis—Nashville. One of our big clients, Columbia, had moved its headquarters there in 1997, and there was a great concentration of health care companies there to which we could apply our health care experience. Plus it was a hotbed of venture capital at the time, so we felt it was a natural fit for our business plan and our areas of expertise." So the firm moved into Middle Tennessee in 1997.

And to the north, Cincinnati, Ohio was the logical choice. The firm already had a toehold just across the river in Covington, Kentucky, and there were existing relationships in Ohio that could be nurtured and grown if the firm had an Ohio address. "Bill Robinson and I had decided, as early as 1995, that we could not succeed in Cincinnati and points north working from the south side of the Ohio River," Anderson says. "The river there is a psychological boundary. It's becoming less so, but it remains a dividing line. If you're not an "Ohio" lawyer, with an office in downtown Cincinnati, there are certain things you just can't do in Ohio." So the move into Cincinnati occurred in 1998.

⤸

Expansion often breeds expansion, and it wasn't long before the firm pushed its boundaries out even further. The firm now has offices in seven cities, adding Frankfort, Kentucky, in 1999 and Washington, D.C., in 2001.

Diversification into new areas of law and new locations means more than mere growth. A regional firm is more able to weather economic downturns, address localized business problems, and stay flexible with the waxing and waning of certain practice areas. For example, when business and transactional work declines due to recession or other uncertainty, bankruptcy and litigation work increases. The firm has always been able to balance itself by staying versatile, full-service, and innovative. Rick Anderson explains that "many offices give us more places to drop our line. If one area is down, the others may be up. We've had years in which one office didn't have a particularly good year, but the other offices balanced it out by doing well. Yes, there's a little added expense to having more offices, but it's marginal, and we've had tremendous success in each of our new cities. They've helped increase our client base, our productivity, and our reputation, all of which drives success."

⤸

Louisville
The Louisville office remains the firm's headquarters and traditional seat of the Managing Partner. Since 1973 the firm has

had its offices downtown in the building now called the National City Tower, gradually expanding to accommodate the growing roster of attorneys, paralegals and staff. By 1997 the 60 lawyers in the Louisville office and the 110 staff members who supported them worked on three floors in 60,000 square feet of office space. By the end of 2001 the firm had grown to 105 lawyers and 135 staff, but still occupied the same 60,000 square feet on three floors and a part of a fourth in the Tower.

In January 2002 the firm announced plans not only to expand its square footage in the building but also to totally rebuild and redesign its space in a bold new way. "The Louisville office was getting tight," Anderson says, "and we were falling all over each other. We hadn't remodeled the place in over a decade. The original lease was up, and the time was right to build ourselves state-of-the-art space that we could live in for the next 20 years."

The expansion will essentially double its office space to 100,000 square feet, occupying floors 32 to 36 and floor 15. Under the new arrangement, floor 35 will be the public greeting and welcome area, with meeting rooms of various sizes. Floor 15 will house the administrative and support personnel. All other space will be devoted to private offices and conference rooms for each Practice Group, with state-of-the-art videoconferencing and computer technologies built in. "Plasma screens that come out of the walls, data ports everywhere — we're going to be on the cutting edge of technology," Anderson says with obvious relish, and with a clear nod to his predecessor who put such emphasis on technology.

Completion of the build-out and the renovations will be completed in late 2003.

≈

Lexington, Job D. (Darby) Turner, 1986
Lexington is the second home of the firm, and the place

of origin of Angus McDonald, one of the three name partners in the firm. Lexington is the firm's gateway to the northern, eastern, and southern quadrants of the Commonwealth, and has been a vital player in matters relating to Kentucky's traditional industries—horses, coal, oil and gas, and minerals. The Lexington office is known particularly for its premier cadre of environmental lawyers, whose expertise nationwide is considered world-class.

Job D. "Darby" Turner, a Woodberry Forest, University of Kentucky, and University of Kentucky Law School graduate, is the Member-In-Charge of the Lexington office today. From 1973 to 1983 he was a do-it-all attorney in his father's Lexington firm, Wallace, Turner & Trigg. In '83 he left that firm to start another firm that eventually merged into Greenebaum when the Toyota work was cresting in 1986. He had known Phil Scott, Van Alford and Angus McDonald in the Lexington legal community, and when the scope of Toyota work demanded more sure hands, Turner was amenable to joining the Greenebaum family.

Today Turner's practice revolves around corporate work and deal structuring for many of Lexington's premier businesses and institutions, essentially serving as outside general counsel for many of them. Of particular interest to Turner is the revitalization of downtown Lexington which he assists through Housing Authority work. Turner assumed the helm of the Lexington Chamber of Commerce in 2003, solidifying his strong ties to Lexington business and his mark as a community leader.

⌒

Nashville, Jim Beckner, 1997

The firm's move to Nashville in 1997 was a natural extension of the firm's long-standing relationship with, and expertise in, the health care industry, which is now firmly rooted in the Tennessee capitol. Just as Cincinnati was seen as a regional commercial engine, so Nashville was flexing its muscles as a growing and important business center in the midwest and upper South. There were capital markets there that held great promise for the firm, and it was soon understood that true regionality for the firm would be impossible without having a presence there.

Anderson began to look for ways to establish the firm there. "Late in 1996 we talked to a lot of people and smaller firms, to see if perhaps they would want to join us. We actually got pretty far down the line with one firm, but we just couldn't reach a satisfactory agreement with them." So Anderson changed tactics and concentrated on finding the right individuals around whom to build the office from scratch. James L. Beckner was one of those core attorneys, and today he is Member-In-Charge of the Nashville office. "We now have ten excellent lawyers there, with a growing practice," Anderson says, "so giving it a go with Jim was clearly the right thing to do."

Beckner is a Hampden-Sydney and Vanderbilt Law graduate with deep ties to the business and social infrastructure of Nashville, specializing in structuring mergers and acquisitions and venture capital transactions. He was with the Baker firm in Nashville for many years, and was contemplating a move into the private venture capital business when a friend asked him if he might be interested in heading up the Nashville office of a Louisville law firm. "Don't tell me which one," Beckner told his friend. "Let me think about it first." When he decided he was interested, Chaz Lavelle called, and a few months later, in June of 1997, the firm had its lead Nashville attorney.

Under Beckner, the Nashville office is involved in the financing and structuring of many of the new companies incubating in the fertile Middle Tennessee entrepreneurial zone, and for this reason the firm's business plan makes Nashville a high priority. "We're looking for significant growth there," says Anderson, "and we're working hard at it. We feel that Nashville and central

Tennessee are the southern boundary of our active market, with Cincinnati and southern Ohio at the northern end. That geographic expanse gives us a nice regional footprint. There are many large, sophisticated businesses that are of interest to us in both those cities, and we are representing a growing portion of them."

The Nashville office is in the American Center complex in the West End facing Vanderbilt University. "We started in the Sun Trust Center downtown," Anderson explains, "but we moved to our current near-city location because there is a lot of legal infrastructure in the area, and because clients like the parking convenience and campus setting of the near-West End." The lawyers like it too, because it is a comfortable but sophisticated space, but still close to the courthouse downtown.

✑

Cincinnati, Wm. T. (Bill) Robinson III, 1998

Cincinnati is the financial center of the Ohio Valley, with significant financial institutions and the headquarters of many large national companies. The Ohio River, which separates Cincinnati from Covington, Kentucky, has always been the cultural and jurisdictional dividing line in the region. So the firm's move to Covington in 1990 was designed as a first step to eventually becoming a player on both sides of the river. No firm from south of the Ohio River had ever moved into Cincinnati, so the idea was to establish the firm in Northern Kentucky, raise the firm's visibility, build in size, make a mark for itself with significant clients, and then, at the appropriate time, open another Greenebaum office in Cincinnati proper. It was only a question of time. In 1998 the firm made that move into the Queen City. It was a vision that Rick Anderson and Bill Robinson had had for many years.

They had predicted the growth surge in the region, and to

validate how well-focused their vision turned out to be, one has merely to notice two major companies who have moved to the Northern Kentucky/Cincinnati area—Toyota (a major Greenebaum client) and Ashland Oil (a major Greenebaum client).

The two Northern Kentucky/Cincinnati offices, which now have about 40 lawyers, operate as one unit of the firm called the Greater Cincinnati office, with one Member-In-Charge (Bill Robinson), one office manager, and so on. The Covington office is located in the River Center office complex, which anchors Covington's revitalized riverfront. The Cincinnati office is located in the Chemed Center in the heart of the city's central business district.

Frankfort, 1999

With a growing number of Greenebaum attorneys involved in governmental affairs, legislation, regulation, and industry advocacy, an office in Frankfort, the seat of Kentucky state government, looked like a good add in 1999. Located in a former distillery that is now an historic building, the Frankfort office keeps a close watch on state government, state regulatory agencies, and the legislature on behalf of Greenebaum clients.

"It's an important office for us," says Anderson, "but it started because we had an opportunity to add some great lawyers to the firm who were practicing primarily in Frankfort." Those lawyers included Carl Breeding and Rusty Cress (son of Lloyd Cress of the Lexington office), whose practices and reputations revolved around environmental law and government relations, and David Knox, a former Court of Appeals judge. Breeding, Cress, and some of their colleagues joined the firm in 1999. A Greenebaum office opened in Frankfort when they came on board. This office is now the firm's center for Kentucky governmental affairs, legislative initiatives and advocacy, and especially its Kentucky state tax practice.

Washington, D.C.

The firm opened an office in the District of Columbia in 2001 to better serve clients on the East Coast and to provide a Washington, D.C. presence for all firm clients. The Washington office also handles business transactions in emerging technology and biotechnology businesses, many of which are based in the District and in northern Virginia.

The D.C. office resulted largely from the addition to the firm of Ray Stewart in 2000. Ray, originally from Cincinnati, had practiced corporate, securities, and tax law in Washington, D.C. for two decades with one of the largest firms in the country. He had and continues to have a major practice among clients in the Washington area. It was determined that Stewart could continue to serve his clients better with a D.C. office location, and that it would become an access point for all firm clients whose businesses are affected by federal legislation and regulation, as well as federal tax considerations. "We felt it was prudent," says Anderson, "to establish a presence there to give Ray a base to continue to serve his clients, but also to serve other clients' needs as they arose. Plus, a permanent office would possibly attract traditional clients from the D.C. area. It gives us another place to show our wares, so to speak, and keeps us close to the capital markets that serve the technology sector in northern Virginia and Maryland."

Many Offices, One Firm

Establishing new offices in cities with accelerating growth rates such as Cincinnati and Nashville has been successful because the sense that pervades the firm is that Greenebaum is one firm, not seven. By current design, each office is not a separate operating unit of the firm—practice groups are the operating units that bridge all the offices and provide uniformity and continuity. The practice group structure is the significant reason why Greenebaum is perceived to be a firm of 180 lawyers in *every* office of the firm, whether in Nashville, Louisville, Lexington, Cincinnati, Covington, Frankfort or Washington D.C. For any particular tax problem in Covington, for example, the tax and employee benefits lawyers, wherever they are physically located, are brought to bear on the client problem through the computer, by email, by teleconference, or by videoconference as needed. Expertise, therefore, is firm-wide, not centralized in one office or another. In that way Greenebaum offices do not compete with one another, but facilitate each other, giving the firm flexibility for growth as opportunities are presented, new clients are developed, and new cities are considered for expansion.

This is the shared understanding in each of the offices and in each area of the law in which the firm practices: by using the best available technologies the firm can operate as one in all its locations throughout the United States, much as if the offices were merely on different floors of the same building. There is an ongoing awareness of the challenge to be as present and available as possible to clients in all cities at all times, creating a real-time, on site presence with clients for all attorneys. The firm's credibility in making good on that promise has been a big part of the firm's recent success.

⁀

Technology
Beginning with Larry Leatherman and continuing with Rick Anderson, the firm's enthusiasm for communications and computing technology has been a factor in the firm's growth. It has inarguably been a force multiplier and a transaction accelerator

for the firm, as well as a key component of client service.

Today the firm would simply not be the same without the technological tools that power it. Technology for the Greenebaum firm has become a distinguishing characteristic that simply reflects how important the firm thinks it is for clients to be able to reach their attorneys literally anytime, anywhere. Accessibility and availability are the hallmark of the kind of professional service the firm delivers to clients, and digital devices — cell phones, pagers, Blackberry devices, streaming video via computer— make it possible. Bill Robinson says, "Whenever we are blessed with a new piece of business from another part of the country, I never end our initial conversation without giving them my home phone number and my cell phone number and invite them to call me in the evening or on weekends. They are often pleasantly surprised that I would be willing to do that. They will try it every once in a while, and find out that we really do want to stay in touch, especially when there is a problem."

As reported by Ric Manning, the "Gizmo Page" reporter for *The Courier-Journal*, in a January 6, 1996 article, "Greenebaum, Doll & McDonald was the first Kentucky firm to hang a shingle in cyberspace with a home page created by Kinetic Corp." This fact not only underlines the firm's commitment to technology, it also affirms that the Greenebaum firm moves quickly to incorporate new ideas and techniques. While other law firms were being circumspect about the World Wide Web, Greenebaum was busy building its site, adding a complete listing of attorneys, a collection of press releases and announcements, information about all Practice Groups and specialty practice areas, and all back issues of the firm's newsletter. Today the web site is both an information and communication system, allowing web browsers to contact the firm generally or by direct communcation with individual attorneys.

The new Greenebaum offices in Louisville, planned to be

completed in late 2003, will be "smart" offices and will reflect the same emphasis most cutting-edge businesses today place on technology. In addition to computers with state-of-the-art speeds and capacities, and docking facilities for visiting lawyers and clients, the firm will continue its commitment to video and satellite delivery systems (first introduced in the 1990s) which will serve two functions — real-time teleconferencing to enable face-to-face meetings between Greenebaum offices, and video productions that are becoming powerful components of evidence presentation, testimony delivery, and situation re-creation in civil and criminal court cases.

⁖

Growth

From a three-man firm in 1952, the firm today has grown to 180 lawyers and about 250 support personnel in seven locations. In Louisville alone the firm has grown since 1997 from 60 to 105 lawyers. Clearly the growth curve has turned sharply upward in recent years, and this is attributable to the sheer amount of work the firm has been able to generate, abetted by smart management of resources and the concentration of personnel on profitable areas of business, some of which are new and developing, such as biotech and environmental law.

But the firm has never been about just the numbers. There still is a dedication to excellence required of all new associates, and a certain amount of drive. The influence of the younger generation is present, and management has discovered that there must be new ways to inspire young people to excellence. But the Greenebaum firm has managed to retain its basic personality through all the generational additions.

⁖

Ed Perry Retirement

As the new faces continue to arrive at the firm in increasing numbers, the firm's pioneers—the men and women who set the standards of excellence in the 1950s and 1960s—begin to retire.

In November, 2000 Ed Perry retired, and his retirement dinner demonstrated the kind of generational transfer of ideals that the firm has been able to accomplish for half a century. Peggy Lyndrup, who had the honor of planning the dinner for her mentor, said, "In addition to all the members in the firm, I invited the young associates in the corporate and commercial group, to let them participate in a bit of firm history." And what a nice moment it was, capped by Bob Doll's presentation to Perry of a pair of cufflinks that Sam Greenebaum had given him many years earlier. It was an emotional and symbolic gesture, signifying, of course, more than just the passing of an artifact—it represented the passing of wisdom and trust and institutional tradition from person to person. It was just the kind of meaningful ritual Lyndrup had hoped the associates could see and feel. "They were so touched by the whole experience," Lyndrup said. "The next morning some of the guys thanked me for including them. They did not know Sam Greenebaum, and barely knew Bob Doll, but when they saw that obvious affection, it meant a lot to them."

Lyndrup's poem that night contained a stanza that communicates not just Perry's style but also the firm's:

> And much of what we are today,
> fine corporate lawyers of broad array,
> we owe to Ed and his famous spiel,
> "Negotiate well and do the deal!"

"Doing the deal" is as fitting a characterization of Greenebaum Doll & McDonald as one could imagine. The firm has always been about the successful, timely conclusion of transactions, ever since Sam Greenebaum and Barney Barnett started the firm.

⌒

The old firm in the modern perspective

Rick Anderson is sincere when he says, "As I get older I look back on the good old days, but in reality these are the good old days." From an economic perspective no one could argue with that assertion. But what about the collegiality of the firm, the closeness and common-mission thinking that pervaded its earlier decades? Is it still intact?

There is no doubt that the large, modern firm is different from the firm of the past. "But it's not as big a difference as you might think," says Rick Anderson. "We make every effort to bring people together—dinners, outings, anything to have a little fun together and get to know each other better."

Having multiple offices can be an impediment to familiarity among lawyers, but the Practice Group organization helps foster camaraderie by creating meeting frequency and interaction between personnel in all locations. Also, video conferencing can provide face-to-face communication frequently, which can create bonds that are very nearly as good as personal meetings.

"We try to make it as 'human' as it was in the 1960s," says Anderson. "It will never be exactly as it was, but most of the basic things that made us successful are still the same."

The young lawyers

One of those success factors has always been the recruitment of smart, highly motivated young lawyers who are willing to work hard, to excel, and to devote themselves to client service. "That's the kind of people we hire," says Rick Anderson, "and that's the message we send to them."

A new generation always has goals different from their predecessors—different approaches and different perspectives on all matters, legal or otherwise. But the Greenebaum firm has had remarkably little dissonance with its new waves of lawyers. Anderson thinks "we've been successful in melding the Greenebaum work ethic and commitment to excellence into our young people. I think they're fairly happy."

Part of that happiness must be attributed to an even more pro-active and helpful attitude toward young associates among the senior lawyers. Today the veterans try to give the newcomers as much feedback as possible. Anderson says, "We insist that their managers evaluate them and let them know how they're doing—that's what they want the most."

Greenebaum University

Another important factor in the smooth integration of new talent is Greenebaum University. The brainchild of Jeff McKenzie, the "University" is essentially a series of classes that are virtually mandatory for all new lawyers, but are open to anyone who wants to attend. The classes are not strictly about the law; they deal with the full range of knowledge a young lawyer must have to be a success in the modern legal industry—business etiquette, client development, time management, technology, networking, civic involvement, writing skills, and even international practices and protocols. The teachers can be Greenebaum professionals, but often an outside expert is brought in. The classes are always well-attended, and they contribute not just skills and proficiency, but also confidence and camaraderie among students.

"And it's not just a one-way street," says Anderson. "We also ask the associates what they'd like to learn. So while they are picking up specific skills they ant to acquire, they're also starting to understand what we feel is important."

The "look" of the firm

Other firms may tout their current diversity, but only one—Greenebaum, Doll & McDonald—has the record to prove its diversity. Greenebaum was the first major Louisville firm to have a woman partner—Ellen Pedley—and women and racial minorities have been part of the lawyer mix well in advance of other big firms. A class picture of the firm's lawyers today would not be appreciably different from one taken forty years ago.

Rick Anderson says, "When I first came down here from Cleveland, I always felt that one of the things that made Greenebaum interesting was its diversity. It was composed of folks of different religions, genders, races, and backgrounds, and most weren't from Louisville's Old Guard." That was not so much the case in the other large firms in those days. "It was, and is, one of our strengths," says Anderson.

Anderson messages

Perhaps more than any previous Managing Partner, Rick Anderson looks out over the whole firm and thinks about more than just business. He sees something valuable and important in interrupting the business frenzy once in awhile to count blessings. "We work so hard," he says, "and we're so focused, that when there are occasions to sit back and take stock, usually around the Thanksgiving and Christmas holidays, I think it's worthwhile to think about the relationships we have with everybody in the firm. Because of the crush of business, we forget to thank people, and appreciate them for what they do. We are blessed with great success, and I just think we should all count our blessings and give thanks for them on the proper occasions."

One of those occasions occurred on the fourth of July, 2002. On that day Anderson sent a memo to everyone in the firm that recalled the topical memos of Sam Greenebaum:

"Although we have not sent a Fourth of July message in prior years — perhaps because we, like most Americans, have taken our freedoms and our system of government for granted — it seems to me almost essential, perhaps a duty even, that we all take special notice of Independence Day and its meaning this year in light of the circumstances prevailing since the attack of September 11th. While it has become fashionable to scoff at patriotism and criticize the United States of America for its real and imagined imperfections — historical and current — it seems to me, based on any reasonable judgement, that we ought rather to remember, celebrate and give thanks for our founders and forebears, and the great sacrifices they made — many lost their lives, families and fortunes in the struggle for independence and later to keep us free — and especially for the system of government which they created in the very early years of our existence, a stroke of genius in the history of humankind that remains the envy of the world and which causes millions to seek entry to our nation so that they might live under it. All our freedoms and our prosperity are, ultimately, the result of these sacrifices and genius, and, particulalry in these times, it is fitting that we remember this and be thankful for it as we go about our Fourth of July celebrations. Please have a safe holiday and God bless you."

A 50th Year Snapshot

Fifty years since the firm's inception, the art of doing the deal has created a law firm fully poised to launch a new era of productivity and unprecedented success. A snapshot of the firm in its 50th year shows the following:

Excellent Financial Performance

The firm's revenues have grown admirably over the past several years, even during the last two years when the economy has slowed appreciably.

Financial performance is undeniably an important factor

in measuring success, but how the firm stacks up with its competitors is a particularly telling marker. On that score the firm compares very well with larger firms in bigger markets such as Seattle, Minneapolis, Columbus, Cleveland, Milwaukee, Atlanta and Dallas.

More than anything else this is a productivity result—Greenebaum lawyers getting more out of an hour's work than their competitors—and it has always been that way, going back to the very beginning of the firm. Guiding that hard work, though, is Rick Anderson's operating philosophy that emphasizes the firm's strengths, and focuses on sophisticated, high-end legal work—the kind that lawyers enjoy doing and clients are anxious to get. The firm will continue to expand practices that generate sophisticated work—the complex and often technical work that requires upper-end, leading-edge specialists in such fields as intellectual property, tax, healthcare, labor, litigation, and most corporate and finance work.

Continued Expansion in the Newest Markets

The reliance on one location—Louisville—to bring in the bulk of firm revenues has long been a thing of the past. Under Rick Anderson's leadership the firm intends to continue its regional growth, concentrating on expansion in Cincinnati and Nashville, increasing market penetration in these two excellent economic centers, where the Greenebaum firm is still a relatively new player in comparison to those cities' longer-lived firms.

If history is a teacher, the firm will become a solid part of the entrepreneurial/new company environment in those cities, just as it did in its home city of Louisville a half century ago. "That's one thing that distinguishes us," Rick Anderson asserts. "We are a highly capable law firm when dealing with growth companies and start-ups. We have earned our reputation as an entrepreneur-oriented firm. After all, many of the top public companies in Kentucky were either incubated at the firm, were started and managed by lawyers connected with the firm, or were guided and represented by us. Think Humana, Vencor, Papa John's, Atria, Ventas, and more. And in rising entrepreneurial towns like Nashville and Cincinnati, we've got a lot to offer."

The growth of both those offices will be the centerpiece of the firm's strategic objectives in the years ahead. There are possible future expansions to the east and west, but Anderson says, "Though we haven't closed the door to other opportunities to expand, we're not actively looking right now. When the right situation comes along, we'll act."

New Practices

In keeping with the firm's tradition of staying on the leading edge of the expertise curve, several new practice teams are in place to offer clients services in rapidly developing areas of the law. The Health and Insurance Group formed a Privacy Task Force to help clients cope with the confusing and costly new privacy laws and regulations coming out of Washington D.C., including Gramm-Leach-Bliley and HIPPA. The tax group formed the State and Local Tax Team—the "SALT" team, lead by Mark Sommer, intended to provide focused state and local tax services to clients in a variety of business situations. A Biotech team led by Vickie Yates Brown and Jeff McKenzie will focus on that growing industry. The Japan, Asia, international, and emerging technologies teams continue to attract clients and grow those practices.

Continued Community Service

The firm's attorneys—in fact, all of its employees—continue to serve the communities in which they live and work, contributing considerable effort, money and time to civic and charitable organizations and initiatives in all markets. In addition to serving their churches, synagogues, youth sport leagues and supporting other personal civic and community interests, Greenebaum attorneys and employees serve on the boards of over 100 charitable and civic organizations in seven markets, and chair many of them. The firm has always supported civic and charitable organizations all across our region, contributing well over $1 million over the past three years.

The firm is also continuing its strong tradition of *pro bono* efforts. Many attorneys have made significant *pro bono* contributions over the years, especially Maggie Keane, who received awards in both Louisville and Lexington for her work. The firm contributes hundreds of hours each year to *pro bono* clients of all types.

Reeves to the Federal Bench

The firm took great pride in 2002 in the appointment of Danny Reeves of the Lexington office as Judge of the United States District Court for the Eastern District of Kentucky.

Judge Reeves started with the Greenebaum firm in the summer of 1983 in the Lexington office. He was in the Litigation Department from the beginning, working mostly with Phil Scott and John West on cases ranging from FDIC-related bank closings, to equine cases for the Maktoums, to injunctive work for the Kentucky High School Athletic Association, whose caseload extended to over 200 matters throughout the 1980s and 1990s.

When Phil Scott stepped down as head of the Lexington Litigation Department in the mid-'90s, Reeves was appointed to that job and held it until December 31, 2001, at which time he assumed his duties on the federal bench.

Reeves had always enjoyed working on federal cases during his career, and when he was told in early 2001 that there were to be judgeships coming open in the Eastern District of Kentucky, Reeves contacted the offices of Kentucky's senators, and began a two-month process of questionnaires that resulted in an invitation to come to Washington, D.C. for interviews. The senators' positive responses led next to an interview with the President's general counsel, Al Gonzalez, then to testimony before the Senate Judiciary Committee, and finally to confirmation in December, 2001.

A Greenebaumer to the core, Reeves worked in the Greenebaum offices until 5:00 p.m. on December 31, 2001, then resigned and was sworn in as District Judge at 5:30. "I was out of work for a whole half-hour," he says.

Today Reeves is seated both in London, Kentucky and Pikeville, Kentucky, and occasionally presides over federal cases in Covington, Lexington, and Frankfort, Kentucky.

"Best Lawyers In America" 2003-2004

An astonishing twenty-seven lawyers in the firm were honored as among the "Best Lawyers in America" for 2003-2004. They are: Richard S. Cleary, Labor and Employment Law; Mark F. Sommer, Tax Law; Wm. T. (Bill) Robinson III, Business Litigation and Personal Injury Litigation; Carl W. Breeding, Environmental Law; Michael L. Ades, Real Estate Law; John C. Bender, Environmental Law; Carolyn M. Brown, Environmental Law; Lloyd R. Cress, Environmental Law; Bruce E. Cryder, Natural Resources Law; Marcus P. McGraw, Natural Resources Law and Environmental Law; John W. Ames, Bankruptcy and Creditor-Debtor Rights Law; Thomas A. Brown, Tax Law; John R. Cummins, Health Care Law and Trusts and Estates; Ivan M. Diamond, Corporate, Mergers and Acquisitions, and Securities Law; A. Robert Doll, Corporate, Mergers and Acquisitions, and Securities Law; Mary G. Eaves, Employee Benefits Law; Charles Fassler, Tax Law; Michael M. Fleishman, Real Estate Law; Margaret E. Keane, Business Litigation; Suzanne P. Land, Trusts and Estates; Charles J. Lavelle, Tax Law; Peggy B. Lyndrup, Corporate, Mergers and Acquisitions, and Securities Law; William R. Patterson, Jr., Personal Injury Litigation; Edwin H. Perry,

Corporate, Mergers and Acquisitions, and Securities Law; Glenn A. Price, Jr., Real Estate Law; Michael G. Shaikun, Real Estate Law; and Paul B. Whitty, Real Estate Law.

CLIENT AND CASE HIGHLIGHTS
OF THE ANDERSON ERA

New Clients

The firm's already impressive client list continued to grow during the Anderson Era, with the addition of several multinational companies and important regional and local businesses and institutions as well. During this period, Sears Roebuck and Co., The Kroger Company, General Electric Co., Ford Motor Company, Home Depot, Siemens, Fifth Third Bank, Atria Communities, Lexington Trots Breeders Association (The Big Red Mile Horse Track), Multi-Color Corporation, Joseph Beth Booksellers, Inc., Associated Industries of Kentucky, Jewish Hospital of Louisville, and the Procter and Gamble Company became clients of the firm. The firm's leadership believes that its regionalization strategy has been, and will continue to be, a prime reason for its engagement by prestigious businesses like these.

The Corporex Case

In a $40 million case that demonstrated all the new ways trial lawyers present compelling evidence to judges and jurors, the firm handled and won a major civil case for its client,

Corporex, in 2000-2001. The case involved a dispute between the firm's client, a Northern Kentucky/Cincinnati real estate developer, and a national investment firm over a commercial mortgage loan arrangement. Bill Robinson and Mark Hayden who headed the Corporex litigation showed off the firm's technology expertise in the new Federal Court House in Covington by deploying dramatic and graphically dynamic electronic presentations that utilized that District Court's new computer-based audio and video systems. Using laptop computers to generate all trial exhibits, the firm's team was able to make a jury understand the complexities of commercial financing and deliver a quick verdict.

This was an historic "paperless" trial involving computer monitors for the judge, jurors, witnesses and attorneys, additional monitors for spectators, digital cameras, touchscreen technology on the witness and attorney monitors, with the ability to print paper copies of any display on the witness and attorney monitors for evidentiary purposes and review by the jury. Despite involving 15 trial witneses and over 180 trial exhibits, the technology accelerated trial time, and the verdict was delivered in only six days. The firm also applied the excellent appellate skills of Bill Robinson, Mark Hayden, John West, Brent Baughman and others on an appellate brief that almost certainly facilitated the ultimate settlement of $27.5 million, which brought the firm the largest single fee in the history of the firm.

Louisville Slugger Returns Home
While Hillerich & Bradsby's corporate offices had always been in Louisville, the manufacturing plant for its famous professional wood bats had long been in Jeffersonville, Indiana. John A. "Jack" Hillerich III, then Chairman and CEO, determined to make a lasting contribution to the home state of the Louisville Slugger bat, decided in 1994 to move the wood bat manufacturing

facility to Louisville, and to also build the Louisville Slugger Museum. H&B's new home would be at 800 West Main Street.

Peggy Lyndrup headed the legal team, including Mark Ament, Brad Dillon and others, which sold the Indiana plant, acquired the Louisville site, and constructed the office, manufacturing and museum complex. Negotiations for the new site included obtaining an extended ground lease for the facility. Lyndrup recalls Jack Hillerich's long-term thinking during this process. "He was delighted," Lyndrup says, "when I told him we had obtained a 99-year ground lease. But then he asked, 'What happens after that?'" She went back to the negotiating table to ask the state for a renewal option for another 99 years. "Are you serious?" she was asked. "Dead serious," she replied. The state agreed to the option. Jack Hillerich was happy, and Louisville Slugger was on its way home.

The Perconti Case

With Eric Ison at the helm, the Greenebaum litigation team argued several high profile cases and won significant judgements for its clients.

In June of 2001 Ison, Christie Moore and the Greenebaum trial team prevailed in a four-week jury trial involving Louisville businessman Paul Perconti and his former employer, Thornton Oil, in a dispute over ERISA benefits withheld from Mr. Perconti. (In a related matter, Perconti's holding companies also sued Thornton Oil for payment of the value of two separate joint business ventures with Thornton Oil.) Presentation of evidence to the jury in this complex case, involving hedge trading, energy commodities and the like, was facilitated by computer projection of scanned documents onto overhead video screens, which obviously was received favorably by the jurors who delivered a favorable judgment to Perconti on the ERISA issues. The award—in excess of $3,000,000—is on appeal.

Kentucky Kingdom

The Perconti success followed another high-profile, media-intense case of the late 1990s involving Ison, Kentucky Kingdom, and WHAS-TV. A two-week trial of the defamation case filed by Kentucky Kingdom Amusement Company against WHAS-TV culminated on March 2, 1998 with a Jefferson Circuit Court jury returning a verdict awarding Kentucky Kingdom $3,975,000 against WHAS-TV. The judgment is the largest libel award ever won in Kentucky. As Ison stated in his closing argument, the case was about freedom and responsibility — freedom of the press and the media's duty to exercise this freedom responsibly.

Ed Hart, CEO of Kentucky Kingdom and the driving force behind the litigation, was extremely gratified with the result, saying "Winning a First Amendment case is nearly impossible, but we did it. Eric gave an unbelievable closing argument. Trying a case like this is time-consuming and draining on everybody. Your lawyer needs to be a zealot and a believer, and Eric Ison was a believer."

As of this writing the case is still on appeal to the Kentucky Court of Appeals.

The Toyota Decision

On the labor and employment front the firm won the landmark Toyota decision — the Americans with Disabilities Act case which the firm originated and took through the appellate stage, and which resulted in the U.S. Supreme Court's affirming the firm's position and rendering a nationally-reported decision in favor of Toyota. The Supreme Court held that, in order for an individual to be substantially limited in the major life activity of performing manual tasks, he or she "must have an impairment that prevents or severely restricts the individual from doing activities that are of central importance to most people's daily lives." The plaintiffs claim of disability was based on an inability to perform extended, repetitive work with hands and arms extended at or above shoulder level, which the Court ruled was not "central to most people's lives." According to the Court, therefore, an impairment that precluded the performance of an isolated and/or unimportant manual task was not sufficient for an ADA claim.

Jeff Savarise designed and managed the case from the outset, and his efforts resulted in a great victory and national visibility for the labor practice group and the firm. Jeff worked closely with two Greenebaum alums, Pat Nepute and Stepanie Prewitt.

The Union Underwear/Fruit of the Loom Case

The labor team also prevailed in the Union Underwear case in which the Kentucky Supreme Court drastically and properly limited the reach of the Kentucky Civil Rights Act. The Kentucky Supreme Court overturned a $1 million jury award and reversed a unanimous Court of Appeals panel which had affirmed the jury award. The Supreme Court decided for the first time that the KCRA did not have extraterritorial application, meaning that the provisions of KCRA are extended to individuals only within the state of Kentucky. Brent Baughman and Rich Cleary represented Fruit of the Loom before the Kentucky Supreme Court, and won another important decision for Greenebaum business clients.

Labor and Employment Practice Successes

Throughout the 90's and into the 21st century the labor group continued its string of important litigation victories and a rapidly expanding roster of prominent clients.

In addition to the victories for Toyota and Union Underwear discussed earlier, the group was instrumental in establishing important precedent in a broad range of cases under the FMLA, ADA, Title VII, NLRA, FLSA, ADEA and various state civil rights acts. Below is a sampling of these cases:

Price v. Marathon Ashland Petroleum, Inc.

In a case of first impression, the court held, in a class action filed against various employers operating in maritime, that the Fair Labor Standards Act preempted the overtime provisions of the Kentucky Wage and Hour Act insofar as it related to seaman who were employed on line haul boats that operated in interstate commerce. The court determined that application of the state overtime provisions to seaman working in interstate commerce would provide excessive interference with maritime law uniformity.

Epelbaum v. Elf Atochem N. Am., Inc.

In a case of first impression, claims of national original discrimination, harassment and wrongful death brought by the estate of an ex-employee who had committed suicide, the Sixth Circuit upheld the district court's grant of summary judgment to the employer, finding that the plaintiff failed to present evidence that the decedent was "offended" by conduct on which the harassment claim was based and, further, that suicide was a superceding, intervening event breaking the chain of liability on the wrongful death claim.

United Steelworkers of America, AFL-CIO-CLC v. Commonwealth Aluminum Corporation

In a case of first impression, Sixth Circuit held that medical eligibility determinations are not arbitrable under the parties' labor contract.

Norsworthy v. The Kroger Co.

The Sixth Circuit affirmed summary judgment to the employer under the ADA, holding that an employer is not obligated to create light duty work or continue light duty assignments indefinitely. The court further held that an employer who exceeds the requirements of the ADA with respect to one individual is not obligated to do so in other cases to comply with its legal obligations.

Audubon Regional Medical Center

The NLRB declined to adopt an Administrative Law Judge's recommended order that the hospital be required to bargain with AFSCME. In a break from long-standing precedent, the Board held that the passage of time and turnover in management staff rendered a bargaining order inappropriate.

David Stephen Brown, et al v. JC Penney Company, Inc.

In the first decision issued within the Sixth Circuit addressing the enforceability of a company's mandatory arbitration procedure based solely upon an employee's receipt of arbitration materials (without a signed release) and consideration based upon continued employment, the Court granted JC Penney's motion to compel Plaintiff Brown to arbitrate his claims under the Company's mandatory arbitration system.

MHC, Inc. v. International Union, United Mine Workers of America

In one of the first cases addressing the use of RICO in the context of a labor dispute, the federal district court addressed the question of whether a RICO action is preempted by the NLRA when the alleged predicate acts can be classified as unfair labor practices. The court found that the LMRA did not preempt the civil RICO claim against the union in a case involving strike violence.

Neweagle Industries – Acguisition of RAG

In 1997, the firm represented Neweagle Industries and its 50% shareholder, International Industries, in the sale of an 80% interest in Neweagle to the U.S. arm of RAG Aktiengesellschaft. RAG is the sole German coal producer, and this acquisition marked its first large investment in U.S. coal properties. The transaction was valued at approximately $115 million. Michael Brown, a member of the firm's Greater Cincinnati office, negotiated the last couple of big deal points in Aachen from a balcony overlooking the border with Belgium. He recalls, "As we talked about the deal, the Chairman of RAG coal companies pointed out where one of his predecessors watched the Allied invasion of Germany, and, if I recall the story correctly, was grazed by a stray bullet."

LG&E Energy Corp. – Big Rivers Electric

In July of 1998, the firm assisted LG&E Energy Corp., the Louisville-based diversified energy company, in completing one of the largest hostile takeovers out of bankruptcy in U.S. history. In that transaction, LG&E Energy successfully forced and won an auction for control over approximately 1,700 megawatts of electric generation capacity owned or controlled by Big Rivers Electric Corporation in Western Kentucky, following Big Rivers' voluntary filing for Chapter 11 protection. The transaction was valued in excess of $900 million.

Big Rivers had sought, through its bankruptcy filing, to complete a twenty-five year lease of that generating capacity to Pacificorp (a West Coast energy services company and principal competitor of LG&E Energy in the wholesale power market), coupled with a twenty-five year commitment from Pacificorp to provide energy to Big Rivers to meet the needs of approximately 90,000 residential, commercial and industrial customers in Western Kentucky. Through its efforts before the bankruptcy court and in protracted negotiations with Big Rivers, its member distribution cooperatives and principal creditors, LG&E Energy was successful in blocking the proposed Pacificorp transaction and, ultimately, in completing a similar 25-year lease transaction with Big Rivers and those other constituents.

A team of attorneys drawn from Greenebaum's corporate, finance, tax, bankruptcy, environmental, employment and regulatory practice groups assisted LG&E Energy in completing this historic and complex transaction, bringing one of the largest bankruptcies in U.S. history to a successful conclusion in record time.

Major Bankruptcy Transactions

In the $1.5 billion AGFI case, the firm's professionals were employed as debtor counsel without any current officers and directors to assist in the reorganization of the debtor. Teaming with Jay Alix and Associates (now Alix Partners), one of the premier turnaround management firms in the country, an innovative Chapter 11 plan was confirmed, binding some 240,000 tort claimants and accomplishing a successful reorganization.

In another unique Chapter I I transaction, the combination of Greenebaurn as debtor's co-counsel, with a premier crisis management firm, Bridge Associates, LLC, resulted in the debtor's assets, consisting of some 54 newspapers and 15 radio stations around the country, being sold for excellent values. The sale did not come easily, with very competitive bidding taking place around-the-clock in Greenebaum's offices over a 50-hour period. John Ames, mimicking Danny Glover in "Lethal Weapon," said, "We're too old for this stuff."

Seattle Slew Case

Seattle Slew was one of the great race horses and sires in the history of thoroughbred racing and breeding. He was also the focal point of a high profile and hotly contested action in the Federal Courthouse in Lexington. Dr. James Hill engaged the firm to sue his partner, Mickey Taylor, for fraud and a proper accounting. Phil Scott and Peggy Miller tried the case, which lasted three weeks and resulted in Dr. Hill recovering several million dollars and attorney fees. The case is cited today as the basis of the obligations one partner has to the other in the equine industry.

Cheyenne Resources Case

Greenebaurn attorneys, led by Bruce Cryder, a Lexington member, obtained a $14,500,000 jury decision in favor of our client, Cheyenne Resources, Inc. This case resolved the issue that development work done on the property by Cheyenne constituted "commencement of mining" within the meaning of the lease. This case has had a significant effect on the relationship between lessors and lessees under hundreds of mineral leases in Kentucky.

Acquisition of The Red Mile Race Track

The firm represented a group of standardbred owners and breeders who purchased the famous Red Mile standardbred tract and the associated Tattersall sales facility in Lexington. The Red Mile has conducted racing at the same location for over 100 years and is a venue of great historical significance to the standardbred community.

Humana Inc.'s Acquisition of ChoiceCare Corporation

The firm represented its long-time client, Humana, Inc., in Humana's 1997 $250 million acquisition of ChoiceCare Corporation, a publicly held company based in the Cincinnati, Ohio area. Greenebaum assisted Humana in the formulation and implementation of Humana's strategy to expand within the Cincinnati and Northern Kentucky region, and in the negotiation of the acquisition, all on an extremely tight timetable with other potential acquirers also vying to acquire ChoiceCare. The transaction team, lead by Michael Hawthorne of Louisville, and Michael Brown of Cincinnati, involved members from three of Greenebaum's offices.

Humana, Inc.

Dan Fisher, a Louisville member, assisted Humana, Inc. in its $125 million sale of all the capital stock of PCA Property and Casualty Insurance Company. This sale was conditioned on the contemporaneous completion of a complicated, and politically sensitive, leveraged buy-out of a subsidiary engaged in third-party administrative management services to PCA Property and Casualty Insurance Company by the internal management team of the subsidiary. Greenebaurn successfully closed both transactions in early 200 1.

LifeTrust America, LLC

In September 2002, Dan Fisher, a Louisville-based member of Greenebaum, assisted LifeTrust America, LLC in its multi-state acquisition of nine assisted living facilities, valued at approximately $61.25 million. LifeTrust financed the transaction through a combination of issuing approximately $6.25 million in its securities, assumed loans from the U.S. Department of Housing and Urban Development in the amount of approximately $28 million, and refinanced approximately $27 million in debt.

Aerial Communications

Michael Hawthorne, a Louisville-based member of the firm, learned that Aerial Communications had engaged two nationally known investment bankers to find Aerial a joint venture partner. The investment bankers spent a year and a half looking for a joint venture partner and failed. Greenebaurn made the connection at a CTIA convention in San Francisco with representatives of Sonera, the potential joint venture partner. A series of meetings followed in Chicago, Tampa Bay, Washington, D.C., New York City and Helsinki. Sonera made a $200 million investment and follow with another $ 1.1 billion. In the end, both parties made ten-digit returns on their investments, and Aerial was able to get enough investment capital to grow its business and be successful.

Gallatin Steel

Jeff McKenzie, a Louisville member, received a call from an engineer, who asked that he meet him and two new clients at a fast food restaurant on 1-71 to discuss a property purchase. After waiting almost an hour, four limousines pulled in and disgorged more than a dozen executives. As he was introduced to, and exchanged cards with, Bill Shields, the CEO of one of the two new client companies, Bill glanced at his card, clapped the engineer on the back and remarked in a thick British accent, "Good for you Steve, you found a Scot in Kentucky! He'll buy the property right! " From that meeting (and our clients' determination), Gallatin Steel arose—a four hundred million dollar steel plant located on the Ohio River in Kentucky.

University of Louisville – Papa John's Cardinal Stadium

The firm represented the University of Louisville in the development of its new football facility, Papa John's Cardinal Stadium. The firm's work for the University covered all aspects of the stadium development, including a land swap with CSX Transportation to acquire the site, bond and private financing used to develop the site, construction and related contracts and the completion of the largest brownfields reclamation project in Kentucky's history.

Series of Acquisitions for Multi-Color Corporation

Greenebaum commenced representation of Multi-Color Corporation, one of the world's leading label makers for consumer products in 1997. The firm now serves as outside counsel for virtually all of Multi-Color's legal needs.

Greenebaum assisted Multi-Color with the acquisitions of- Buriot International, Inc. a manufacturer of pressure-sensitive labels in December 1999; Uniflex, a manufacturer of shrink sleeve labels located in Las Vegas, Nevada in June 2000; Premiere Labels, Inc., a manufacturer of pressure sensitive labels located in Troy, Ohio in October 2001; Quick Pak, Inc., a contract packaging company located in suburban Cincinnati in May 2002.

Nashville Health Care Transactions

Stephen T. Braun, former Senior Vice President and General Counsel of Columbia/HCA Healthcare Corporation has been a Member in the firm's Nashville office since 1998. Since joining the firm he has lead the firm's healthcare transaction practice in middle Tennessee and represented many of Nashville's most prestigious health care companies in transactions important to their growth. Among these transactions:

• United Surgical Partners International, Inc.

In February 2001, for United Surgical Partners International, Inc., Braun completed an acquisition by merger of Ortholink Physicians Corporation (a physician practice and surgery center company) with a consideration of $ 100 million.

• Ardent Health Services, LLC

In September 2002, Braun completed an acquisition by Ardent Health Services, LLC of St. Joseph Health System (which included four hospitals in Albuquerque, NM) with a consideration of $ 100 million.

• Communily Health Systems, Inc.

• In January 2003, Braun completed an acquisition of

seven hospitals from Methodist Healthcare in Memphis by Community Health Systems, Inc. for a consideration of $140 million.

Corporate and Securities Practice

During the Anderson Era, the firm continued to lead the region in sophisticated corporate finance work, handling major public offerings and securities transactions, including:

• Atria Communities, Inc., October, 1997, $143,750,00; 5% convertible note offering; Rule 144A.

• Vencor, Inc., July, 1997; $750,000,000; senior subordinated notes issued pursuant to Rule 144A

• CTBI Preferred Capital Trust 11; January, 2002; $25,000,000

• Atria Communities, Inc.; July, 1997; $96,600,000; 6,900,000 shares of common stock

• Atria Communities, Inc. (IPO); August, 1996; $57,500,000; 5,750,000 shares of common stock

• Vencor, Inc. (IPO); September, 1989; $14,450,000; 1,700,000 shares of common stock

• Papa John's International, Inc.; May, 1996; $46,500,000; 1,550,000 shares of common stock

• PJ America, Inc. (IPO); October, 1996; $25,875,000; 2,070,000 shares of common stock

• Papa John's International, Inc.; June, 1993; $18,850,000; 1,450,000 shares of common stock

• Rally's Hamburgers, Inc.; March, 1993; $83,000,000, 9-7/8% senior notes

• PJ America, Inc.; September, 2002; $35,000,000 "going private" tender offer and merger

The Firm's Support Staff

A history of Greenebaum would not be complete without appropriate mention of the support staff whose dedication contributed to the success of the Firm and its attorneys.

Commitment to client service has been exemplified in all of the Firm's ranks. The contribution of its paralegals and secretaries, its accounting staff, librarians, technology staff, office managers, its administrative staff, its service center personnel and its receptionists are admired and recognized.

"We would need another book to document the contributions of those who have supported our attorneys' and our clients' successes," said Rick Anderson. "But a few stories may give you the flavor of the meaning of 'Team Greenebaum,' especially some from the early days."

Roberta Jenkins, a long-time receptionist with the Firm, was always the first person at work in the morning. She would endear herself to the young lawyers with wake-up calls, so that they would not miss a court appearance or meeting. She would sew a missing button on a partner's jacket and return it quietly to his office. She was always a recruiter and promoter of the Firm in every way. Peggy Lyndrup fondly recalls the day as a summer associate that she received an offer of full time employment from the Firm. "Roberta called me over as I walked through the 33rd floor reception area and said that she had heard I had received an offer, and wanted to know was I going to accept. I told her I certainly was going to consider it." Smiling, Roberta said, '*Good, I have just one thing to say – You can go down from here but you can't go up from here.*' I knew then that my fate was sealed."

The Firm's senior legal secretary is Linda Hunter, who joined the Firm in 1966. Except for an 18 month stint at the beginning of her career working for Tom Brown and Mike Shaikun, she has supported the Firm's senior lawyer, Bob Doll, since. Bob says of Linda – "Linda Hunter has been an exceptional Secretary for me and the firm for over 37 years. She is very bright, and hardworking, which is quite a combination. She has seen the firm progress from a handful of personnel to our current status, and she has made a major contribution to our growth and success."

Cindy Hamilton followed shortly thereafter, and Ed Perry, with whom she has worked for over 35 years recounts her contribution. "I could not have done it without Cindy. Her incredible memory and unparalleled dedication has served our clients and inspired our young lawyers." Lyndrup seconds the motion. At a celebration for Cindy at Ed Perry's a few years ago, a stanza from a poem Lyndrup wrote honoring Cindy, demonstrates Cindy's contributions to young lawyers:

"She Perryized my work,
and guided me
so that I could pass
his scrutiny."

Pat Evans, the Firm's Accounting Manager, celebrated her 30th year of service in 2002, along with Carolyn Davis, the Firm's General Accounting Supervisor, with 25 years of service. Debbie McCoy, with over 22 years of service, serves as the Firm's Senior Accountant. Pat, Carolyn and Debbie typify the commitment that Greenebaum's administrative staff have given the Firm over the years. Bob Doll recounts their loyalty and service as part of the Greenebaum family as extraordinary.

Sandra French joined the Firm over 22 years ago and has distinguished herself not only as a legal secretary to Maggie Keane and others, but also as an accomplished playwright. In 2001, she received the "Scribe Award" for her original play, "The Movement," in The Procter & Gamble Dreambuilder Celebration. "The Movement" was subsequently developed into a screenplay and filmed as a television movie which aired regionally. In April,

2002, "The Movement" was awarded five Emmys by the Ohio Valley Chapter of the National Academy of Television Arts & Sciences, including the category "Outstanding Achievement for Individual Craft-Writing."

Vera Gebhardt, legal secretary to John Cummins, also joined the Firm in 1980. Her work was so valuable to the Firm that in the late 1990's she became a legal assistant in the Trusts and Estates area as well.

The Firm's longest serving paralegal, Dana Martin, joined the Firm in 1981. She has ably assisted in many litigation wins for the Firm over the years and currently is a paralegal in the Health Care Practice Group.

Pat White, the most senior Legal Secretary in Lexington, joined the Firm in 1980, two years after the merger. Phil Scott, with whom she has worked for many years, recalls that Pat White first joined the firm as a temporary secretary while the Firm was located on Market Street. Her temporary position has now reached almost 23 years. Pat had no legal experience when she came on board. "Self taught," she now handles virtually every-thing our practice requires. She has worked through weekends, nights and over holidays and always been intensely loyal to our firm and its clients. At one point Pat even kept the financial records for the Maktoum farms. She is the source of firm history for Lexington and has a wonderful recall of where to find things. Clients tend to want to talk with Pat on a regular basis as they recognize she gets them to the correct attorney and provides a fast response to their inquiry. We have indeed been fortunate to have Pat as a member of our team."

Lynn Fogle, the Firm's Head Librarian, has been with Greenebaum for over 17 years. She is credited with assisting the move of many of the Firm's legal publications from hard copy to the on-line versions now used by attorneys.

Rick Anderson's secretary, Lori Hayden, was hired in

1989 and went right to work for Anderson when he was heavily engaged in the Firm's corporate, mergers and acquisitions practice. She worked long hours on M&A deals Anderson was handling and fit right into the Firm's work ethic. Anderson says, "she has saved me hundreds of times, and is an excellent secretary and assistant. She has two uncanny abilities; she can read my handwriting, still important even in these days of high tech practice, and, more importantly, my mind."

Rosemary May, legal secretary to Bill Robinson, joined the Firm at the time of the Covington merger and has been with the Firm ever since. She is the senior most secretary in the Covington office. She was joined by Chris Houp, who is currently secretary to Rob Hudson, Luanne Devine and Paul Wilhelm, and Tara May, who is Central Files Supervisor in the Covington Office. Jackie Pate, Service Center Supervisor in Covington, also joined the Firm at the time of the Covington merger.

Other support staff who joined the Firm in the 1980's and continue to serve the Firm today include:

Catherine C. Marksbury	Legal Secretary
Teri L. Barnett	Real Estate Paralegal
Patricia J. O'Brien	Legal Secretary
Lucille M. Luckett	Legal Secretary
Teeny Apple	Risk Manager
Sandra J. Leep	Legal Secretary
Susan F. Bailey	Legal Secretary
Diana L. Smith	Legal Secretary
Dianna G. Moore	Litigation Paralegal

"The Firm is fortunate, indeed, for their loyalty and service," said Eric Ison, Member-in-Charge of the Louisville Office. "They are an integral part of our successful practice."

A 50-Year Summary

Sam Greenebaum surely could not have imagined that his three-man firm in 1952 would become, after 50 years, one of the dominant law firms in the Midwest. He may have hoped it, and may even have thought his new men, Bob Doll and Larry Leatherman, were capable of great things. But 180 lawyers? Seven locations? Tens of millions of dollars in billings? It would have been a giant leap of faith for him to think it were possible.

But it has happened. The Greenebaum firm has grown through many changes—personnel, management, firm names, locations, clients, organizational structure—but in the end it has remained solid because it has had a constant goal to sustain it—the pursuit of excellence. Sam Greenebaum encouraged it; Bob Doll insisted on it; Larry Leatherman demanded it; and Rick Anderson now expects it from everyone in the firm.

This premium on excellence is the heart of the organization, but excellent legal product alone would not have been enough to create a powerhouse without a complementary devotion to client service. The firm has always put its emphasis in the right place — on the client side, where needs arise, trust is built, loyalty accrues, and business begins. "I'll never forget," Rick Anderson says, "Bob Doll said that the thing that always distinguished us from other firms was the fact that we always found a way to break through the usual morass of problems to get a deal done. You know, lawyers used to be regarded as the "beavers" of any deal, damming things up, causing and creating problems, keeping things from happening. The Greenebaum philosophy is this: we're going to tell our clients how to break through the logjams and get the deal done. That's the trademark of the Greenebaum firm."

In the spring of 2003 the firm stops briefly to reflect on its past, and the people and clients who have made the trip so memorable. But then it's back to work. For Greenebaum Doll McDonald, it's always been about the work — pursuing excellence relentlessly around the clock, burning the midnight oil, pushing clients' interests when others might have called it a night.

From a three-lawyer beginning, Greenebaum Doll McDonald now strides across state borders, regions, and even nations. But in the background rings the simple, guiding admonition of founder Sam Greenebaum:

"I am determined that those of you who are associated with this office conduct yourselves like persons who are attempting to achieve ability, success, maturity and advancement in the practice of law."

In its 50th anniversary year, the firm's success and growth proves its Members' acknowledgment of, and adherence to, Mr. Greenebaum's words. The new millennium awaits; the Greenebaum past is merely prelude to new work, new victories, and new attainments in the fields of life and law.

The Members of
Greenebaum Doll & McDonald PLLC
In its 50th Year

MICHAEL L. ADES
Member, Lexington

Areas of Concentration
Real Estate Development, Planning and Zoning

Education
Edinburgh University, Scotland, 1961
University of Pennsylvania, B.S., Economics, 1962
Yale Law School, LL.B., 1965

Admitted to Practice
Kentucky, 1965

Achievements in Areas of Concentration
Director of Citizens Advisory Commission on
    Planning and Zoning, 1972-73
Chairman of Mayor's Advisory Task Force on
    Growth Planning, 1977-80

Professional Memberships
Fayette County Bar Association
Kentucky Bar Association
American Bar Association

Associations
Lexington Home Builders Association
Lexington Apartment Association
Member and Past President of Commercial
    Property Association of Lexington
Member and Past President of Central Kentucky
    Jewish Federation
Member and Past President of Ohavay Zion
    Congregation
Member of Temple Adath Israel
Optimist Club of Lexington
Director of Blue Grass Community Foundation

LAWRENCE R. AHERN III
Member, Nashville

Areas of Concentration
Bankruptcy, Commercial Litigation and
  Transactions (creditors' and debtors' interests,
  trustees, indenture trustees and creditors'
  committees)
Banking, Lending (esp. asset-based and workout
  transactions, troubled institutions and debtor-
  in-possession financing)
Complete reorganizations and acquisitions (esp.
  leveraged buyouts, distressed businesses and
  bankruptcy transactions)

Education
Vanderbilt University, B.A., 1969
Vanderbilt University, J.D., 1972

Admitted to Practice
Tennessee, 1972
Federal: all Districts in Tennessee Sixth Circuit,
  1977
U.S. Supreme Court, 1979
Eastern District of Michigan, 1998
U.S. Court of Appeals, Third Circuit, 1999

Achievements in Areas of Concentration
Fellow, American College of Bankruptcy
Certified since 1994 as a business bankruptcy
  specialist by the American Board of Certification
  and the Tennessee Commission on CLE &
  Specialization
The Best Lawyers in America, Woodward/White,
  Inc.: listed 1989- present; Business Reorganiza-
  tion, Creditors' Rights, and Bankruptcy
  Litigation

Publications
Author, "Workouts" Under Revised Article 9: A
  Review of Changes and Proposal for Study, 9
  Am. Bankr. Inst. L. Rev. 115 (2001)
Author, Anti-Trustee Act or Full Employment
  Program: 15 Things Trustees Need to Know
  About Revised Article 9, 17 NAB Talk 43 (No.
  3, Fall, 2001)
Author, Secured Transactions, 14 and 14A West's
  Legal Forms (West Group, scheduled for
  publication, 2003)
Co-author, Bankruptcy Procedure Manual (West
  Group 5th ed. 2002)
Co-author, Bankruptcy Jury Manual (West

Group 5th ed. 2001)
Co-author, Bankruptcy, 6, 6A & 6B West's
  Federal Practice Forms (West Group 2000)

Presentations
National Conference of Bankruptcy Judges
American Bankruptcy Institute
National Association of Bankruptcy Trustees
Turnaround Management Association
Mid-South Commercial Law Institute
Tennessee Bar Association
Tennessee Bankers' Assoc. & Vanderbilt Owen
  School of Management, Banking Faculty

Professional Memberships
American College of Bankruptcy
American Bankruptcy Institute: Director
American Board of Certification: Director
Turnaround Management Association: Director;
  President, Tennessee Chapter
Mid-South Commercial Law Institute: Director,
  1983-2002; President, 1987-88
Tennessee Commission on Continuing Legal
  Education & Specialization: 1995-2000;
Tennessee Bar Association: House of Delegates,
  1991-95; Section of Commercial, Banking and
  Bankruptcy Law, Chair, 1995-96; Conclave on
  Legal Education in Tennessee, 1996-97; 1996
  Joint Study Committee on UCC
American Bar Association: Business Law Section

MARK S. AMENT
Member, Louisville
Corporate and Commercial Practice Group
Health and Insurance Practice Group
Co-Chair Emerging Technologies Group

Areas of Concentration
Start-ups and Venture Funding
Emerging Technology
Higher Education
Mergers & Acquisitions
Health Care Transactions

Education
Northwestern University, B.A. Urban Studies, 1973
Duke University School of Law, J.D., 1976
University of Miami School of Law, LL.M.
(Taxation), 1977

Admitted to Practice
Kentucky, 1976
Florida, 1977

Publications & Presentations
Co-author, "The Health Care Quality
Improvement Act and the National
Practitioner Data Bank," Chapter 10, *Kentucky
Health Law, 3rd edition*, published by the
University of Kentucky
"Business Organizational Structures," University
of Kentucky College of Law
"Financing The Growing Business," Kentucky
Society of CPA's
"Condominiums and Planned Unit
Developments," University of Kentucky
College of Law
"Condominiums," University of Louisville School
of Law
"Business Organizational Structures, Selecting the
Most Suitable
Alternative for Equine Businesses," University of
Kentucky College of Law
"The Right of Publicity in Horses," Louisville
Lawyer

Professional Memberships
Louisville Bar Association
Kentucky Bar Association
The Florida Bar
American Bar Association (Business Law Section,
Venture Capital and Private Equity Committee;
Health Law Section)

Kentucky Reporter, Commercial Financial
Services Committee of American Bar
Association Business Law Section
American Health Lawyers Association
National Association of College and University
Attorneys (Publications Committee)

Associations
Secretary and Board of Directors, Evans Furniture
Co.
Board of Directors, Jewish Family and Vocational
Services
Board of Directors, Northwestern University
Alumni Association
Member, Entrepreneurship Committee, Greater
Louisville Health Enterprises Network
Vice President, Central Agency for Jewish
Education, 1992- 1995
Past Member, City of Louisville Mayor's Task Force
on Low-Income Housing
Advisory Board - Mideastern Center for Private
Adjudication
Past Member, Board of Trustees, Congregation
Adath Jeshurun
Commissioner, City of Robinswood, Kentucky,
1984-1999
Merger Committee, City of Indian Hills
Past President, Northwestern Club of Kentuckiana
Thoroughbred Owners and Breeders Association

JOHN W. AMES
Member, Louisville
Real Estate and Finance
Corporate Reorganization, Bankruptcy, Creditors
  Rights

Education
University of Louisville, B.A. International Affairs
  1967
University of Louisville School of Law, J.D., 1973
International Legal Courses, Hebrew University,
  Jerusalem, Israel; Thessaloniki, Greece

Admitted to Practice
Kentucky, 1974

Military Service
United States Marine Corps 1967-1972, Captain

Achievements in Areas of Concentration
Director, American Bankruptcy Institute
Named to Best Lawyers in America (Bankruptcy)
  1989-1990, 1991-1992, 1992-1993, 1994-95,
  1996-97
First Class of Certified Business Bankruptcy
  Specialists, American Bankruptcy Board of
  Certification; Recertified 1997
Vice President, American Boards of Certification
President, Counsel for Certified Bankruptcy
  Specialists
First Annual Publications Award, American
  Bankruptcy Institution Journal, 1994

Publications & Presentations
Contributing Editor "Norton Bankruptcy Law and
  Practice, 2nd Edition" 11 Volume Treatise, Clark
  Boardman and Callaghan, 1997
Co-Author "Advanced Chapter 11 Bankruptcy
  Practice," Six volume treatise; Wiley Law
  Publications 1996
Co-Author "Kentucky Construction Law,
  Mechanics Lien and Bankruptcy Manual"
Co-Author "A New Chapter in Bankruptcy Law:
  Chapter 12"
Co-Author 1991, 1995 Annual Survey of
  Bankruptcy Law, published by Callaghan & Co.
Contributing Editor and Author for
  Environmental and Bankruptcy Column,
  "Toxins-ARE-Us," ABI Journal
Featured Speaker, Tucker Law Forum,
  Washington and Lee Law School, Lexington, VA

Academic Achievements
Magna Cum Laude Law School
Who's Who in American Colleges and
  Universities

Professional Memberships
Professor at the University of Louisville Law
  School (Debtor-Creditor Rights) 1976-1996
Lecturer of Political Science; University of
  Louisville, 1973-1975, 1989-1991
Director, U.S. Marine Corps Toys for Tots
  Campaign 1997
Director, Kentucky Marine Corps Coordinating
  Committee
Past President, University of Louisville Alumni
  Association
Member of Crane House, Louisville, Kentucky
1991 Leadership Louisville Class
Past Chairman Kentucky Bar Association
  Bankruptcy Section
Past Chairman National Guidelines in
  Bankruptcy for Accountants Project, American
  Bankruptcy Institute Professional Fees &
  Compensation Committee
Co-Chairman Professional Fees and
  Compensation Committee for American Bar
  Institute 1990-1998
Past-Chairman, Louisville Bar Association
  Bankruptcy Committee
Executive Committee, American Bankruptcy
  Institute, Southeast Bankruptcy Workshop 1995

P. RICHARD ("RICK") ANDERSON, JR.
Member, Louisville
Chairman, Executive Committee

Areas of Concentration
Corporate; Mergers & Acquisitions; Securities;
International Law

Education
University of Maryland, B.A., 1969
Marshall-Wythe School of Law, College of
William and Mary, J.D., 1973

Admitted to Practice
Ohio, 1973
Kentucky, 1980

Military Service
United States Marine Corps and USMC Reserve,
1969-1975

Achievements in Areas of Concentration
Structuring and Negotiation of Domestic and
International Business Acquisitions and
Dispositions for Public and Privately-Owned
Businesses

Publications & Presentations
"Structuring Alternative Dispute Mechanisms in
Business Transactions," Kentucky Bar
Association Annual Convention, June, 1995
"Buying and Selling a Business," National
Business Institute, Cincinnati, Ohio, 1992,
1993, 1994
"Anatomy of a Business Acquisition," Kentucky
Bar Association Convention, June, 1990
"Buying or Selling A Business," University
of Kentucky Law School, Chairman-Moderator,
1988
"Legal Considerations in Buying or Selling a
Business," Louisville Chamber of Commerce,
October, 1988

Academic Achievements
Senior Editor, *William and Mary Law Review*,
1972-73; *William and Mary Law Review*, 1971-
1973

Professional Memberships
Louisville Bar Association

Kentucky Bar Association (Section of Business
Law)
Ohio Bar Association
Cleveland Bar Association
American Bar Association (Section of Business
Law, Section of Law Firm Management)

Associations
Board of Directors and Executive Committee,
Greater Louisville, Inc. (Chamber of
Commerce)
Board of Directors and Executive Committee,
Kentucky Opera
Board of Directors and Executive Committee,
Louisville Fund For the Arts
Board of Directors, Center for Leadership in
School Reform
Anchorage Presbyterian Church, Elder
Pendennis Club
Alumni, Phi Sigma Kappa Fraternity
Director, William and Mary Law School Annual
Fund
Leadership Louisville

TODD H. BAILEY
Member Cincinnati

Education
Duke University (J.D. May, 1976 (With
  Distinction)
Miami University, Oxford, Ohio B.A. May, 1973,
  Magna Cum Laude
Secondary schooling in Australia

Admitted to Practice
U.S. District Court, Southern District of Ohio
Eastern District of Kentucky
Sixth Circuit Court of Appeals
Ohio

Achievements in Areas of Concentration
Concentration in the areas of intellectual property
litigation, commercial litigation, trade secret
misappropriation, unfair competition, and
products liability

Publications & Presentations
ADR Techniques
CPR Institute for Dispute Resolution (June
1996)

Academic Achievements
J.D. (With Distinction)
Scholarship recipient, Phi Beta Kappa
Awarded departmental honors
Founder of Miami University Student Founda-
  tion
Honorary Doctor of Law (1992), Miami
  University

Professional Memberships
Defense Research Institute (Commercial
  Litigation Section)
Industrial Designers Society of America (affiliate
  member)
Collaborative Law Center member
Adjunct Instructor, Miami University, Depart-
  ment of Finance, 2002-2003 (400 level
  intellectual property and e-commerce courses
  taught to seniors)
Speaker: ABA Annual Meeting 2002: Collabora-
  tive Law: Solving Problems of Business with
  Non-Court Solutions Covenants Not to
  Compete and Trade Secrets (1997, 1998, 1999,
  2001), Speaker Commercial Damages (1999),
Speaker Ethics and Professionalism (2000 and 2001)

Speaker National Institute for Trial Advocacy
  faculty member (10 years)
Advisory Council to the Dean of Arts & Sciences,
  Miami University (2002)
Volunteer mediator in the United States District
  Court, S.D. (1996 to date)
Trained as mediator by Center for Dispute
  Settlement, Washington DC
Federal Bar Association 2004 Annual National
  Convention, Planning Committee Chair
  Volunteer Lawyers for the Poor
Board Member Ohio Children's Trust Fund,
  Local Advisory Board for Hamilton County
  Chair (oversees an annual budget of $200,000
  in grants for child abuse prevention programs)

Associations
Federal Bar Association (Cincinnati Chapter, Past
  President)
American Bar Association (Intellectual Property
  and Litigation Sections)
Ohio State Bar Association (Litigation and
  Intellectual Property Sections)
Cincinnati Bar Association (Chair, IP Litigation
  Committee)
Ohio Association for Civil Trial Attorneys

BRENT R. BAUGHMAN
Member, Louisville

Areas of Concentration
Labor and Employment Law

Education
University of Louisville, B.A., 1984
Indiana University, M.B.A., 1988
Indiana University, J.D., 1988

Admitted to Practice
Illinois, 1988
Kentucky, 1990
U.S. District Court, Western District of
  Kentucky, 1993
U.S. District Court, Eastern District of Kentucky,
  1993
U.S. Court of Appeals, Sixth Circuit, 1994
U.S. District Court, Eastern & Western Districts
  of Arkansas, 1994
U.S. Supreme Court, 1995

Publications & Presentations
Kentucky Employment Law Letter, M. Lee Smith
  Publishing Co., Contributing Editor, 1993-
Employment Law in the Private Sector, University
  of Louisville Labor-Management Center, Panel
  Member, March 1995
*Preventing and Defending Sexual Harassment
  Claims in Kentucky*, National Business Institute,
  Co-Author, November 1995
*Sexual Harassment Litigation — Ex Parte Contact
  with an Adverse Party's Employees*, Louisville Bar
  Association, Author, December 1995
Employment Law Issues Facing Public Employers,
  Kentucky Public Human Resources Association,
  Author, May 1996
*Ex Parte Contact with an Adverse Party's Current
  and Former Employees*, University of Louisville
  School of Law Carl Warns Labor & Employment
  Law Institute, Author, June 1996
Union Avoidance for Kentucky Employers,
  Associated Industries of Kentucky, November
  1996
How to Conduct an Internal Investigation, Council
  on Education in Management, February 1999
*Punitive Damages Under the Kentucky Civil Rights
  Act: Myth and Reality*, Louisville Bar Association
  Bar Briefs, Author, March - May 1999

*Privacy Issues in the Workplace (including e-mail
  and Internet policies)*, Greenebaum Doll &
  McDonald 1999 Update on Labor &
  Employment Issues, Author, September 1999
Discipline and Discharge in Arbitration, ABA
  Labor & Employment Section, ADR in Labor
  & Employment Law Committee, Contributing
  Author, 1999

Associations
Louisville, Kentucky and American Bar
  Associations
President, University of Louisville Woodcock
  Society, 1993-
Chair, Louisville Bar Association Labor &
  Employment Section, 2000
Barrister, American Inns of Court, 1996-1999

WINIFRED "WENDY" L. BRYANT
Member, Lexington

Areas of Concentration
Employment Law

Education
University of Richmond, Virginia, B.A., 1972
Middlebury College, M.A., 1976
University of Kentucky College of Law, J.D., 1981

Admitted to Practice
Ohio, 1981
Kentucky, 1983
U.S. District Court, Eastern District of
    Kentucky, 1984
U.S. Court of Appeals, Sixth Circuit, 1984

Achievements in Areas of Concentration
Planning Committee for Cincinnati Bar
    Association Regional Employment Law
    Institute, 1996
Co-Chair, University of Kentucky CLE
    Employment Law Handbook Planning
    Committee, 1992, 1994
Co-Chair, KBA Labor and Employment Law
    Section, 1992-93

Presentations
Presenter, "Workplace Discrimination: Sexual,
    Gender and Racial Harassment," UK 7th
    Biennial Employment Law Institute, 2000
Presenter, "Family Medical Leave Act: Update
    and Current Issues," Fayette County Bar
    Association Labor & Employment Law Section,
    2000
Presenter, "Employment at Will in the 21st
    Century," Lorman Education Services, 1999
Presenter, "Employee Handbooks in Kentucky:
    Drafting and Enforcing Sound Policies,"
    National Business Institute, 1999
Presenter, "Workplace Harassment," University
    of Kentucky Continuing Legal Education,
    1998
Presenter, "Workplace Violence," Kentucky
    Housing Authority, 1998
Presenter, "Sexual Harassment," Madison County
    Industrial Club, 1998
Presenter, "Happy Birthday You're Fired!
    Identifying and Controlling Today's Hottest
    Forms of Discrimination," Council on
    Education in Management, 1997

Presenter, "Managing Your Future Workforce," J
    & H Marsh & McLennan, 1997
Presenter, "Overview of the Family & Medical Leave
    Act," Fayette County Bar Association, 1997
Presenter, "Problems & Pitfalls in Employer-
    Employee Relations," Greenebaum Doll &
    McDonald PLLC, 1996

Publications
"Evaluating Employee Performance," *Legal
    Handbook for Business, 2000*
"Workplace Harassment: Sexual, Racial and
    Gender" (with Julie K. Hackworth), *UK-CLE
    Monograph*, 1998
"Discrimination on the Basis of Disability" (with
    Richard G. Griffith), *UK-CLE Employment Law
    Handbook*, 1992

Academic Achievements
Staff Member, *Kentucky Law Journal*, 1980-81
Award for Best Survey Article, Award for Best
    Writing, 1981 Graduating Class
American Jurisprudence Award for Antitrust Law,
    1981

Professional Memberships
Kentucky Bar Association (Labor and
    Employment Law Section)
American Bar Association (Labor and
    Employment Law Section)
Fayette County Bar Association

JAMES L. BECKNER
Member-in-Charge, Nashville
Member, Family Business Practice Group

Areas of Concentration
Corporate; Mergers and Acquisitions; Venture
Capital; Securities Transactions; Business
Negotiations

Education
Hampden-Sydney College, B.A. 1968
Vanderbilt School of Law, J.D. 1971

Admitted to Practice
Tennessee, 1971
U.S. District Court, Middle District of
Tennessee, 1971

Professional Memberships
American Bar Association
Tennessee Bar Association
Nashville Bar Association

Associations
Former Member, Board of Trustees, Hampden-
Sydney College
Chairman, Ambassadors Committee, Partnership
2000, Nashville Chamber of Commerce
Former Chairman, Board of Directors Nashville
Institute for the Arts
St. George's Episcopal Church, former member of
Vestry and Jr. Warden
Counsel, Nashville Symphony Association

Achievements in Areas of Concentration
Negotiating and structuring numerous mergers
and acquisitions, venture capital transactions,
asset acquisitions, divestitures, related
financings, and other transactions.
Public and private capital formation and related
transactions.
Counsel to privately-held corporation with more
than $200 million in revenues and in excess of
100 shareholders, with numerous foreign
subsidiaries, in its acquisition through merger
by another corporation, forming a holding
company having in excess of 10 international
subsidiaries and with revenues in excess of $500
million.
Counsel for purchaser in all cash asset acquisition
in excess of $90 million with related acquisition
financings in excess of $100 million.

Counsel in formation of insurance holding
company with intrastate public offering of stock
and subsequent formation of insurance
company subsidiary.
Counsel to venture capital firm and investors
purchasing preferred stock in health care
company in private placement in aggregate of
$16.3 million.
Counsel for venture capital firm in private
placement of equity in aggregate amount of $30
million in health care industry.
Counsel for venture capital company in numerous
health care investments and transactions.
Counsel to company in formation of non-bank
affiliate of bank holding company, including
formation of corporation and private placement
of $1.5 million in debt; counsel to company in
relation to matters involving approval of
Comptroller of the Currency.
Counsel to investment limited partnership in
acquisition of Australian insurance holding co.
Counsel to company in placement of $250 million
in revolving trade receivables purchase facility.
Counsel to company in placement of in excess of
$200 million in revolving trade receivables in
state tax shelter purchase facility.
Counsel to international corporation pertaining
to its acquisition of seat on commodities
exchange in Singapore.
Counsel for financial institutions in more than
300 loans and other financing transactions.

JACK C. BENDER
Member, Lexington

Areas of Concentration
Environmental Law and Litigation

Education
Pennsylvania State University, B.S., Mining
  Engineering, 1978
University of Kentucky, College of Law, J.D.,
  1987

Admitted to Practice
Kentucky, 1987

Academic Achievements
Order of the Coif, University of Kentucky
Articles Editor, *Journal of Mineral Law & Policy*,
  1986-87

Professional Memberships
Fayette County Bar Association
Kentucky Bar Association
Air & Waste Management Association
Editor, *Kentucky Air Quality Review*, a quarterly
  newsletter published since March 1998 by
  Greenebaum Doll & McDonald PLLC

Selected Publications & Presentations
Citizen Suit Litigation, 4th Annual Kentucky
  Environmental Permitting & Reporting
  Conference, Lexington, KY, August 10, 2001.
"Mid-America's Hot Air Permits Issues –
  Kentucky Permitting Issues," Manufacturers'
  Education Council's 10th Annual Business and
  Industry's Environmental Symposium,
  Cincinnati, OH, March 22, 2001.
"Kentucky Air Permits and Compliance,"
  Manufacturers' Education Council's
"Water Quality-Based Permitting," Kentucky
  Chamber of Commerce, Environmental
  Permitting Seminar, August 13, 1999.
"EPA's Objections to Kentucky's Environmental
  Audit Privilege & Civil Penalty Amnesty Law,"
  Kentucky Chamber of Commerce, Business
  Bulletin, Volume 13, Number 5, June/July 1999
"Kentucky Water Quality Issues,"
  Manufacturers' Education Council's 8th
  Annual Business and Industry Environmental
  Symposium, Cincinnati, OH, March 1999

"Kentucky Division of Water Initiates Triennial
  Review of Water Quality Regulations,"
  Kentucky Chamber of Commerce, *Business
  Bulletin*, January 1999
"Mid-America's Hot Air Permits Issues –
  Kentucky Permitting Issues," Manufacturers'
  Education Council's 10th Annual Business and
  Industry's Environmental Symposium,
  Cincinnati, OH, March 22, 2001.
"Permits for Water Control, Pollution Control,
  and Environmentally Distressed Property," NBI
  Land Use Law Update in Kentucky Seminar,
  February 1998
"EPA Adopts Final Rule for Compliance
  Assurance Monitoring Under the Clean Air
  Act," Kentucky Chamber of Commerce,
  Environmental Newsline, Vol. VII, Issue 12,
  December 1997
"Antidegradation Review Under Kentucky's Water
  Quality Standards," Business and Industry
  Seminar, Cincinnati, OH, April 1997
"Kentucky Issues Emergency Regulation for
  Permitting of Air Contaminant Sources,"
  Kentucky Chamber of Commerce, *Business
  Bulletin*, Vol. 10, Number 8, August 1996
"Considerations for Title V Permitting of Air
  emission Sources in Kentucky," 12th Annual
  Environmental Law Institute, University of
  Kentucky College of Law, March 1996

AMY B. BERGE
Member, Louisville

Areas of Concentration
Trademark and Trade Dress Law
Copyright Law
False Advertising and Unfair Competition
International Intellectual Property Law
Software Licensing Agreements
Internet Agreements
Privacy

Education
Auburn University, B.S. Business Administration,
 High Honors, 1984
University of Louisville, J.D., Magna Cum
 Laude, 1988

Admitted to Practice
Kentucky, 1988
U.S. Court of Appeals, Sixth Circuit
U.S. District Court, Eastern and Western Districts
 of Kentucky, Southern District of Indiana

Achievements in Areas of Concentration
Extensive U.S. and International Trademark
 Prosecution and Registration
Experience before the U.S. Trademark Trial and
 Appeal Board
Federal Court Experience

Publications
Co-Author, Kentucky Chapter, *State Trademark
 and Unfair Competition Law*
"Online Privacy Compliance," *Bar Briefs*,
 Louisville Bar Association, August, 2001
"Intellectual Property in the Information Age,"
 Business First Legal Handbook for Business,
 November, 2000
"Trade Dress Protection: What's Left for the
 States?" 27 *N. Ky. L. Rev.* (2000)
"Who Owns the Ads and Logos You Create or
 Buy?" *Communique*, Advertising Club of
 Louisville, March, 2000
"Negotiating Software Licenses," *Law Letter*,
 Greenebaum Doll & McDonald PLLC, August,
 2000
"Who's Watching Your Trademarks?" *Law Letter*,
 Greenebaum Doll & McDonald PLLC, April,
 2000
"International Trademark Protection," *Law Letter*,
 Greenebaum Doll & McDonald, Dec., 1999

Various articles on trademark, copyright, and
 privacy issues featured in small business column
 for Louisville's *The Courier-Journal*

Presentations
"Copyright Protection of Computer Programs,"
 The Louisville Bar Association, May 16, 2002
"Beyond HIPPA, Other Privacy Rules," Greater
 Louisville Health Enterprises Network Seminar,
 October 17, 2001
"UCITA Uniform Computer Information
 Transactions Act,"Kentucky Chapter Special
 Libraries Association, May 22, 2001
"The Long Arm of the Law of the Internet,"
 National Business Institute, October 27, 2000
"Cyberlitigation Trademark Conflicts," The
 Louisville Bar Association, September 28, 2000
"International Trademark Protection," The
 Louisville Bar Association, May 12, 2000
"Protection of Trade Dress," Intellectual Property
 Law 2000 Symposium, Salmon P. Chase
 College of Law, Northern Kentucky University,
 February 5, 2000
"Domain Names and Trademark Conflicts,"
 Terralex North American Conference,
 September 17, 1999

Academic Achievements
Brandeis Society
Journal of Family Law, Member

THOMAS J. BIRCHFIELD
Member, Louisville

Areas of Concentration
Labor and Employment Law, Mediation

Education
Indiana University, B.S., 1985 (with distinction)
Indiana University, J.D., 1988

Admitted to Practice
Kentucky, 1988
Indiana, 1988
Sixth Circuit Court of Appeals
U.S. District Court
    Western District of Kentucky
    Eastern District of Kentucky
    Northern District of Indiana
    Southern District of Indiana

Professional Achievements
International Center for Dispute Resolution, Certified Mediator, 2002
Chairman, Labor and Employment Law Section, Louisville Bar Association, 1998
Vice Chair, Labor and Employment Law Section, Louisville Bar Association, 1997
Labor Relations Counsel, State of Indiana, 1991-1992
Field Examiner, National Labor Relations Board, Region 25, 1984-1985
Business First's Forty Under 40, 2000
Leadership Kentucky, Member Class of 1999
Louisville Bar Association
Society for Human Resources Management, Kentucky State Council Member, 1999 to present

Publications & Presentations
Kentucky Employment Law Letter, M. Lee Smith Publishing Co., Contributing Editor, 1992-pres.
"Untangling the Confusing – and Often Conflicting – Web of Leave Laws: FMLA, ADA and Workers' Comp." – Council in Education Management, August 2001
"A Better Way? Choosing Mediation to Resolve ADA Disputes" – Access Center Partnership, October 2000
"Telecommuting and What it Means for the Human Resources Professional" – Indiana University Southeast and Society for Human Resources Management Breakfast Briefing, November 2000

"The Americans with Disabilities Act in Kentucky: Cutting Edge Issue and Developments" – National Business Institute, April 1999
"Advanced FMLA Update: Legally Managing Employee Leave with Incomplete or Insufficient Facts" – Council on Education Management Personnel Law Update, March 1999
"All Hands On Deck: Navigating Return to Work Issues" –Access Center Partnership, March 1999
"Drug-Testing: A Management Perspective" – Louisville Labor- Management Committee, January 1999
"Temporary or Contingent Employees: No Panacea for Avoiding Liability Under Employment Law" – Louisville Bar Association, Dec. 1997
"Hiring, Firing and Coping In Between" – Kentucky Nursing Home Association, July 1997
"NLRB Considers Employer Use of Temporary Help"–Louisville Bar Association, *Bar Briefs,* April 1997
"Emerging Issues in Employment Law" – Kentucky Homes and Services for the Aging, March 1997
"The Clinton Administration's Legislative Agenda 994" – Society for Human Resources Management – Kentucky Chapter, Annual Meeting, March 1994
"Special Issues Under the American with Disabilities Act of 1990" – Louisville Bar Association

C.R. "CHIP" BOWLES, JR.
Member, Louisville

Areas of Concentration
Bankruptcy
Debtor/Creditor Relations

Education
University of Kentucky, B.A. in History "With
High Distinction" 1981
University of Kentucky College of Law, J.D.
"With High Distinction" 1984

Admitted to Practice
Kentucky, 1984
Ohio, 1987
U.S. District Western District of Kentucky, 1985
U.S. District Southern District of Ohio, 1988
U.S. District Eastern District of Kentucky, 1988
U.S. District Southern District of Indiana, 1999

Previous Government Employment
Law Clerk, Honorable Merritt S. Deitz, Jr.,
United States Bankruptcy Judge for the Western
District of Kentucky, United States Courthouse
– Louisville, Kentucky, 1984 - 1986
Career Law Clerk to the Honorable Henry H.
Dickinson, United States Bankruptcy Judge for
the Western District of Kentucky, United States
Courthouse – Louisville, Kentucky, 1992 -1999

Achievements
Kentucky Bar Association's Award for service as
first Editor of Bankruptcy Section's Quarterly
Newsletter, *The Broken Bench & Bar*, 1994
Kentucky Bar Association's Continuing Legal
Education Award, 1994
Hartzell United Methodist Church's recognition
for serving as Chairperson of Finance
Committee, 1992
KBA Section Secretary, 2001

Professional Membership
American Bar Association
Ohio Bar Association
Kentucky Bar Association
Louisville Bar Association
Association of Trial Lawyers of America
Kentucky Academy of Trial Attorneys
American Bankruptcy Institute

Associations
Member of Ohio CLE Institute's Bankruptcy
Planning Commission, 1990 - Present
The Kentucky Bar Association (KBA) Bankruptcy
Section, Treasurer 1994 - 1995, Secretary 1995
- 1996, Vice Chair 1996 - 1997, Chair 1997 -
1998, Chair 1999 - 2000
Member of KBA's CLE Committee, 1994 - 1995
Editor of KBA Bankruptcy Section's Quarterly
Newsletter, 1993 - present
Member, Federal Alternative Dispute Resolution
Council, 1994 - present
Member, Midwestern Regional Bankruptcy
Seminar Advisory Committee, 1995 - present
Chair, Bankruptcy Section Louisville Bar
Association, 1993, 1994, 1997, 1998
Member, Local Rules Committee United
States Bankruptcy Court for the Western
District of Kentucky, 1990 - 1991
Judge, Moot Court, University of Louisville
1988, 1996-1998
Program Chair University of Kentucky CLE
Consumer Bankruptcy Seminar, 1994, 1996,
1998 and 2000
Judge, Moot Court Bankruptcy Competition
Team, University of Louisville, 1999

246

STEPHEN T. BRAUN
Member, Nashville

Areas of Concentration
Corporate Law
Mergers and Acquisitions
Securities Transactions
Health Law and Insurance

Education
St. Cloud State University, B.A., with high
  honors, 1978
University of Notre Dame Law School, J.D., *cum
  laude*, 1981

Admitted to Practice
Texas, 1981
Minnesota, 1987

Achievements in Areas of Concentration
Former Senior Vice President and General
  Counsel, Columbia/HCA Healthcare
  Corporation
Negotiated numerous hospital and other health
  care facility acquisitions, dispositions and joint
  ventures
Provided guidance in terms of compliance with
  federal and state regulations relating to health
  care matters
Developed various corporate compliance
  programs
Negotiated definitive agreements and securities
  work on five transactions valued at more than
  $1 billion each
Private and public capital raising, including initial
  public offerings, secondary offerings and shelf
  registrations
Represented issuers and underwriters in debt and
  equity offerings in a variety of industries
Reviewed and implemented various stock-based
  compensation programs, including omnibus
  programs

Academic Achievements
Administrative Editor, *Notre Dame Law Review*

Professional Memberships
State Bar of Texas

Publications & Presentations
"Acquisition of Exempt Hospitals by Investor-
  Owned Companies" (ABA 1995)
"Healthcare Mergers and Acquisitions: General
  Counsel Perspective" (ABA 1997)

CARL L. BREEDING
Member, Lexington

Areas of Concentration
Environmental Law
Governmental Affairs

Education
Transylvania University, B.A., 1976
University of Kentucky, College of Law, J.D.,
1979

Admitted to Practice
Kentucky, 1979
U.S. District Courts,
    Eastern District of Kentucky, 1982
    Western District of Kentucky, 1982
U.S. Sixth Circuit Court of Appeals, 1982
U.S. Supreme Court, 1984

Achievements in Areas of Concentration
Kentucky Bar Association (Natural Resources and
    Environmental Law Section, Vice Chairman
    (1992-1993); Chair-Elect (1993-1994); and
    Chair (1994-1995)
American Bar Association (Natural Resources,
    Energy and Environmental Law Section)
American Bar Association Dialogue on Incentives
    for Voluntary Compliance Programs, participant
Brownfields and Voluntary Cleanup Program
    Focus Group, participant with the Kentucky
    Natural Resources and Environmental
    Protection Cabinet and the City of Louisville
Kentucky Water Quality Standards Review Panel
Risk Analysis Regulation Development Advisory
    Group
Air Toxics Advisory Panel
Member of Governor's Groundwater Advisory
    Committee
Listed in "The Best Lawyers in America"

Publications & Presentations
Co-Author, Natural Resource Damages Under
    CERCLA: A New Beginning? 20 N. Ky. L.Rev.
    23 (1992)
Frequent speaker on environmental, legislative,
    and regulatory issues

Professional Memberships
Kentucky Bar Association
American Bar Association
Fayette County Bar Association

Associations
Associated Industries of Kentucky - General
    Counsel
Kentucky Chamber of Commerce Environmental
    Committee, Former Legislative Committee
    Chair

CAROLYN M. BROWN
Member, Lexington
Chair, Environmental and Natural Resources
  Practice Group

Areas of Concentration
Environmental Law; Litigation

Education
University of Kentucky, B.S., 1979
University of Kentucky School of Law, J.D., 1982

Admitted to Practice
Kentucky, 1985
U.S. Court of Appeals, Sixth Circuit, 1986
U.S. District Court, Western District of
  Kentucky, 1987
U.S. District Court, Eastern District of Kentucky,
  1987
Texas, 1982
U.S. District Court, Northern District of Texas,
  1982
U.S. Court of Appeals, Fifth Circuit, 1984
U.S. Court of Appeals, for the District of
  Columbia Circuit, 2000

Achievements in Areas of Concentration
Member, Local Emergency Planning
Committee for Fayette County
Past Chair, Natural Resources Law
Section, Kentucky Bar Association

Publications & Presentations
Speaker, "Practical Compliance with EPA
  Regulations," Kentucky Chamber of
  Commerce Seminar, 1997
Moderator, "Environmental Law Update,"
  Kentucky Bar Association Convention, 1997
Speaker, "Environmental Justice and
  Redevelopment of Brownfields," Kentucky Bar
  Association Convention, June 1995
Speaker, "Kentucky Water Quality Issues," 1995
  Business & Industry's Environmental
  Symposium, April 1995
Speaker, "The Resource Conservation and
  Recovery Act," Executive Enterprises, Inc.,
  Environmental Regulation Course, June 1992
Speaker, "Current Issues in Kentucky Real Estate
  Leases: Negotiating and Drafting Environmental
  Provisions," National Business Institute
  Seminar, May 1992

Speaker, "Environmental Law Update," Kentucky
  Bar Association Annual Convention, April 1992
Speaker, "The Resource Conservation and
  Recovery Act" and "SARA Title III: Emergency
  Planning and Community Right-to-Know Act
  of 1986," Executive Enterprises, Inc.
  Environmental Regulation Course, May 1991
Speaker, "Regulation of Storm Water Discharges
  Associated with Industrial Activity," Kentucky
  Chamber of Commerce Environmental
  Seminar, March 1991
Speaker, "Summary of Environmental Laws that
  Affect Real Estate Transactions," NBI
  Environmental Seminar, October 1990
Speaker and Paper, "Environmental Liabilities
  and the Innocent Landowner," Eastern Mineral
  Law Foundation, 10th Annual Institute, 1989
Speaker and Paper, "1987 Clean Water Act,
  Revised Water Quality Standards, State
  Implementation," Sixth Annual Current
  Environmental and Natural Resource Issues in
  Kentucky Seminar, University of Kentucky,
  April 1989

Achievements
Moot Court Board
Staff, *Kentucky Law Journal*
Order of the Coif
Listed in *The Best Lawyers in America*

MICHAEL H. BROWN
Member, Cincinnati
Member, Corporate and Securities Practice
  Group and Tax and Employee Benefits Practice
  Group
Law Firm Technology Member

Areas of Concentration
Corporate Law
Mergers, Acquisitions and Divestitures
Corporate Finance Law
Federal Income Tax Law

Education
Notre Dame Law School, J.D., 1981
Xavier University, B.S.B.A. (Accounting), 1978

Admitted to Practice
Kentucky, 1981
Ohio, 1982
United States Tax Court, 1982

Professional Activities
Lecturer on Law in Law and Accounting,
  University of Cincinnati College of Law, 1983-
  1987
Speaker on tax and legal technology issues: Tax
  Research using Internet Tools, February 1999,
  16th Annual Advanced Estate Planning
  Institute; Prepare for EDGAR, January, 1993;
  32nd Annual Southwestern Ohio Tax Institute,
  December, 1991; Current Issues for Corporate
  Counsel, June 1991; CapSoft Development
  Users Conference, January 1992, January 1991
Humana Inc.; acquisition of the outstanding stock
  of Choice Care Corporation; October 1997
Neweagle Industries, Inc.; sale of 80% of the
  outstanding stock of Neweagle Industries, Inc.
  to RAG EBV Aktiengesellschaft and formation
  of corporate joint venture; September 1997
Liebel-Flarsheim Company; sale of 100% of the
  outstanding stock of Liebel-Flarsheim
  Company to Mallinckrodt Medical, Inc.;
  January 1996
International Industries, Inc.; acquisition of
  496,272 shares of ESOP Common Stock by
  the International Industries, Inc. Employee
  Stock Ownership Plan and senior bank debt
  refinancing; November 1995

Southwestern Ohio Steel, Inc.; acquisition of
  remaining 50% of the partnership interests of
  Southwestern Ohio Steel, L.P. by Itochu
  International, Inc. and formation of Southwestern Ohio Steel, Inc.; December 1994

Tax Litigation
*Worldvision Enterprises, Inc. and Subsidiaries v.
  Commissioner,* Tax Court Docket No. 45721-
  86 (foreign tax credit on income from film
  distribution business IRS conceded after trial)
Franks v. Commissioner, T.C. Memo 1988-245
  (advanced coal royalties)
Collins v. Commissioner, T.C. Memo 1988-245
  (advanced coal royalties) (consolidated with
  Franks v. Commissioner)
Mafco Equipment Company v. Commissioner, T.C.
  Memo 1983-637 (capital gain vs. ordinary
  income on sales in a heavy equipment rental
  business)

ROBERT L. BROWN
Member, Louisville

Areas of Concentration
Antitrust and Unfair Competition; Corporate and Securities; E-Commerce, Economic Development; Encryption; Finance; Immigration; Intellectual Property; International; Mergers and Acquisitions; Product Distribution; Start-Ups; Telecommunications

Education
University of Louisville, B.A., International Studies, 1971

University of Louisville, M.S., Community Development, 1972

Escuela Libre de Derecho, Mexico City, Certificate, Latin American Trade, 1973

University of Louisville, J.D., M.B.A., 1974

Jochi University, Tokyo, M.S., Japan Business, 1982

Cambridge University, UK, Ph.D., Japanese Privatization, 1997

Admitted to Practice
Kentucky, California, District of Columbia, New York

Japan (Foreign Attorney), 1991-1994

England and Wales (Solicitor)

Hong Kong (Solicitor), 2000

Positions
General Counsel, Tiernan Communications, Inc., San Diego

Principal, Brown & Gutterman, San Francisco

International Partner, Pillsbury Madison & Sutro, San Francisco and Tokyo

Special Counsel, Heller Ehrman White & McAuliffe, San Francisco

Senior Counsel/USA; Foreign Legal Counsel/Japan, Mitsui & Co., New York and Tokyo

Publications & Presentations
Doing Business on the Internet. Aspen/Harcourt Brace.

Financing Start-Ups. Aspen/Harcourt Brace.

Equity Finance: Venture Capital, Buyouts, Restructurings and Reorganizations (2001 Supplement). Aspen

Limited Liability Companies Guide. Aspen/Harcourt Brace.

Powerlink. West Group.

"Incorporation and Bylaws." *California Transaction Forms.* Bancroft Whitney.

"Letters of Credit." *California Transaction Forms.* Bancroft Whitney.

Managing Your e-Business/Hong Kong. Contributor. CCH.

Commercial Laws of East Asia. Sweet & Maxwell.

Intellectual Property Laws of East Asia. Sweet & Maxwell.

Asian Economic and Legal Development. Kluwer.

Professional Memberships
Louisville Bar Association

Kentucky Bar Association

California Bar Association

District of Columbia Bar Association

Association of the Bar of the City of New York

State of New York Bar Association

American Bar Association, Section of International Law and Practice, Committee Co-Chair, Telecommunications, Privatization, Asia-Pacific Law

Law Society of England and Wales

Hong Kong Law Society

THOMAS A. BROWN
Member, Louisville

Areas of Concentration
State and Federal Taxes

Education
Bellarmine College, 1955-58
University of Louisville School of Law, BSL,
1959; LLB 1961

Admitted to Practice
Kentucky, 1961
U.S. District Courts of Kentucky, 1967

Military Service
U.S. Army, 1956 and 1961-62, Active Duty
U.S. Army Reserve, 1956-62

Achievements in Areas of Concentration
Lead counsel in numerous Kentucky tax matters
relating to sales and use tax, corporate income
and license tax, coal tax and constitutional
issues
Lead counsel on tax related issues in matters of
the energy exemption, pollution control facility
exemptions and recycling credits
Lead counsel in negotiations that resulted in the
certification of an entire manufacturing plant as
a pollution control facility
Counsel on a significant number of private
rulings by Kentucky Revenue Cabinet which
provide a considerable body of unpublished
case reference for current client work
Member, Kentucky Revenue Cabinet Liaison
Committee, 1995 to present
Tax Liaison between Kentucky Bar Association
and Kentucky Revenue Cabinet, 1996 to
present
Technical Member, Governor's Tax Reform Study,
1994-1995
Member, Tax Committee, Kentucky Economic
Development Corporation, 1988-1994
Attorney, Office of Chief Counsel, Internal
Revenue Service, 1962-1966
"Best Lawyers in America" Taxation (Woodward/
White, Inc.)

Publications & Presentations
Multiple Louisville and Kentucky Bar
Associations Seminars

Professional Memberships
Louisville Bar Association; Member and Past
Chair of Tax Section
Kentucky Bar Association; Founding Member of
Tax Section and Past Chairman in 1980 and
1989; former Vice Chair
American Bar Association

VICKIE YATES BROWN
Member, Louisville
Chair, Health and Insurance Practice Group
Co-chair Biotech Team
Co-chair Privacy Task Force

Areas of Concentration
Health Care and Health Insurance Law
Government Affairs
Mediator-Certified in Kentucky

Education
Georgetown College, B.A., Magna Cum Laude
University of Kentucky School of Law, J.D.

Admitted to Practice
Kentucky
U.S. Court of Appeals, Sixth Circuit
U.S. District Court, Eastern District of Kentucky

Professional Associations
American Bar Association
Kentucky Bar Association
Louisville Bar Association
American Health Lawyers Association

Boards and Associations
Council Member and Chair, Government Affairs
Committee of the ABA Health Law Section
Board of Directors and Chair of Government
Affairs Committee of Greater Louisville Inc.'s
Health
Member of Founding Board of Directors of
Hospice of Louisville Foundation (2002-
Present)
Appointed as ABA Health Law Section's liaison to
the ABA Commission On Women in the
Profession (2000-2002)
Vice President, Alumni Advisory Board of
Georgetown College
Member, MasterWorks Chorale of the Louisville
Orchestra (1995-1996)
Member, Choral Arts Society (1996-1997) and
Bach Society (1994-1996)
Board of Directors and President of the Alliance
of Community Hospices and Palliative Care
(1996-2002)
Board of Directors and Executive Committee,
Partners for a Healthy Louisville (1996-
Present)

Board of Directors (1997-2002) and Executive
Committee (1998) of Kentucky Opera
Association
Appointed as Chair of the Greater Louisville, Inc.
Health Care Task Force, 1994 to 2001.
Appointed to the Health Care Reform
Implementation Team Coordinated by Seven
Counties Services, Inc. for 1994-1995 and
appointed to chair the Administrative
Regulation Subcommittee, 1994-1998.
Member of Board of Trustees of Kentucky
Medical News (2002-   )
Member of the Greater Louisville, Inc. Legislative
Affairs Committee.
Member of the Board of Directors of the
Olmstead Parks Conservancy.

Achievements
Appointed to ABA Health Law Section Task
Force to draft comments concerning the 1999
proposed HHS HIPAA privacy regulations and
in 2001 comments to the final regulation.
Member of the Greater Louisville, Inc. Legislative
Appreciation Dinner Committee in 1999.
"Outstanding Young Career Woman of the Year,"
Spencer County Business Professional Woman's
Club, 1980.
Law Clerk for Supreme Court of Kentucky;
Justice J. Calvin Aker, 1979-1980
Who's Who in American Colleges and
Universities

JOHN K. BUSH
Member, Louisville

Areas of Concentration
Complex and Appellate Litigation (including
Antitrust, Securities,
    Financial Institutions, Intellectual Property
and Product Liability
    Disputes)

Education
Vanderbilt University, B.A., *summa cum laude*,
1986
Harvard Law School, J.D., *cum laude*, 1989

Admitted to Practice
Kentucky, 1996
District of Columbia, 1992
Arkansas, 1989
U.S. District Court, Western and Eastern
    Districts of Kentucky, 1996
U.S. District Court, Southern District of Indiana,
    1996
U.S. District Court, District of Maryland, 1994
U.S. Court of Appeals, Fourth Circuit, 1997
U.S. Court of Appeals, Sixth Circuit, 1996
U.S. Court of Appeals, Federal Circuit, 1993
U.S. Court of Appeals, Fifth Circuit, 1991
U.S. Court of Appeals, Eighth Circuit, 1990
U.S. Supreme Court, 1994

Achievements in Areas of Concentration
Antitrust advice to clients relating to mergers and
    acquisitions, distribution, franchiser-franchisee
    disputes and pricing.
Represented defendants in securities class actions,
    including prevailing parties in *Lampf, Pleva,
    Lipkin, Prupis & Petigrow v. Gilbertson* (U.S.
    1991), and *Plaut v. Spendthrift Farm, Inc.* (U.S.
    1995), and the Securities Industry Association
    as *amicus curiae* in *Central Bank of Denver v.
    First Interstate Bank of Denver* (U.S. 1994).
Represented parties in disputes and litigation
    involving alleged trademark infringement and
    misappropriation of publicity rights.
Represented parties in product liability cases at
    the trial level and on appeal.
Represented parties successfully challenging
    constitutionality of punitive damage awards in
    several cases, including defendants in *Life
    Insurance Co. of Georgia v. Johnson* (Ala. 1996),
    and *Continental Trend Resources, Inc. v. OXY*

USA, Inc. (10th Cir. 1996), and *amici* in
BMW of North America, Inc v. Gore (U.S.
1996).
Represented thrift investors in several cases
    successfully challenging government regulators'
    enforcement of FIRREA, including *amici* in
    United States v. Winstar (U.S. 1996).
One of former President Reagan's attorneys
    during the Iran-contra investigation.
One of the attorneys who represented former Los
    Angeles Police Sergeant Stacey Koon in his
    successful sentencing appeal to the U.S.
    Supreme Court in the Rodney King case.

Significant Publications
"Sixth Circuit Rejects Claims that Honeywell Has
    Illegal Tying Arrangement," Corporate Counsel
    News, Summer 1997
"A Better Approach to Civil Litigation Reform,"
    The National Law Journal, May 26, 1997
"Two Recent High Court Cases List GVR
    Criteria," The National Law Journal, July 29,
    1996
"Amid Increased Public And Congressional
    Debate Over Punitive Damages, Supreme
    Court of the United States Agrees To Hear
    Another Punitive Damages Case," Century City
    Lawyer, May 1995
"The End of the Section 10(b) Aiding and
    Abetting Liability Fiction," Insights, June
    1994

DANIEL P. CHERRY
Member, Louisville

Areas of Concentration
Litigation and Trial Practice
Construction Law

Education
Western Kentucky University, B.A., Government,
1983
University of Louisville, School of Law, J.D.,
1990

Admitted to Practice
Kentucky, 1990
U.S. District Court, Western District of
Kentucky, 1990
U.S. District Court, Eastern District of Kentucky,
1992

Achievements in Areas of Concentration
Member, Attorney General's Task Force on Older
Kentuckians
Director, Kentucky Bar Association Construction
Law Section

Academic Achievements
Pi Sigma Alpha, National Political Science Honor
Society

Professional Memberships
Louisville Bar Association
Kentucky Bar Association
American Bar Association
Association of Trial Lawyers of America
Kentucky Academy of Trial Attorneys

Associations
University of Louisville School of Law Alumni
Association
Delta Theta Pi, International Law Fraternity

ANNE A. CHESNUT
Member, Lexington

Areas of Concentration
Civil Litigation, including commercial,
employment, franchising   disputes

Education
Western Kentucky University, B.A., (magna cum
laude), 1976
University of Kentucky College of Law, J.D.,
1979

Admitted to Practice
Kentucky, 1980
U.S. District Court, Eastern District of Kentucky,
1981
U.S. Court of Appeals, Sixth Circuit, 1981
U.S. Supreme Court, 1992

Publications & Presentations
KBA Federal Practice Update, Fall 1992 and
1993
"Kentucky Civil Practice Before Trial," U.K./
CLE, Contributing Author, 1989
"Motion Practice in Kentucky," U.K./CLE
Seminar, 1989
Comment, "Keeping Kidnapping In Its Place:
When Does Kentucky's Exemption Apply?" 66
KLJ 448

Achievements
Law Clerk to the Honorable Eugene E. Siler, Jr.,
then District Judge, United States District
Court for the Eastern & Western Districts of
Kentucky, 1979-81
Managing Editor, *Kentucky Law Journal*, 1978-79
Best Feature Writer 1976, Kentucky
Intercollegiate Press Association

Professional Memberships
Fayette County Bar Association
Kentucky Bar Association
American Bar Association (Forum on
Franchising: Section of Litigation)
Henry Clay, American Inns of Court
Lexington Journal Club

Associations
Community Bank of Lexington, Inc. Organizing
Director and former Advisory Director

Former Title III, Local Emergency Planning
Committee
Hunter Presbyterian Church, Elder

RICHARD S. CLEARY
Member, Louisville
Chairman, Labor & Employment Practice
  Group

Areas of Concentration
Labor and Employment Law

Education
Washington and Lee University, B.A., Economics
  (cum laude), 1978
Georgetown University Law Center, J.D., 1981

Admitted to Practice
Kentucky, 1981
District of Columbia, 1992
U.S. District Court, Western District of
  Kentucky, 1981
U.S. District Court, Eastern District of Kentucky,
  1989
U.S. Court of Appeals, Sixth Circuit, 1983
U.S. Court of Appeals, Seventh Circuit, 1993
U.S. Supreme Court, 1990

Professional Achievement
Listed in *The Best Lawyers in America*
  (Woodward/White Inc.)

Professional Memberships
Co-Chair (Management), Committee on the
  Development of the Law Under the National
  Labor Relations Act, American Bar Association,
  1999-2002
Program Co-Chair (Management), Committee
  on the Development of the Law Under the
  NLRA, American Bar Association, 1996-99
Kentucky and Louisville Bar Associations
  (Chairman, LBA Labor & Employment Law
  Section, 1994)

Publications & Presentations
The Developing Labor Law, BNA, Co-editor,
  2000, 2001 and 2002 Supplements; Associate
  Editor, 1997-1999; Assistant and Contributing
  Editor, 1987-1996
Kentucky Employment Law Letter, M. Lee Smith
  Publishing Co., Editor, 1991-present
"National Labor Relations Board Update,"
  Speaker, ABA Annual Meeting, August 13,
  2002
National CLE Conference, "The Year In Review:
  An Update of the Most Significant NLRA

Decisions of 2001," Steamboat Springs,
  Colorado, January 2002
University of Louisville Labor-Management Center,
  "Technology, The Workplace and Legal Issues,"
  December 2001
Society for Human Resource Management:
  "Workplace Privacy," August 2001
"National Labor Relations Board Update,"
  Speaker, ABA Annual Meeting, August 7, 2001
"Developments at the National Labor Relations
  Board".
Speaker, ABA Annual Meeting, July 9, 2000
"National Conference on Labor - Management
  Relations: Labor Law in the Year 2000 and
  Beyond", Speaker, June 8, 2000, Washington,
  D.C.
"Labor Arbitration Advocacy Institute,"
  Instructor, December 13, 1999, Louisville,
  Kentucky.

Associations
National Alumni Board, Washington and Lee
  University, 1997-2001
Alumni Board, Georgetown University Law
  Center, 1992-96
American Heart Association, Louisville Chapter
  Board of Directors, 1996-2001
Management Representative, Advisory Board,
  University of Louisville Labor-Management
  Center, 1986-present
Leadership Louisville

H. BUCKLEY COLE
Member, Nashville

Areas of Concentration
Trial Practice
Commercial Litigation
Labor and Employment Law
Construction Law
Family Law

Education
University of Virginia, B.A., English (with
distinction), 1976
University of Virginia, J.D., 1981

Admitted to Practice
Tennessee, 1986
Pennsylvania, 1981
Virginia, 1984

Professional Memberships
Nashville Bar Association
Tennessee Bar Association
American Bar Association

Associations
Exchange Club of Nashville, (Past Secretary and
Board Member)
University of Virginia Alumni Associations of
Middle Tennessee (Past President)
St. Luke's Community Housing Programs (Past
Board Member)
Child Abuse Prevention of Tennessee (Past Board
Member)
Exchange Club Antiques and Garden Show (Past
Board Member)
Nashville Young Leaders Council
Christ Episcopal Church (Capital Campaign
Committee)

Publications and Presentations
Real Estate Litigation in Tennessee, National
Business Institute, 1998
Trial Practice Seminar, Nashville Bar Association,
1997
Valuation of Closely Held Businesses in Divorces,
Nashville Bar Association, 1995
Impact of Tennessee Small Schools Case, Tenn.
Assn. Of County Attorneys, 1993

LLOYD R. ("RUSTY") CRESS, JR.
Member, Frankfort

Areas of Concentration
Environmental Regulatory and Compliance
Government Relations

Education
University of Kentucky, B.G.S., 1988
University of Kentucky, College of Law, J.D.,
1991

Admitted to Practice
Kentucky, 1991
U.S. District Courts
Eastern District of Kentucky, 1992
Western District of Kentucky, 1993

Civic Activities
1996-1997 - Member, Fayette County Board of
Education Equity Council
1996-Present - Member, LFUCG Hazardous
Materials Technical Advisory Commission

Kentucky Bar Association - Chair, Natural
Resources Law Section (1998-1999)

Achievements in Areas of Concentration
Planning Committee, ABA/Region 4 EPA
conference - 1998
Chair, KBA Natural Resources Section - 1998-
1999
Planning Committee University of Kentucky
Mineral Law Center Environmental Conference
- 1993-2000
AIK/CIC Representative for Clean Air Act Task
Force Meetings, 1996-Present

Publications & Presentations
*"Natural Resources Damages Under CERCLA: A
New Beginning?"* 20 N. Ky. L. Rev. 23 (1992)
Co-Author, KBA Convention, Kentucky
Legislative Update - 1998
Speaker, Kentucky Environmental Regulatory
and Legislative Updates - 1994-2000
Speaker, UK Mineral Law Center, Kentucky's
Groundwater Regulation - 1995
Speaker, TSCA: Hot PCB Issues - 1993
Speaker, Environmental Considerations in the
Medical Industry -1992

Professional Memberships
American Bar Association - Section of Natural
Resources, Energy, and Environmental Law

BRUCE E. CRYDER
Member, Lexington

Areas of Concentration
Mineral and Environmental Law; Commercial
Law; Litigation

Education
Ohio University, B.A., (cum laude), English,
1968
Ohio State University, J.D., (cum laude), 1972

Admitted to Practice
Ohio, 1973
U.S. Supreme Court, 1976
Kentucky, 1981

Professional Activities
Board of Trustees, Eastern Mineral Law Foundation
Editorial Advisory Board, *Journal of Natural
Resources and Environmental Law*
Listed in Best Lawyers In America, 1997 – present

Publications & Presentations
"Legal Right of Entry for Coal Mining Permits in
Kentucky," Fourteenth Annual Kentucky
Professional Engineers in Mining Seminar, 2001
"Ownership of Coal Refuse and Underground
Voids," 26th Mineral Law Conference,
University of Kentucky Mineral Law Center,
2001
"Real Property Co-Ownership and Natural
Resources Development," Eastern Mineral Law
Foundation Annual Institute, 1997
"Environmental and Regulatory Aspects of Mine
Closings," Eastern Mineral Law Foundation
Special Institute, 1995
"Lessor Liability for Reclamation Under the
Surface Mining Control and Reclamation Act,"
Eastern Mineral Law Foundation Special
Institute, 1994
"Coal Mining in Wetlands," University of
Kentucky Mineral Law Seminar, 1991
"Concurrent and Successive Ownership of Coal
Property," 11 Eastern Mineral Law Institute,
1990
"Subsidence Law," University of Kentucky
Mineral Law Seminar, 1990
"Alternative Dispute Resolution in the Mineral
Industry," University of Kentucky Mineral Law
Seminar, 1988

"What's Left of the Broad-Form Deed?",
University of Kentucky Mineral Law Seminar,
1984
"Strip Mining: The Ohio Experience," *Capital
University Law Journal*, 1975

Professional Memberships
Fayette County Bar Association
Kentucky Bar Association
Ohio Bar Association
American Bar Association

JOHN R. CUMMINS
Member, Louisville
Chair, Trusts and Estates Practice Group
Chair, Family Business Group

Areas of Concentration
Estate, Trust and Business Planning and
    Administration; Health Law

Education
Brown University, A.B., 1972
Harvard University Law School, J.D., 1975

Admitted to Practice
Kentucky, 1976
U.S. Court of Appeals, Fourth Circuit, 1976
U.S. Court of Appeals, Sixth Circuit

Achievements in Areas of Concentration
Listed in *Best Lawyers in America* Woodward/
    White, in both Trust and Estates and Health
    Law
Member, American College of Trust and Estate
    Counsel
ABA Estate & Gift Tax Committee, 1983-
    Chairman, Valuation Subcommittee, 1986-
    1991
Chairman, Employee Benefits Subcommittee,
    1984-86
Chairman, Liquidity Subcommittee, 1983-84
Selected for American Medical Association
    National Physician Advisory Network
Selected for National Directory of Healthcare
    Consultants and Attorneys by American Society
    of Plastic and Reconstructive Surgeons

Publications & Presentations
"Recent Developments in Estate Planning,"
    University of Kentucky Annual Estate Planning
    Seminars, 1981-1985, 1987
"Handling Distributions from Qualified Plans,"
    Midwest Tax & Estate Planning Seminar, 1985
"Retained Power to Substitute Corporate
    Trustees," 119 *Trusts & Estates* 42, Co-Author,
    April 1982
"The Active Business Requirements for Estate Tax
    Deferral; How Little Activity Qualifies?" 59 *Taxes*
    647, September, 1981
"Tax Planning for the Coal Miner's Daughter's
    Father," 120 *Trusts & Estates* 55, October, 1981
"Making a Timely Section 754 Election after a
    Partner's Death," *Taxation for Accountants*,

August, 1982
"The Equine Partnership Freeze: How to Win
    the Estate Tax Stakes," *Kentucky Bench and Bar*,
    October, 1982
"Current Attitudes Toward Estate Tax Discounts
    for Restricted Securities and Underwriting
    Fees," 10 *Estate Planning* 276, September, 1983
"Section 6166 Legislation: Interpreting TCA '82
    and Treasury's Response to S. 1251, "122 *Trusts
    & Estates* 39, October, 1983
"Passive Assets: New Changes to the Deferral
    Rules," 123 *Trusts & Estates* 29, September,
    1984
"Proposed Regulations Explain Some Limitations
    on Stock Redemptions to Pay Taxes and
    Expenses, 12 *Estate Planning* 8, January, 1985

Achievements
Phi Beta Kappa
Editor-in-Chief, Greenebaum Doll & McDonald
    PLLC *Law Letter*, 1985-1998
Founder and Editor-in-Chief, Greenebaum Doll
    & McDonald PLLC *Health Letter*, 1990-1998
Leadership Louisville, 1989-90

Professional Memberships
Louisville Bar Association
Kentucky Bar Association
American Bar Association (Sections of Taxation,
    Real Property, Probate and Trust)

LUANN DEVINE
Member, Covington

Areas of Concentration
Labor and Employment

Education
State University of New York at Plattsburgh, B.S.
  (Magna cum laude), 1979
University of Cincinnati, College of Law, J.D.,
  1994

Admitted to Practice
Georgia, 1995
Kentucky, 1996
United States District Court, Eastern District of
  Kentucky, 1996
  Western District of Kentucky, 1996
United States Court of Appeals, Sixth Circuit,
  1996

Academic Achievements
Order of the Coif
American Jurisprudence Award, Legal Research
  and Writing American Jurisprudence Award,
  Conflicts of Law

Prior Experience
Judicial Clerk for the Honorable William O.
  Bertelsman, Chief Judge, Eastern District of
  Kentucky, 1994-95

Publications
Contributing Editor for the Kentucky
  Employment Law Letter, M. Lee Smith
  Publisher, 1995 to present
Contributing Editor for Hiring & Firing
  Handbook, 1997 Edition

Seminars
Author, "Privacy In The Workplace," 1996
Remedies Under The NLRA presented by
  Richard S. Cleary to the Labor And
  Employment Section of the American Bar
  Association July 2000

Associations
American Bar Association
Kentucky Bar Association
Northern Kentucky Bar Association
Vice Chair For Labor And Employment Section
  of the Kentucky Bar Association

IVAN M. DIAMOND
Member, Louisville
Chair, Corporate & Securities Practice Group

Areas of Concentration
Corporate; Securities, Bank Acquisitions and
Regulatory Matters

Education
University of Florida, B.A., (cum laude), 1962
University of Florida, J.D., 1964

Admitted to Practice
Florida, 1964
District of Columbia, 1966
Kentucky, 1969
U.S. Court of Appeals, Sixth Circuit, 1969

Achievements in Areas of Concentration
Attorney, Securities and Exchange Commission,
   Washington, D.C., 1964-68
Represented companies in connection with
   numerous public offerings of equity and debt
   securities, and mergers and acquisitions,
   totaling billions of dollars.
Counsel to large bank holding company with
   respect to only Kentucky "stake-out" merger
   agreement and unique
      financing through redeemable debentures and
   stock purchase contracts.
Represented numerous financial institutions in
   connection with organization, holding
   company formation, mergers, acquisitions,
   capitalization, and savings and loan
   conversions.
Corporate planning including "golden
   parachutes," director liability limitation and
   "poison pills."
Private and public capital raising, including initial
   public offerings, secondary offerings and shelf
   registrations.

Publications & Presentations
"Anti-Takeover Strategies-Shark Repellents"
"How Regulators Look at Bank Holding
   Company Acquisitions"
"Private Placements of Securities"
"Insider Trading: Recent Developments"
"Business Judgment Rule - Recent Development
   in Kentucky and Other Jurisdictions"

"Securities Law Issues for Smaller Firms"
"Exemptions from the 1933 Act"
"Bank-Holding Company Acquisitions"
"Strategic Planning for Acquisitions"
"Bank Mergers & Acquisitions - Anti-trust Law
   Considerations"
"Attorney's Due Diligence in a Securities
   Offering"
"Summary of Kentucky Banking Laws",
   Southern Region Banking Legislation Group,
   Co-Author
"New Techniques for Limiting Bank Director
   Liability", The Business of Banking, co-author

Achievements
Editorial Board, Florida Law Review
Louisville Chamber of Commerce
Louisville Strategic Economic Development Plan-
   Co-Chairman, Service Sector Task Force
Securities Law Committee, Kentucky Bar
   Association

Professional Memberships
Louisville Bar Association
Kentucky Bar Association
Florida Bar Association
American Bar Association

263

BRADLEY E. DILLON
Member, Louisville

Areas of Concentration
Environmental
Risk Management
Nuclear Licensing, Compliance

Education
University of Louisville, B.A., 1973
University of Louisville, J.D., 1975
University of Southern California,
 Environmental Management Institute, 1980
 (Pursuant to U.S. EPA grant)
Insurance Institute of America, Associate in Risk
 Management, 1987

Admitted to Practice
Kentucky, 1976
Western Kentucky District, 1980

Publications & Presentations
 Kentucky Chamber of Commerce,
 "Environmental Justice Update," November
 2000
Louisville Bar Association, "Update on
 Environmental Legislation," April 2000
Kentucky Chamber of Commerce,
 "Implementation of Ambient Air Quality
 Standards in Light of the *American Trucking*
 Decision," November 1999
Louisville Bar Association, "NOx Sip Call and
 Other Clean Air Act Matters," August 1999
GD&M - "The Use of Expert Witnesses in
 Environmental Disputes," November 1998
Kentucky Chamber of Commerce, "Wetlands
 Permitting," July 1998, October 1998
Wetlands Seminar, October 1998
The Kentucky Environmental Marketing
 Association (KEMA) - "Bridging the Gap -
 What Industry Wants from Environmental
 Consultants," June 1998
Kentucky Chapter of the American Waste
 Management Association, "The Credible
 Evidence Rule - Is it Credible or Relevant?"
 May 1998
GD&M, "Title V Air Permitting," October 1997
GD&M/Presnell Associates, Inc./Micro-
 Analytics, Inc., "OSHA Asbestos Regulatory
 Compliance," June 1997
"Toxics In Packaging Legislation - Don't Be
 Boxed In," Environmental Corporate Counsel

Report, 1995
Kentucky Bar Association Seminar - Current
 Issues in Environmental Law presentation -
 "Selected Federal and State Issues Under the
 Clean Air Act," April 1995
Environmental Corporate Counsel Institute,
 Washington, D.C., "Sword vs. Shield: How To
 Take the Offensive By Using Existing
 Environmental Insurance Policies to Cover
 Compliance Costs," May 1993
Louisville Area Chamber of Commerce -
 Presentations 1993 "Implications of
 Noncompliance with Environmental Laws"
 "Clean Air Act - Necessity for Accurate Record
 Keeping" "Clean Water Act - Costs of
 Implementation"
Environmental Corporate Counsel Institute,
 Washington, D.C., "In House Perspective on
 Environmental Claims," Nov. 1992
Insurance Claims for Environmental Damage,
 Washington, D.C., Executive Enterprise, "An
 Insured's Perspective on Environmental
 Claims," November 1990
Department of Energy - Annual Conference on
 Low Level Disposal, "Facility Operator's
 Viewpoint on Nuclear Insurance," Denver, 1987

Professional Memberships & Associations
Kentucky Bar Association
Kentucky Chapter of Hazardous Material
 Managers

LAUREL S. DOHENY
Member, Louisville

Areas of Concentration
Domestic Relations
Civil Litigation

Education
University of Louisville, B.A., 1989
University of Louisville School of Law, J.D., 1992

Admitted to Practice
Kentucky, 1992
U.S. District Court, Western and Western
   Districts of Kentucky, 1993

Publications & Presentations
Note, Schutz v. Schutz, *Journal of Family Law*,
   Vol. 31, No. 1,
   1992-93
Divorce Education program, Center for Women
   and Families
Family Law Practice for Paralegals, "Gathering,
   Organizing and
      Using Financial Information in Divorce
   Cases"
Case Law Updates,
      Louisville Bar Association
      Franklin Bar Association
Kentucky Bar Association presentation,
   "Investigating and Developing Your Case: The
   Attorney's Responsibility in Commencing
   Litigation"

Achievements
Former Chair; Member, Louisville Bar
   Association, Family Law Section
Former Chair; Member, Louisville Bar
   Association, Pro Bono
      Consortium
Secretary and Member, Legal Aid Society Board
Member, Louis D. Brandeis American Inn of
   Court
Member, Citizens for Better Judges
Member, Focus Louisville Alumni Group
Member, Brandeis Society
Member, Journal of Family Law
Member, Psi Chi Psychology Honorary Society

Professional Memberships
Kentucky Bar Association
Louisville Bar Association

JAMES C. EAVES, JR.
Member, Louisville

Areas of Concentration
Patent Law; Intellectual Property Law; Trademark
Law; Copyright Law; Licensing; Unfair
Competition; Litigation and Dispute
Resolution; International Law; Internet Law
and E-Commerce; Corporate and Commercial;
Biotech

Education
University of Louisville, J.D., cum laude, 1991
University of Dayton, 1988-1989
Webster College, M.A., Government, 1978
Air Force Institute of Technology, B.S.E.E., 1974
University of Kentucky, B.S., Mathematics, 1968

Admitted to Practice
U.S. Patent and Trademark Office, 1990
Kentucky, 1991
U.S. District Court, Western District of
Kentucky
U.S. District Court, Eastern District of Kentucky
U.S. District Court, Southern District of Indiana
U.S. District Court, Northern District of Illinois
U.S. Court of Appeals, Sixth Circuit
U.S. Court of Appeals, Federal Circuit

Military Service
United States Air Force, 1968-1988
    Communications Engineer 1974-1988
    Radar Maintenance, 1968-1972

Achievements in Areas of Concentration
Registered Patent Attorney, 1990, Reg. No.
34,589
Registered Professional Engineer, Ohio, 1984

Publications & Presentations
"Patented Invention Could Infringe on Other
Patents", *The Courier-Journal*, June 2, 2002
"Patent Law Update", Louisville Bar Association,
2002
"Patent Practice in Light of <u>Festo</u>", Louisville Bar
Association, 2001
"International Patent Protection", Louisville Bar
Association, 2000
"Patent Applications Will Go Public", *The
Courier-Journal*, December 17, 2000
"Patent Rights are Country Specific", *GDM Law
Letter*, June 2000

"International Patent Options", *The Courier-
Journal*, June 22, 2000
"Patent Pending", *The Courier-Journal*, January
16, 2000
"Ownership and Protection of Intellectual
Property – Do You Need an Employer/
employee Agreement?" *GDM Law Letter*,
December 1999
"Holders of trademarks can seek INTERNET
name", *The Courier-Journal*, August 29, 1999
"Does a World Wide WebPresence Mean World
Wide Jurisdiction?" *LBA Bar Briefs*, August
1999
"Jurisdiction on the INTERNET", TerraLex
North American Conference, 1999
"Protecting Your Intellectual Property - Before
You Disclose That Invention", *GDM Law
Letter*, June 1999

Academic Achievements
Adjunct Lecturer, Louis D. Brandeis School of
Law, University of Louisville: Patent Law,
Internet Law, Patent Practice and Procedure

Associations
American Bar Association, Section of IP Law
Kentucky Bar Association
Louisville Bar Association, Intellectual Property
Section, Chair 1999, Vice-Chair 1998
American Intellectual Property Law Association
International Trademark Association

MARY G. EAVES
Member, Louisville

Areas of Concentration
Employee Benefits

Education
University of Kentucky, B.A., (with high
  distinction),
  Political Science, 1972
University of Dayton, Masters in Public
  Administration, 1974
Washington University, J.D., 1983

Admitted to Practice
Kentucky, 1990
Ohio, 1983

Achievements
Phi Beta Kappa
Order of the Coif
Listed in *The Best Lawyers in America,* Employee
  Benefits (Woodward/White, Inc.)

Professional Memberships
Louisville Employee Benefits Council
Southern Employee Benefits Conference
Secretary and Steering Committee Member
Louisville Bar Association
Kentucky Bar Association
Dayton Bar Association
Ohio State Bar Association
American Bar Association

Presentations
HIPAA & Medical Records Privacy Seminar,
  Medical Educational Services, Inc., Louisville,
  Kentucky, November 29, 2001
Nuts and Bolts of 401(k) Plans, Lorman Education
  Services, Louisville, Kentucky, October 24,
  2001
Privacy Seminar for HealthCare Industry, Firm and
  Health Enterprises Network of Greater
  Louisville, Inc., Louisville, Kentucky, October
  17, 2001
Update of Health Law Aspects of ERISA, Kentucky
  Academy of Trial Attorneys, Lexington,
  Kentucky, March 9, 2001
*New Rules on Electronic Administration of
  Qualified Plans,* Louisville Employee Benefits
  Council, Qualified Plans Subcouncil Meeting,
  Louisville, Kentucky, September 26, 2000

Understanding HIPAA and its Impact on Employers,
  Louisville Bar Association, Louisville, Kentucky,
  September 8, 2000
IRAs - New Rules and Attractive Options, National
  Association of Women Business Owners,
  Greater Cincinnati and Northern Kentucky
  Chapter, Covington, Kentucky, March 10,
  1998
*Welfare Benefit Plans Subject to ERISA and Recent
  Changes in Health Care Law,* Louisville Bar
  Association, Louisville, Kentucky, August 28,
  1997
Legal Environment of Welfare Plans, Louisville
  Area Chapter of the International Society of
  Certified Employee Benefit Specialists,
  Louisville, Kentucky, March 19, 1997
*Retirement Planning under the $150,000
  Compensation Limitation,* Kentucky Society of
  Certified Public Accountants, Louisville,
  Kentucky, December 1, 1994
Dependent Care Assistance Plans, Sixth Annual
  Paralegal Forum, Louisville, Kentucky,
  November 4, 1994
Dependent Care Assistance Plans, 1994 Employee
  Benefits & Pension Law Conference, Law
  Education Institute, Inc., and The Bureau of
  National Affairs, Inc., Lake Buena Vista,
  Florida, March 4, 1994
*New Approaches to Executive Compensation:
  Opportunities and Challenges for 1994,*
  University of Louisville, October 22, 1993

LOUIS K. EBLING
Member, Cincinnati

Areas of Concentration
U.S. and Foreign Trademark: Counseling,
Clearance, Prosecution and Enforcement Large
Trademark Portfolio Logistics and Manage-
ment
U.S. and Multinational Transactions Involving
Intellectual Property
Trademark, Character, and Merchandise
Licensing
Trademark/Trade Dress Issues in Product
Labeling
Intellectual Property Audits

Education
University of Michigan, J.D.
Albion College, A.B. with Honors, Magna Cum
Laude

Admitted to Practice
Ohio Illinois (Inactive)
Northern District Illinois

Associations
International Trademark Association, Meetings
Committee

Representative Matters
Among the most active in domestic prosecutions
among Midwest attorneys with over 400 U.S.
filings in the last 30 months.
Active international practice with established
associations in 140 countries around the world.
Consolidation and management of 3000 mark
international portfolio of Fortune 1000
consumer products company.
Representation of award-winning consumer
products start up focused on strategic
acquisition of established and undervalued
brands.
Representation of Fortune 1000 consumer
products company in connection with the
granting of a security interest in a large
portfolio of trademarks.
Representation of Fortune 1000 international
service provider in connection with a complex
international trademark licensing program

Publications & Presentations
"Buy 4, get 11 Free: New Law Makes Trademark
Registration, Always Essential, Now a Bargain
in Europe", Corporate Counsel's International
Adviser, 21, June, 1996
"Dilution is Remedy for Internet Mark Misuse",
The National Law Journal, May 18, 1998
(with K. Kreider)
"Searching and Clearance of 'Non-Traditional'
Marks", INTA Annual Meeting, May, 1999
"Protecting your Good Name Through Trade-
marks", Fayette County Bar Association Bar
News, July/August, 1999
"Registering Trademarks", Clermont Chamber of
Commerce Intercom, June, 1999
"Understanding Basic Trademark Law Principles",
Lorman Education Services, February 10, 1999

HIRAM ELY III
Member, Louisville
Past Member, Firm Executive Committee

Areas of Concentration
Commercial and tort litigation, including
product liability, antitrust, securities, business
and personal torts, contract disputes and tax
court litigation

Education
Centre College of Kentucky, B.A., 1973
Washington & Lee University School of Law,
J.D., 1976

Admitted to Practice
Kentucky, 1976
U.S. District Court, Western District of
Kentucky, 1976
U.S. District Court, Eastern District of Kentucky,
1979
U.S. Supreme Court, 1979
U.S. Court of Appeals, Sixth Circuit, 1979
U.S. Court of Claims, 1979
U.S. Tax Court, 1984

Achievements in Areas of Concentration
Business and tort litigation in both federal and
state courts in numerous jurisdictions
In addition to bench trials, over 50 jury trials
Product liability claim prevention and defense for
several firm clients, including the management
of all pending product liability litigation
nationwide and the institution and management
of preventive counseling programs
Negotiations and litigation between insurance
companies, clients and injured parties
Representation of clients in various forms of
alternate dispute resolution, including
mediation and arbitration

Publications & Presentations
"Seminar on Trial Advocacy," Nice, France
"How to Handle Expert Witnesses," Lexington,
Kentucky
"How to Handle the Newsworthy Case,"
Louisville, Kentucky
"Planning to Avoid (Or Win) Business
Litigation," Honolulu, Hawaii
"How to Be a Better Witness," Louisville,
Kentucky

"Annual Insurance Law Update," Louisville,
Kentucky
"Report of the Kentucky Attorney General's Task
Force on Election Fraud," Frankfort, Kentucky
"Assessment of Liability," Establishing and
Proving Causation" "Legislative Update,"
Louisville, Kentucky
"The 1988 Omnibus Election Reform Act,"
Louisville Lawyer, Winter, 1989
"Jury Trials of the Future," Louisville, Kentucky

Other Achievements
Law Clerk to Hon. James C. Turk, Chief Judge,
U.S. District Court, Western District of Virginia
Chairman, Kentucky Attorney General Fred
Cowan's Special Task Force on Election Fraud
Leadership Louisville
Leadership Kentucky
Young Lawyers Club of Louisville, President
Vice-Chairman, Policy Committee, Louisville
Central Area Downtown Action Plan
One of "Top Ten Outstanding Young
Kentuckians," Kentucky Jaycees
Board of Directors, Centre College of Kentucky
Alumni Association

Professional Memberships
Louisville Bar Foundation, Board of Directors,
President
Kentucky Defense Lawyers
Defense Research Institute

PHILIP C. ESCHELS
Member, Louisville

Areas of Concentration
Labor and Employment Law

Education
Concordia College, River Forest, Ill., B.A., 1974
Ball State University, M.A., 1977
Indiana University Law School, J.D. (with honors), 1983

Admitted to Practice
Kentucky, 1985
Indiana, 1984
U.S. District Court, Southern District of Indiana, 1984
U.S. District Court, Western District of Kentucky, 1985
U.S. District Court, Eastern District of Kentucky, 1986
U.S. Court of Appeals, Sixth Circuit, 1988

Publications & Presentations
"Avoiding Employment Litigation," Southeastern Regional Council, National Association of Housing and Redevelopment Officials, November 16, 1992
"Harassment — It's Not Just Sex Anymore," Paducah Area Employee Relations Association, April 27, 2000
"Avoiding Retaliation Claims," American Bar Association EEO Basics Seminar, Louisville Bar Association, December 13, 2000
Kentucky Employment Law Letter, M. Lee Smith Publishers, Contributing Editor, 1990-present
2001 Cumulative Supplement, Employment Discrimination Law, Third Edition, Barbara Lindemann and Paul Grossman, American Bar Association, Chapter Editor
"Human Resources In Cyberspace: Telecommunications, E-Mail Monitoring And Discovery Issues," Four Rivers SHRM, Minding Your Company's Business: Strategies To Assist Human Resources In Limiting Liability And Bringing Value To The Bottom Line, March 15, 2002
"Avoiding Employment Litigation From Disciplinary Actions, Terminations And Harassment," SERC-NAHRO Annual Conference, Managing Your Workforce In 2002, June 18, 2002

"Workplace Harassment," Kentucky Society for Human Resource Management Conference, September 2002
"How to Avoid Legal Problems in Hiring and Firing in Kentucky," Co-Author, Greenebaum Doll & McDonald, 2002

Achievements
Leadership Louisville, Class of 1997
Bingham Fellows 2000
Leadership Kentucky, Class of 2001

Professional Memberships
Louisville Bar Association (Section of Labor and Employment)
Kentucky Bar Association (Co-Chair, Section of Labor and Employment, 1992)
Indiana Bar Association (Section of Labor and Employment)
American Bar Association (Committee on Equal Employment Opportunity, Section of Labor and Employment)

Associations
Actors' Theatre of Louisville, Board of Directors, Executive Committee
President, Concordia Lutheran Church
Member, Junior League of Louisville Community Advisory Board
Indiana University Southeast, Mentoring Program Advisory Council

CHARLES FASSLER
Member, Louisville

Areas of Concentration
Taxation; Partnership; Limited Liability
Company; Corporation; Executive
Compensation; Real Estate; Family Business

Education
Brooklyn College, City University of New York,
B.S., Accounting, 1967
University of Wisconsin Law School, J.D., 1970
New York University School of Law, LL.M.
(Taxation), 1974

Admitted to Practice
Kentucky, 1976
New York, 1971
U.S. Tax Court, 1972

Professional Memberships
Louisville Bar Association
Kentucky Bar Association
American Bar Association

Publications & Presentations
"Kentucky Limited Liability Company, Forms and
Practice Manual," Data Trace Publishing Co.
Kentucky Editor, "State Limited Partnership
Laws," Aspen Law & Business
Kentucky Editor, "State Limited Liability
Company and Partnership Laws," Aspen Law
& Business
Equity Compensation in Partnerships," American
Bar Association, Section of Taxation, January,
2002
"Tax Issues in Drafting Operating Agreements,"
Kentucky Bench & Bar, July, 2002
"Tax Issues on the Sale of a Business," Kentucky
Bar Association, June, 2000
"LLCs in Kentucky: Organization, Operations
and Opportunities," Lorman Education
Services, June, 2000
"New Developments in LLCs and LLPs,"
Professional Education Systems, Inc., June,
1998, July, 1999
"Taxpayer Relief Act of 1997, Selected Federal
Income Tax Provisions," Louisville Bar
Association, February, 1998
"ABC's of Tax-Free Reorganizations," Kentucky
Society of Certified Public Accountants, May,
1998

"Special Tax Considerations and Strategies,"
Kentucky Partnership Law, 1996
"Specifics of Drafting: The Limited Liability
Company Operating Agreement's Treatment of
Financing, Distributions and Control Issues,"
University of Kentucky, February, 1995.
"Choice of Entity - Income Tax Considerations"
and "Federal Income Tax Aspects of Operation
of Limited Liability Companies in Kentucky,"
University of Kentucky CLE, 1994
"Tax Issues in Coal Acquisitions," ALI-ABA,
February, 1982
"Selected Tax Consequences of Advanced Coal
Royalties," Kentucky Mineral Law, 1986

Achievements in Areas of Concentration
Kentucky Revised Uniform Limited Partnership
Act, Draftsman
Kentucky Limited Liability Company Act,
Drafting Committee
Listed in "Best Lawyers in America," Tax Law,
Woodward/White, since 1989

Associations
Congregation Adath Jeshurun - Board of Trustees,
1986-1992; Treasurer, 1989-1990
United States Handball Association - Kentucky
Commissioner, 1985-2000

271

NICHOLAS W. FERRIGNO, JR.
Member, Covington and Cincinnati
Areas of Concentration
Employee Benefits Law & Litigation

Education
Salmon P. Chase College of Law, Northern
  Kentucky University, J.D. (*cum laude*), 1995
University of Rhode Island, B.S.B.A. (Finance),
  1982

Admitted to Practice
Kentucky, 1995, Ohio 2002
U.S. District Court - Eastern District of KY
U.S. Court of Appeals for the Sixth Circuit

Professional Memberships
Federal Bar Association
Kentucky Bar Association
Northern Kentucky Bar Association
Cincinnati Bar Association, Employee Benefits
Greater Cincinnati Compensation & Benefits
  Assoc.
American Society of Pension Actuaries
The ESOP Association

Publications
ERISA Facts (electronic and print publication),
  Co-Author (The National Underwriter Co.,
  1998-2002 Editions)
*The Insider's Guide to DOL Plan Audits - How to
  Survive an Employee Benefit Plan Audit*, (print
  publication), Co-Author (The National
  Underwriter Co.)
Benefit Facts (print publication), Co-Author (The
  National Underwriter Co., 2000-03 Editions)
Benefitslink.com Website, ERISA Question &
  Answer Column, Co-Author, 1999-2001
"Retirement Plans for Small Employers, Parts I &
  II," *Northern Kentucky Business Journal*,
  November/December 1999
"Benefit Briefs," *Lex Loci*, NKBA Bi-Monthly
  Column
"Department of Labor Investigations of
  Retirement Plans– Tips and Traps," Northern
  Kentucky Bar Assoc., March 1999
"Avoiding Employee Benefits Liability," *Northern
  Kentucky Business Journal*, December, 1998
"Department of Labor Service Provider Audits,"
  The Pension Actuary, July-August 1998
"Employers Should Review Plan Asset
  Requirements," *Benefits & HR Advisor*, Vol. 6,

No. 4, Winter 1997, published by Grant
Thornton LLP

Presentations
"Tax and Business Issues for High-Tech
  Companies in Tennessee," Lorman Education
  Services, December 2000
"ERISA Claims and Litigation In Ohio" Lorman
  Education Services, November 2000
"Overview of ERISA," National Association of
  Insurance Women, June 2000

Achievements
Recipient, Forty Under 40 Business Leaders of
  Cincinnati Chartered Life Underwriter (CLU)
Chartered Financial Consultant (ChFC)
Appointed to Government Affairs Committee,
  Sub-Committee on DOL Enforcement-
  American Society of Pension Actuaries
Appointed to the Great Lakes Area TE/GE
  Council to the Internal Revenue Service
Internship with Honorable J. Gregory Wehrman,
  United States District Court for the Eastern
  District of Kentucky
Eagle Scout - District Advancement Chair,
  Daniel Boone District

Associations
Board of Governors, Salmon P. Chase College of
  Law Alumni Assn.

DANIEL E. FISHER
Member, Louisville

Areas of Concentration
Mergers and Acquisitions; Securities Transactions; Venture Capital; Corporate and Commercial Transactions; Energy Law

Education
Wittenberg University, A.B. in Business Administration, with Emphasis in Accounting; Political Science Minor, 1983
University of Cincinnati College of Law, J.D., 1986

Admitted to Practice
Kentucky, 1986
U.S. Tax Court, 1986

Achievements in Areas of Concentration
Structured and negotiated numerous mergers and acquisitions, divestitures and other transactions for publicly and privately-owned businesses
Structured and completed several private offerings of securities for closely-held businesses and venture capital transactions; frequent advisor on private capital formation strategies
Counsel to a national energy services company in an approximately $1 billion dollar acquisition of a bankrupt rural electric cooperative
Counsel in all cash sale of stock of insurance company in excess of $125 million
Counsel to large assisted living company in numerous domestic acquisition and divestiture transactions, including an all cash sale of assets of assisted and independent living facilities in excess of $65 million
Extensive experience in representing clients in the restaurant industry, including franchising, restaurant development, and mergers and acquisitions in anticipation of initial public offerings

Publications and Presentations
"Significant Legal Developments for In-House and Corporate Counsel," Louisville Bar Association, March, 2000
"Selecting The Proper Form Of Business Organization," Louisville Bar Association Tax Section Seminar, June, 1988
"Tired Of The Tax Time Shakedown," *Bar Briefs*, September, 1988

Academic Achievements
Lutheran Scholarship Award, Wittenberg University
Phi Eta Sigma Freshman Honorary
Tau Pi Phi Business Honorary, Wittenberg University
Dean's Honors List, University of Cincinnati, 1983-86
Internship, Internal Revenue Service, Office of District Counsel

Professional Memberships
Louisville Bar Association
Kentucky Bar Association

Associations
Board of Trustees, The Council for Retarded Citizens of Jefferson County
Session Member, Highland Presbyterian Church
Alumni, Beta Theta Pi Fraternity

MICHAEL M. FLEISHMAN
Member, Louisville
Chair, Business and Commercial Practice

Areas of Concentration
Zoning
Real Estate Development, Syndication and
Financing Transactions
Commercial Financing Transactions
Mergers & Acquisitions
Venture Capital

Education
Clemson University, B.A. (with honors), 1966
Tulane University of Louisiana School of Law,
J.D., 1969

Admitted to Practice
Kentucky, 1969

Achievements in Areas of Concentration
Listed in *The Best Lawyers in America*, Real Estate
Law, Woodward/White, 1989 and Subsequent
Years

Publications & Presentations
"1969 Tidelands - Definition of 'Inland Waters'
as used in the Submerged Lands Act," 42
Tulane Law Review, 1967-68
"Federal Taxation-Section 2035, Internal Revenue
Code of 1954-Life Insurance Proceeds-Revenue
Rule 67-463," 43 *Tulane Law Review*, 1968-69
Lecturer, University of Louisville School of Law,
1970-72
Numerous speeches at seminars sponsored by Bar
Associations, Real Estate and Lending Groups
and Organizations

Achievements
Member, *Tulane Law Review*, 1967-69
Member, Board of Directors, Chi-Chi's, Inc., and
Chairman of its Finance Committee, 1983-
1988
Member, Presidential Search Committee, Chi-
Chi's, Inc. 1986
Member, Board of Directors, Rally's Hamburgers,
Inc.
Member, Board of Trustees, Bellarmine College,
1989-1995
Member, Presidential Search Committee,
Bellarmine College, 1989

Member, Advisory Board of Paul Semonin
Realtors

Professional Memberships
Louisville Bar Association
Kentucky Bar Association
American Bar Association

DAVID A. FRENCH
Member, Lexington

Areas of Concentration
Commercial Litigation
Civil Rights & Constitutional Law
Legal Ethics

Education
David Lipscomb University, B.A., summa cum
laude, Political Science, 1991
Harvard University J.D., cum laude 1994

Admitted to Practice
Supreme Court of Tennessee, 1994
Supreme Court of Kentucky, 1997
U.S. Court of Appeals for the Sixth Circuit, 1999
U.S. District Court for the Eastern District
of Kentucky, 1998
U.S. District Court for the Western District of
Kentucky, 1998

Achievements
Valedictorian, David Lipscomb University, 1991
Editor, Harvard Journal of Law & Public Policy,
1992-1993
Teaching Experience Lecturer, Cornell Law
School, 1999-2001– instructor in legal ethics
and legal methods.

Publications (Legal)
"A Season for Justice: Defending the Rights of the
Christian Home, Church and School"
(Broadman & Holman) (June 2002 release)
"Foundation for Individual Rights in Education:
Guide to Religious Liberty on Campus" (Fall
2002 release).
Co-author, "Religious Freedom Handbook
(InterVarsity) (2000)

Publication (Fiction)
David & Nancy French, "South Pacific Journal
(Broadman & Holman) (1999) – historical
fiction novel.

Presentations
Panelist, Teaching Ethics in a Pluralist Demo-
cratic Society" – symposium sponsored by the
Cornell Christian Faculty/Staff Forum. (2001).
Panelist, "I Came To a Fork in the Road." –
Ethics CLE program sponsored by the New
York State Bar Association (2001).

V. THOMAS FRYMAN, JR.
Member, Lexington

Areas of Concentration
Litigation

Education
Harvard College, B.A., 1962
Harvard Law School, L.L.B., 1966

Admitted to Practice
Kentucky, 1988
New York, 1967
U.S. Supreme Court, 1970
U.S. Court of Appeals, Second Circuit, 1967
U.S. Court of Appeals, Sixth Circuit, 1988
U.S. Court of Appeals, Eleventh Circuit, 2002
U.S. District Court, Western District of
Kentucky, 1988
U.S. District Court, Eastern District of Kentucky,
1988
U.S. District Court, Southern District of New
York, 1968
U.S. District Court, Eastern District of New
York, 1968

Achievements in Areas of Concentration
Assistant United States Attorney for the Southern
District of New York, U.S. Department of
Justice, 1973-78
Staff Counsel, Select Committee to Investigate
Covert Arms transactions with Iran, U.S.
House of Representatives, 1987

Publications & Presentations
"Proving Federal Crimes," 6th Edition, 1976,
contributor
"Accountants' Legal Liability After Hochfelder,"
The Ohio Society of Certified Public
Accountants, Columbus, Ohio, June 18, 1979
"Accounting Issues Raised by FCPA," The World
Trade Institute at the World Trade Center, New
York City, June 13, 1980

Professional Memberships
Fayette County Bar Association
Kentucky Bar Association
American Bar Association
Association of the Bar of the City of New York
Federal Bar Council (New York City)

Associations
Harvard University Club of Central and Eastern
Kentucky, Inc.
President, 1990-92
Co-Chairman, Schools Committee, 1995-
Harvard Alumni Association
Regional Director for the Ohio Valley, 1992-95
Harvard Law School Class of 1966
25th Reunion Gift Committee
Lexington Philharmonic Society, Inc.
Director, 1993-96, 1999-
Vice President-Development, 1994-95
Vice President-Education, 1995-96
Vice President-Long Range Planning, 2000-02
The Lexington School Board of Trustees, 1998-
2000
Old Washington Renaissance Board Member, 2000-
The University of Kentucky
Library Associates, Executive Committee, 2002-

J. MARK GRUNDY
Member, Louisville

Areas of Concentration
Business litigation and dispute resolution.

Education
University of Kentucky, 1977
University of Louisville, B.A., 1981
University of Louisville, J.D., 1988:
   moot court finalist
   scholastic awards in taxation, legal research,
decedent estates
   member of law journal

Admitted to Practice
Supreme Court of Kentucky
U.S. District Courts, Kentucky
U.S. District Court, S.D. Indiana
U.S. Court of Appeals, Sixth Circuit

Experience
Engaged in full-time litigation practice for past
   fourteen years.
Successfully litigated dozens of cases before
   federal, state, and administrative courts and
   agencies.
Obtained favorable trial judgments and jury
   verdicts.
Significant reported decisions include: Trial that
   established new law dismissing a single asset
   bankruptcy petition. Obtained a $9.6 million
   judgment.
KHC v. Pleasant Point, U.S. Court of Appeals,
   Sixth Circuit -multi-million dollar dispute that
   established new law for interpretation of long
   term supply agreements. KU v. South East
   Coal Co., Supreme Court of Kentucky

Publications, Seminars & Presentations
"A Manufacturer's Guide To Avoiding Products
   LiabilityClaims," the Kentucky, Indiana, Ohio
   Manufacturers Association Journals, Spring 1998.
"The Seven Deadly Sins of Construction
   Lending," Kentucky Banking Association,
   Annual Legal Issues for Financial
   Institutions Seminar, University of Kentucky
   College of Law, April 14-15, 2000.
"Legislative Developments in Computer Law,"
   Annual Computer Law Institute Seminar,
   University of Kentucky College of Law, March
   17, 2000.

Featured speaker on KET *Kentucky Tonight*
   television broadcast regarding impact of federal
   legislation, March 29, 1999.
Regularly conduct seminars regarding litigation
   practice, products liability, construction law,
   computer law, protection of trade secrets, and
   non-competition agreements.

Professional Memberships
Louisville, Kentucky, and American Bar
   Associations
Kentucky Academy of Trial Attorneys
Defense Research Institute

Associations & Activities
Former President, Chairman of Board, Lakeside
   Corporation
Certified airplane pilot, Federal Aviation
   Administration
Former division chairman, Louisville Chamber of
   Commerce

STEPHEN E. GILLEN
Member, Cincinnati

Areas of Concentration
Intellectual Property (non-patent)
Publishing Transactions and Disputes
Software Licensing
Entertainment & Music
Media Law
Advertising
Internet and e-Commerce
ASP Agreements
Development and Hosting Transactions
Privacy Compliance
Content & Database Licensing (in/out)
Character & Celebrity Licensing
Rights Clearance
Pre-Publication/Pre-Broadcast Review
Electronic Aggregation and Syndication
Technology Transfer

Education
Miami University, B.S.B.A., 1975
Salmon P. Chase College of Law, J.D., 1980

Admitted to Practice
Ohio, 1980
Southern District of Ohio, 1980
6th Circuit, 1980

Representative Matters
Representation of book and journal publishers in connection with the sale of their businesses to major international publishing houses

Representation of a regional legal publisher in copyright infringement litigation concerning its flagship title

Representation of music publisher in copyright infringement litigation against advertising agency

Engaged as expert on copyright question in litigation involving renewal rights to a popular card game

Representation of health care businesses in high stakes software implementation transactions

Representation of township in acquisition of E-911/mobile communicationsand dispatch system

Representation of telecommunications company in acquisitions of software and technology and in divestiture of directory business

Representation of international database publisher in licensing transactions (in/out)

Representation of major newspaper in development of electronic aggregation and syndication business

Representation of rightsholders in optioning dramatic and documentary rights to trade books

Representation of museums, libraries, and school systems in connection with web-based archiving, distance learning, and other copyright issues

Representation of authors, artists, photographers, videographers, developers, producers, and other creatives in transactions and dispute

Associations
Text & Academic Authors Assn., Council Member Voyageur Media Group, Trustee
Authors' Guild, Member
Adjunct Instructor, *Media Business and Law*, University of Cincinnati Media Technologies Program
Adjunct Instructor, *Electronic Media Law*, UC College Conservatory of Music

Representative Publications and Presentations
Ten Tips for Your Next Book Deal, SCBWI Bulletin, June/July
If You're Outsourcing Creative Work…, Media & the Law, January 24, 1997
Lawyers on the 'Net, CBA Report, March 1997
Slicing the Electronic Pie, *Folio*, April 1997

278

BARBARA REID HARTUNG
Member, Louisville

Areas of Concentration
Health and Insurance Law

Education
Randolph Macon Women's College, 1964-65
University of Louisville, B.A., History *cum laude*, 1967
University of Louisville School of Law, J.D. *cum laude*, 1981

Admitted to Practice
Kentucky, 1981
U.S. District Court, Western District of Kentucky, 1981
U.S. District Court, Eastern District of Kentucky, 1982
U.S. Court of Appeals, Sixth Circuit, 1982
U.S. Supreme Court, 1989

Publications & Presentations
"Managed Care in the New Millennium," January, 2001, sponsored by KMGMA at Louisville, Kentucky
"Legislative Update and New Developments in the Health Law Field," co-author, appears as Chapter One of Kentucky Health Law, 3d. Ed., University of Kentucky, 2000
"Healthcare Reform in Kentucky: Setting the Stage for the Twenty First Century?" principal author, Northern Kentucky Law Review, Vol. 27, No. 2, 2000
"Arbitration in Managed Care," sponsored by ABA Health Law Section, July, 2000, London, England
Seminar lecturer in September, 1999, "Medicare – Medicaid Fraud and Abuse Compliance, sponsored by KAHSA
Seminar lecturer, "Managed Care Regulations," co-sponsored by ABA and AAHP, Tucson, Arizona, April, 1999
Seminar lecturer in January, 1999, update on HIPAA and Balanced Budget Act, sponsored by Lorman Business Center, Inc., Louisville, KY
"Managed Care Regulation," presented at seminar on "Fundamentals of Managed Care," co-sponsored by ABA and AAHP, April 1998, St. Petersburg, Florida
"Managed Care at the Crossroads - Can Managed Care Organizations Survive Government Regulation?" co-author, Loyola University Chicago School of Law, Institute for Health Law, in *Annals of Health Law*, Fall, 1998
"Welfare Benefit Plans Subject to ERISA and Recent Changes in Health Care Law," presented by Mary G. Eaves and Barbara Reid Hartung, Louisville Bar Association, Summer 1997
Federal Law Update, Kentucky Bar Association Regional Bar Meetings, September 1993, 1994, 1995, 1996, 1997
Presentation at July 18, 1996 seminar on Kentucky Health Care Reform, Louisville, KY

Achievements
CPCU, Chartered Property and Casualty Underwriter, 1987
Who's Who in American College, 1981
Brandeis Society
Editor-in-Chief, *Journal of Family Law*, 1980-81

Associations
Member, Board of Directors, Leadership Louisville Foundation, 1988-1990
Member, University of Louisville Law School Alumni Council, 1995 to present
President, University of Louisville Law School Alumni Council, 2000-2001
Member, University of Louisville Alumni Association Board, 2000 to present

MICHAEL DE LEÓN HAWTHORNE

Member, Louisville
Member, Corporate and Securities Group
Chair, Telecommunications and Technology
  Practice
Member, Family Business Group

Formerly with Sidley Austin Brown & Wood,
  Chicago, Illinois, 1989-1996

Areas of Concentration
Corporate and Securities; Mergers and
  Acquisitions; Venture   Capital; Business
  Negotiations

Education
Denison University, B.S., 1984 (summa cum
  laude)
University of Wisconsin, J.D., 1987

Admitted to Practice
Kentucky, Wisconsin, Illinois and
U.S. District Court for the Northern District of
  Illinois

Professional Memberships
American Bar Association
Friends of the Waterfront
Greater Louisville, Inc. (Metro Chamber of
  Commerce) Kentucky Bar Association
Louisville Bar Association
Southern Indiana Chamber of Commerce
State Bar of Wisconsin
TeN – Technology Network

Achievements in Areas of Concentration
Represented clients in connection with private
  and public capital formation, including public
  offerings, shelf registrations and private
  placements
Represented clients in connection with general
  business matters, mergers, acquisitions,
  divestitures, financings, settlement of litigation
  matters, and Federal and state securities law
  matters
Extensive experience in representing clients
  involved in the telecommunications and
  technology industries

Presentations
Southern Indiana Chamber of Commerce, Business
  Planning through Succession or Sale, 2002

Greater Louisville Inc., Legal Issues for Small
  Business Seminar, 2001
Kentucky ITEC Conference, 2001
Growing Your Company and Raising Capital, I.T.
  Symposium, 2001
Venture Capital, First Union Securities and in
  association with The Enterprise Corporation,
  2000
Venture Capital for the Telecommunications and
  Technology Industries, First Union Securities,
  2000
Raising Capital, First Union Securities, 2000
Plain English Disclosure Rules and SEC Year
  2000 Disclosure Guidelines, 1998
Federal and State Securities Law Issues, University
  of Louisville Telecommunications Research
  Center, 1998
Maximizing Wealth through Shareholder
  Liquidity Alternatives, Houlihan Lokey
  Howard & Zukin, 1997
Securities Law Disclosure Update, 1997

Achievements
Board Member, Cystic Fibrosis Foundation,
  Kentucky/West Virginia Chapter, 1998 - present
Board Member and Treasurer of the Ambassador
  Condominium Association, 1990 -1995
Board Member, Friends of the Waterfront, 2002 -
  present
Member, Finance Committee, Friends of the
  Waterfront, 2002 - present

MARK T. HAYDEN
Member, Cincinnati/Northern Kentucky Office

Areas of Concentration
Trial Practice; Complex Commercial Litigation;
Product Liability

Education
Providence High School, 1979
Indiana University, B.A., 1983
Indiana University, School of Law, J.D. (cum
laude), 1986

Admitted to Practice
Kentucky; Ohio; U.S. District Court, Eastern
District of Kentucky; U.S. Court of Appeals,
Sixth Circuit; and U.S. District Court,
Southern District of Ohio

Achievements
Represents public and private clients in complex
commercial litigation matters
Lead counsel in 19 jury trials to verdict (16 wins
and 3 losses)
Successfully prosecuted and defended multi-
million dollar claims as lead trial counsel
Lead trial counsel in a defense jury verdict in a
$605 million product liability claim-selected by
the *National Law Journal* as a "Big Win" in 1998
Co-lead trial counsel in a plaintiff's jury verdict
awarding $40 million in a commercial claim—
one of the top ten jury verdicts in the history of
Kentucky
Cincinnati Business Courier's "Top Forty under
40" April, 2000
Distinguished Service Award for Fund Raising
from the Campbell County YMCA, 1999
Adjunct Professor of Law, Legal Writing and Oral
Advocacy, University of Kentucky Law School
(August 1993 to 1995)
American Bar Association's "Star Award" for
service to the Product Liability Committee, 1997
American Bar Association's "Leadership Award"
for service to Product Liability Committee, 1997

Publications & Presentations
Speaker & Author, "The Paperless Trial," Kentucky
Academy of Trial Attorneys, Annual Convention
and Seminar, 2000
Speaker & Author, "Discovery Tactics & Abuse,"
Kentucky Bar Association, Kentucky Law
Update 2000, Regional Bar Meetings, 2000

Speaker, "Opening and Closing Statements - A
Defense Perspective," Kentucky Bar Association,
Regional Bar Meetings, 1998
Author, "An Analysis of Selected Portions of the
Proposed Restatement of Products Liability Law
and a Comparison to Existing Kentucky Law,"
Kentucky Bar Association, Bench and Bar, 1997
Speaker, "Direct and Cross-Examination of
Orthopedists-A Defense Perspective," Professional
Education Systems Seminar, 1997
Speaker, "Accident Reconstruction," Presented to
the Kentucky Claims Association, 1994
Author, "Evaluating an Occupant Restraint
System Case - A Practitioner's Perspective," Trial
Diplomacy Journal, September/October 1993

Professional Memberships & Associations
Defense Research Institute, Product Liability
Subcommittee
American Bar Association, Tort and Insurance
Practice (Vice-Chair of The Products General
Liability and Consumer Law Committee, 1996-
1997)
American Bar Association, Product Liability
Committee (Co-Editor of the Newsletter, 1996-
present)
Kentucky Defense Council
Cincinnati, Ohio, and Kentucky Bar Associations
Campbell County YMCA, Board of Directors,
1996-present
Diocese of Covington, Kentucky Pastoral Council

ROBERT D. HUDSON
Member, Covington and Cincinnati

Areas of Concentration
Labor and Employment Law

Education
University of Kentucky, B.S. in Accounting (with High Distinction), 1984
University of Kentucky, College of Law, J.D., 1987

Admitted to Practice
Kentucky
Ohio

Publications
Editorial Board - Sixth Circuit, Labor & Employment Law Digest, 1992-93
Contributing Editor & Author - Ky. Employment Law Letter, 1992-00
Contributing Labor Author - No. Ky. Bar Assn. Lex Loci, 1990-93
"Trusty v. Big Sandy Health Care - A Further Erosion Of the At-Will Doctrine In Kentucky," Kentucky Bar Association Labor Line, 1991
"The Older Workers Benefit Protection Act - An Analysis and Review," Kentucky Chamber of Commerce Newsletter, 1991
"Employee Handbooks in Kentucky," Ky Bar Assn. Labor Line, 1990
"An Employment Law State Legislative Update," No. Ky. Bar Assn., Newsletter, 1990
Contributing Editor - Developing Labor Law, 1994
Editor - The Human Resources File Cabinet, 1999

Presentations
Mr. Hudson has conducted several hundred management training sessions and seminars. Representative presentations include:
Speaker, "Sexual Harassment - A Mock Trial and Demonstration," All-Ohio Human Resource Annual Conference, 1991
Speaker, "Wage and Hour Law," Council on Education in Management, Lorman Seminars, 1993
Speaker, "Wrongful Discharge," Cincinnati Bar Association, 1990
Speaker, "Complying with the Family and Medical Leave Act of 1993," Resource Association, 1993

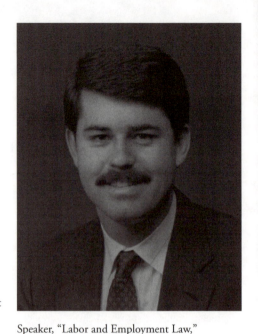

Speaker, "Labor and Employment Law," Kentucky Chamber of Commerce, 1992
Speaker, "The 1991 Civil Rights Act and Sexual Harassment -Evolving Legal Obligations," Ky. Bar Assn. Annual Convention, 1992
Speaker, "Collective Bargaining for School Boards," Kentucky School Board Association, 1992

Achievements and Associations
Industrial Relations Research Association, Cincinnati Chapter, Board Member, 1995-96
Kentucky Bar Association, Labor & Employment Law Section, Management Co-Chair, 1994, Secretary, 1991-92
No. Ky. Bar Assn., Labor and Employment Section, Chairman, 1993-94; Vice-Chairman, 1991-92; Board Member, 1994-98
Northern Kentucky Human Resource Association, President, 1994;Legislative Com., Chair, 1994-97
University of Ky. Alumni Assn. Cincinnati Chapter, Board Member, President, 1996
Northern Kentucky Chamber of Commerce, Chairman, Family/Medical Leave Task Force, 1993; Chairman, Government and Business Relations Council Human Resources Committee, 1996-00; Board of Directors, 2000
Kentucky's Outstanding Young Lawyer, Finalist, 1993
Be Concerned, Inc., Board Member, 1992-96, President, 2000

ERIC L. ISON

Member In Charge, Louisville
Member, Executive Committee
Chairman, Litigation and Dispute Resolution
  Department
Special Justice, Kentucky Supreme Court, 1997

Areas of Concentration
Commercial Litigation

Reported Decisions
*Louisville and Jefferson County Metropolitan Sewer
  District v Douglas Hills Sanitation Facility, et
  al., Ky., 592 S.W.2d 142 (1979)*(Declaratory
  judgment as to relative rights of lot owners,
  developer/owner of private sewage treatment
  plant and city/county sewer district and others
  in and to real property easements and sewage
  collection system).
*Central Adjustment Bureau v. Ingram Associates,
  Inc.*, Ky. App., 62 S.W.2d 861 (1981) (new law
  in Kentucky regarding enforceability of post
  employment covenants not to compete).
*Hammond v. Baldwin and Toyota Motor
  Manufacturing, U.S.A.*, 866 F.2d 172 (6th Cir.
  1989)(dismissal of § 1983 claim for failure to
  state a claim of violation of due process and
  absence of final administrative action on which
  to base deprivation of due process claim).
*Pleasant Pointe Apartments, Ltd. v. Kentucky
  Housing Corporation*, 139 B.R. 828 (W.D. Ky.
  1992) (new law in the Western District of
  Kentucky dismissing single asset Debtor's
    Chapter 11 petition for lack of good faith);
The Kentucky Lottery Corporation v. Casey, Ky.,
  862 S.W.2d 888 (1993)(case of first impression
  construing Kentucky's Lottery statute).
Niehoff v. Surgidev Corp., Ky., 950 S.W.2d 816
  (1997) (no federal pre-emption of state law
  negligence and product liability claims)(author
  of Dissenting Opinion sitting as Special Justice).

Education
University of the South, B.A. (Cum Laude), 1970
Institute of European Studies, Madrid, Spain,
  1968-69
Vanderbilt School of Law, J.D. 1974
Associate Editor, Vanderbilt Law Review.

Admitted to Practice
Kentucky, 1974
Tennessee, 1998

U.S. District Court, Western District of Kentucky
U.S. District Court, Eastern District of Kentucky
U.S. District Court, Southern District of Indiana
U.S. Court of Appeals, Sixth Circuit

Professional Memberships
Louisville Bar Association
Kentucky Bar Association
American Bar Association

Associations
Kentucky Board of Bar Examiners (current)
Board of Directors, Beacon House Aftercare
  Program Inc. (current)
Leadership Kentucky
President, Board of Directors, STAGE ONE: The
  Louisville Children's Theatre
Board of Trustees, University of the South
Attorney Steering Committee, Citizens for Better
  Judges
Supreme Court Historical Society
Committee on Professional Ethics, Louisville Bar
  Association
Councilman, Anchorage, Kentucky

JANET P. JAKUBOWICZ
Member, Louisville

Areas of Concentration
Business and Commercial Litigation
Securities and RICO Litigation and Arbitration

Education
University of Louisville, B.A., 1979
University of Kentucky College of Law, J.D.,
1982

Admitted to Practice
Kentucky, 1982
U. S. District Court
    Western District of Kentucky, 1983
    Eastern District of Kentucky, 1983
U. S. Court of Appeals
    Sixth Circuit, 1986
    Fourth Circuit, 1997
U. S. Supreme Court, 1987
U. S. Tax Court, 1987

Achievement in Areas of Concentration
Successful prosecution and defense of a variety of
    commercial, securities and RICO litigation and
    arbitration mattersinvolving the coal industry,
    banking, brokerage firms, manufacturing and
    retail

Publications & Presentations
"The Executive Branch Code of Ethics," *Election
    Law in Kentucky* (1995)
"Survey Article-Domestic Relations," Vol. 70,
    Kentucky Law Journal, 1981-82
"Practical Ethics Considerations for Your
    Practice," Louisville Bar Association, May 1999
"Conflicts of Interest: It's a Jungle Out There,"
    Louisville Bar Association, June 1997

Achievements
Staff Member, *Kentucky Law Journal*
Moot Court Board
The Woodcock Society
Phi Kappa Phi

Professional Memberships
Association of Trial Lawyers of America
Louisville Bar Association (Member Services
    Committee)
Kentucky Bar Association

American Bar Association (Subcommittee on
    RICO; Subcommittee on Security Trials and
    Takeover Litigation; Section of Corporate,
    Banking and Business Law)

Associations
Member, Citizens for Better Judges
Member, Louisville Bar Association, Board of
    Directors
Chair, Louisville Bar Association, Member
    Services Committee
Member, Louis D. Brandeis Inn of Courts
Trial Commissioner, Kentucky Bar Association
Member, Kentucky Securities Law Advisory
    Committee, Kentucky Department of Financial
    Institutions, Division of Law and Regulatory
    Compliance

MARGARET E. KEANE

Member, Louisville
Executive Committee Member, 2001-2004
[Executive Committee Member, 1994-97]

Areas of Concentration
Trial Practice; Commercial Litigation;
   Employment Law; Products Liability; Family
   Law

Education
University of Kentucky, 1970-73
University of Louisville, B.A. (Dean's scholar,
   High honors), 1979
Louis D. Brandeis School of Law at the
   University of Louisville, J.D. (Magna cum
   laude, Outstanding Senior award), 1982

Admitted to Practice
Kentucky, 1982
U.S. District Court, Western District of
   Kentucky, 1982
U.S. District Court, Eastern District of Kentucky,
   1983
U.S. Court of Appeals, Sixth Circuit, 1984
U.S. Claims Court, 1991
U.S. Court of Appeals, Federal Circuit, 1992
U.S. Supreme Court, 1993

Achievements
Brandeis Honor Society
Omicron Delta Kappa
Phi Kappa Phi
Research Editor, *Journal of Family Law*
Business Associate of the Year (1991), Louisville
   Chapter, American Business Women's Association
Legal Aid Society's "Volunteer Lawyer of the
   Year" (1990)
Louisville Bar Association's Public Service Award
   (1996)
Twice nominated by Judicial Nominating
   Commission for Circuit Court Judge

Publications & Presentations
Presenter, Kentucky Bar Association District Bar
   Meeting, "Interactive Evidence Workshop,"
   (September, 2001)
Coordinator and Presenter, Kentucky Bar
   Association "Orientation on Professionalism"
   for First-Year Law Students, Louis D.
   Brandeis School of Law at the University of
   Louisville (1998)

Kentucky Bar Association 1997 Annual
   Convention "You Be the Judge for the Day:
   Evidence, Interaction and More"
Louisville Bar Association "Evidentiary Problems
   in Dissolution Actions" (1996)
Kentucky Law Update, "Law and the Media"
Lecturer, Louis D. Brandeis School of Law at the
   University of Louisville
"Trade Associations: Industry Advocates or Co-
   Conspirators?" Defense Research Institute (1999)
"Litigating Wrongful Discharge," Professional
   Education Systems, Inc.
"Defendant's Perspective in Handling Employee
   Relations Cases Including Wrongful
   Discharge," Professional Education Systems,
   Inc. Seminar: Kentucky - Litigating Wrongful
   Discharge
"The Current Status of Wrongful Discharge
   Actions in Kentucky," Professional Education
   Systems, Inc.
"Kentucky - Litigating Wrongful Discharge,"
   Professional Education Systems, Inc.

Offices, Boards and Appointments
Louisville Bar Association Delegate to ABA
   House of Delegates 1998-2002
Kentucky Bar Association, Trial Commissioner,
   1998
Louisville Bar Association President, 1997
Kentucky Supreme Court Special Justice (1997)
Graduate, Leadership Louisville

JUNE NALLY KING
Member, Louisville

Areas of Concentration
Securities, Corporate, Banking and Health Care

Education
University of Kentucky, B.M., 1975
University of Kentucky College of Law, J.D., 1979

Academic Achievements
Phi Beta Kappa
Notes Editor, University of Kentucky Law
  Journal, 1978-1979
Order of the Coif

Admitted to Practice
Kentucky, 1979

Professional Honors
Leadership Louisville, Class of 1993
Bingham Fellowship, 1997

Associations
Kentucky Bar Association
Louisville Bar Association

Professional Memberships
Director, The Louisville Orchestra
National Association of Stock Plan Professionals

Achievements in Areas of Concentration
Former Assistant General Counsel at Vencor, Inc.
  Responsibilities with respect to: public offerings,
  SEC reporting, Hilhaven acquisition, issuer
  tender offer, stock repurchase program, Board
  and Stockholder meetings, stock transfer issues
  and stock plan administration

Publications & Presentations
"Ethical and Practical Concerns in Attempts to
  Impose Contractual Limits on Attorney
  Liability," Midwest/Midsouth Securities Law
  Conference, 1994
"Public Announcements and Shareholder
  Communications," Midwest/Midsouth
  Securities Law Conference, 1996
Panelist at Corporate Management Solutions
  User Conference, 1995

SUZANNE LAND
Member, Cincinnati

Areas of Concentration
Trusts and Estates
Family Business
Non-profit Organizations
Elder Care Law

Education
Youngstown State University, 1987, Accounting
and Economics, Summa cum Laude
Case Western Reserve School of Law, 1990,
Summa cum Laude

Admitted to Practice
Ohio, 1990

Achievements in Areas of Concentration
Best Lawyers in America in Trusts and Estates,
2002-2003

Western Reserve Law Review

Publications and Presentations
Adjunct Professor of Law, University of Cincin-
nati Law School, 1998 to present, Teaching
courses in Estate Planning and Drafting of
Estate Plans.
Presenter: "Charitable Tax Strategies," The Jewish
Federation of Cincinnati, Ohio, 1995
Presenter: "Estate Tax and Asset Protection
Strategies," The Greater Dayton Real Estate
Association, 1998 and 2000
Presenter: "Estate Planning and Planned Giving
Strategies," The University of Cincinnati
Foundation, Annual Medical School Alumni
Weekend, 1999, 2000, 2001
Presenter: "Estate Planning with Family Limited
Partnerships and Limited Liability Companies,"
sponsored by Horan and Associates, 2000
Presenter: "Estate Tax and Asset Protection
Strategies," The Greater Cincinnati Real Estate
Association, 2001
Presenter: "The New Generation Skipping Tax
Rules and Duties for Fiduciaries," Fifth Third
Bank Trust Department, 2001
Presenter: "Advanced state Tax Minimization
Strategies," Fifth Third Bank Trust Department
and Private Banking, 2001
Presenter: "Estate Planning in 2002–What to do
Now," AXA Financial Advisors annual meeting,
2002 Academic Achievements Order of the Coif
Edwin Halter Merit Scholar Editor, Case

Professional Memberships
Cincinnati Bar Association
Ohio State Bar Association
American Bar Association

CHARLES J. LAVELLE
Member, Louisville
Chair of Tax & Employee Benefits Practice Group

Areas of Concentration
Federal Income Taxation

Education
University of Notre Dame, B.S., Chemistry
 Conc. (high honors), 1972
University of Kentucky, J.D., 1975
New York University, LL.M., Taxation, 1977

Admitted to Practice
Kentucky, 1975, U.S. Tax Court, 1977
U.S. District Ct. (W. Dist. Ky.) 1977
U.S. Court of Appeals, Sixth Circuit, Federal
 Circuit 1986
U.S. Court of Federal Claims, 1986, U.S.
 Supreme Court, 1989

Reported Decisions - Tax Counsel
*Ocean Drilling & Exploration Company v. United
 States*, 988 F.2d 1135 (Fed. Cir. 1993) —
 substantial unrelated business captive insurance
Humana Inc. and Subsidiaries v. Commissioner,
 811 F.2d 247 (6th Cir., 1989) — "brother
 sister" captive insurance
Resolution of dozens of cases relating to federal
 income, estate, gift and excise taxes, penalties
 and interest involving the health care, insurance,
 natural resources, fast foods, manufacturing,
 equine and other industries, including
 definition of insurance, taxation of HMOs as
 insurance companies, interest computations,
 mitigation provisions, investment credit,
 tax accounting, qualification for cash basis
 accounting, depreciation, accumulated earnings
 tax, air transportation tax, depletion, fringe
 benefits, black lung tax, reasonable
 compensation, valuation, capitalization and
 cost segregation

Achievements in Areas of Concentration
Listed in "The Best Lawyers in America" Taxation
 since 1993, Woodward/White, Inc.)
Chair Southeast Region IRS - Bar Liaison; Past
 Vice-Chair; Secretary
Kentucky Limited Liability Company Initial
 Legislation Drafting Committee
Past Chair, Central Regional IRS - Bar Liaison;
 Vice Chair

Past Member, Regional Counsel Advisory Group
Past Member, Regional Counsel Advisory Group
Past Chair, Kentucky Bar Association Tax Section
Past Chair, Louisville Bar Association Taxation
 Committee
Various committees, American Bar Association
 Tax Section; currently Vice Chair, Law
 Development of the Closely Held Business
 Committee

Achievements
Executive Committee and Director, Kentucky
 Chamber of Commerce
Executive Committee and Director, Leadership
 Kentucky Foundation
Past President and Director, Leadership Kentucky
 Alumni; Director, Secretary and Treasurer,
 KCTCS Foundation
Past Treasurer and Director, Downtown Louisville
 Rotary Club
Planning Committee and Participant, Kentucky
 Conclave on Legal Education
Steering Committee, Kentucky Education Coalition
Visiting Committee, University of Kentucky Law
 School
Past Alumni Senator, University of Notre Dame
 Alumni Senate
Past Kentucky Bar Association Annual
 Convention CLE Committee Member
Past President, Director and Treasurer, University
 of Kentucky Law Alumni Association

MARK LONGNECKER
Member, Cincinnati

Areas of Concentration
Mergers and Acquisitions
Venture Capital
Securities Transactions
Corporate

Education
Denison University, B.A., 1973
Harvard Law School, J.D., 1976

Admitted to Practice
Illinois, 1976
Ohio, 1979

Achievements in Areas of Concentration
Counsel for regional homebuilder in initial public
offering
Counsel for HMO in initial public offering
Counsel for regional crane company in sale of its
assets
Counsel for publicly-held HMO in merger
valued at $250 million
Counsel to numerous public companies in
adoption of poison pill plans
Counsel to publicly-held bank holding company
in tender offer defense
Counsel to numerous start-up companies in
venture capital financing and private placements
Counsel to SIPC in sale of assets of insolvent
broker-dealer

American Red Cross
Director, ST Media Group International
Former Board Member, Ohio Fair Plan Under-
writing Association
Former President, Harvard Club of Cincinnati
Former Elder, Knox Presbyterian Church

Publications & Presentations
Lecturer, Cincinnati Bar Association
Corporate and Securities Law Institute
"Legal Opinions in Business Transactions" (1988)
"How to Buy and Sell A Business - Panel, 1990
Cleveland Securities Institute, "Counter-Tender
Offers, Two-Tier Offers, and Pro-Ration Pools"
(1983)
Lecturer at presentations sponsored by Lorman,
Geneva, Cambridge Institute

Professional Memberships
Ohio State Bar Association
Cincinnati Bar Association

Associations
Advisory Board Member, Salvation Army
Chairman, Financial Development Committee,

JOHN S. LUEKEN
Member, Louisville
Member, Family Business Group

Areas of Concentration
Business, Estate and Trust Planning and
Administration

Education
University of Evansville, B.S., Accounting, *summa cum laude*,
A.S., Computing Science, 1985, University of Louisville

Admitted to Practice
Kentucky, 1992
U.S. Court of Appeals, Sixth Circuit, 1998
U.S. District Court, Western District of Kentucky, 1998

Professional Memberships
Louisville Bar Association, 1997 Probate and Estate Section Chairman
Kentucky Bar Association
American Bar Association

Previous Professional Experience
Certified Public Accountant (formerly with Deloitte & Touche, L.L.P.)

Achievements
2000 Recipient, *Business First* 40 Under 40 Award
Editor-in-Chief, Greenebaum Doll & McDonald PLLC *Law Letter*

Focus Louisville, Leadership Louisville Foundation, February 2000
Louisville Bar Association, 1997 Section of the Year Award
Phi Kappa Phi

Publications & Presentations
"Breaking Up is Hard to Do - The Estate Planner's Guide to Planning for Married Clients," Louisville Bar Association, May 2001.
"Kentucky State Tax Issues Update," Professional Education Systems, Inc., June 2002, July 2000, July 1999, August 1998, July 1997, June 1996.
"Impact of the 1997 Tax Reform Act on Your Estate and Financial Planning," Louisville, Kentucky, October 1997.
"Prudent Investor Rule Opens Doors for

Kentucky Banks and Trusts," *Bar Briefs*, Louisville Bar Association, September 1997, *Kentucky Banker Magazine*, Fall 1996.
"Estate and Disability Planning," YMCA of Greater Louisville, November 1996.
"Selected Topics for Business Owners," Kentucky Financial Group, Inc., October 1996.
"Disability Planning: A Panel Discussion," Louisville Bar Association, August 1995.
"Annual Tax Law Update," Louisville Bar Association, April 1995.
"Private Foundations - A Vehicle for Charitable Giving," Southern Kentucky Estate Planning Council, September 1994.
"Valuation Issues Relating to Business," Louisville Bar Association, May 1993.
"Valuation for Gift & Estate Tax Purposes," Cincinnati Bar Association, February 1993.

Associations
Downtown Louisville Rotary Club, Chairman, *Sparks* Committee, 2002-2003
Estate Planning Council of Louisville
Southern Indiana Chamber of Commerce
Greenebaum Doll & McDonald PLLC Recruiting Committee
Volunteer Lawyer Program, Legal Aid Society, Inc.
Past Treasurer and Board of Directors, Walden Theatre
Past Member, Actors Theatre of Louisville Development Board

PEGGY B. LYNDRUP
Member, Louisville
Chair, Corporate and Commercial Practice
  Group

Areas of Concentration
Corporate Law; Mergers and Acquisitions; Real
  Estate Leases; Contracts; Distribution and
  Licensing

Education
University of North Dakota, B.S., Education
  (magna cum laude), 1969
Kent State University, M.Ed., 1971
University of Louisville School of Law, J.D.
  (summa cum laude), 1979
Harvard Law School, Program of Instruction for
  Lawyers-Business Planning, Taxation of
  Corporate Reorganizations and Corporate
  Law, July, 1982

Admitted to Practice
Supreme Court of Kentucky, 1979
U.S. District Court, Western District of
  Kentucky, 1979
U.S. District Court, Eastern District of Kentucky,
  1981

Achievements in Areas of Concentration
Former V.P. and General Counsel, Meidinger,
  Inc.
Chairman, Corporate Practice Section, Louisville
  Bar Association, 1987
Acquisitions of manufacturing, mining,
  distribution and service companies in a variety
  of industries, including athletic goods, coal,
  chemical, coatings, communications,
  construction, distilled spirits, employee benefit
  consulting, expositions, industrial gas, industrial
  equipment, investment advisors, investment
  management, milling, newspaper, retail, stone
  and gravel and steel fabrication
Member of KBA Committee which revised the
  Kentucky BusinessCorporation Act of 1988

Publications & Presentations
"Fiduciary Duties; Confidentiality and Non-
  Competition Agreements"-University of
  Kentucky 8th Biennial Business Associations
  Law Institute, February 2001
"Annual Update on Corporate Law" - Louisville
Bar Association, March 1999
"Significant Developments in Mergers &
  Acquisitions"-University of Kentucky 6th
  Biennial Business Associations Institute,
  February 1997
"Use of Delaware Corporations and Delaware
  Holding Companies"- University of Kentucky
  College of Law, 1997

Academic and Professional Achievements
Selected to Best Lawyers in America
Valedictorian, University of Louisville School of
  Law
President, Louisville Bar Association, 1989
Recipient, 1984 Bar Service Award of Merit
Recipient, 1989 Distinguished Alumnus Award,
  University of Louisville School of Law
President, University of Louisville School of Law
  Alumni Foundation -1989-91
Board of Directors - Kentucky Bar Foundation -
  1996-99

Professional Memberships
Louisville Bar Association; Kentucky Bar Association;
  American Bar Association (Section on Banking,
  Corporation and Business Law)

Associations
Board of Directors, Waterfront Development Corp.
Board of Trustees, Louisville Free Public Library
  Foundation, 1987-88

MARCUS P. MCGRAW
Member, Lexington

Areas of Concentration
Environmental Law; Mineral Law;
  Environmental, Health and Safety
  Litigation

Education
University of North Carolina, Chapel Hill, B.A.,
  English 1964
George Washington University Law School,
  LL.B. 1967

Admitted to Practice
Kentucky, 1981
District of Columbia, 1968
Maryland, 1969
U.S. District Court, Eastern District of Kentucky
U.S. District Court, District of Columbia
U.S. Court of Appeals, Sixth Circuit

Professional Memberships
Kentucky Bar Association (Natural Resources
  Section)
Kentucky Crushed Stone Association-Health &
  Safety Committee
Kentucky Coal Association - Safety &
  Environmental Committee
National Stone, Sand & Gravel Association Safety
  & Health Committee
Kentucky Ready Mixed Concrete Association
  Environmental Health & Safety Committee
National Mining Association - Safety and
  Environmental Committees

Achievements in Areas of Concentration
Trustee at Large, Eastern Mineral Law
  Foundation
Board of Editors, *Journal of Mineral Law & Policy*,
  UK College of Law, 1985-1992
Board of Editors, *Journal of National Resources &
  Environmental Law*, UK College of Law, 1993
Legal, Environmental and Health and Safety
  Committee, Kentucky Coal Association
Regulatory Editor, *Kentucky Mineral Law
  Handbook*

Publications & Presentations
"Current Regulatory Issues Under the Clean
  Water Act Relating to the Corps of Engineers
  EPA and other Agencies as They Relate to
the Mining Industry," 18th Annual Environmental
  Law Institute, May 17 & 18, 2002.
Kentucky Environmental Law Handbook, Third
  Edition, 2001
"Crisis Management - How to Survive A Serious
  Or Fatal Accident and How to Prepare,"
  Kentucky OSHA Regulation: Does Your
  Construction Site Comply, Lexington July
  27,2001
"MSHA Failed To Heed Warnings About
  Impoundment Charges MSHA Official"
  Kentucky Crushed Stone Newsletter, June, 2001
"Metal Mines and Coal Mines Are Subject To Toxic
  Release Inventory Reporting Requirements But
  Waste Rock Will Not Have To Be Reported As a
  Toxic Release According To Court Decision,
  Kentucky Crushed Stone Newsletter, February, 2001
"Mine Safety & Health Bulletin" Winter, 2000-
  2001
"Coal Mining Regulatory Developments" *Kentucky
  Crushed Stone Newsletter*, December, 2000
"Legal Developments Involving The Coal
  Industry" *Kentucky Crushed Stone Newsletter*,
  August, 2000
"Legal Developments Involving The Coal
  Industry" *Kentucky Crushed Stone Newsletter*,
  June, 2000
"New Corps of Engineer Nationwide Permit
  Rules Will Drastically Tighten Wetland Permit
  Requirements" *Kentucky Crushed Stone
  Newsletter,* May, 2000

JEFFREY A. MCKENZIE
Member, Louisville and Covington
Chairman, Hiring Committee

Areas of Concentration
Business Law; Economic Development;
  Corporations; Real Estate Development and
  Finance; Commercial Lending; Construction;
  Planning and Zoning

Education
Virginia Polytechnic Institute & State University,
  B. Architecture, 1983
University of Cincinnati School

Admitted to Practice
Supreme Court of Kentucky, 1986
Supreme Court of Ohio, 1987
U.S. District Court, Western District of
  Kentucky, 1987
U.S. District Court, Eastern District of Kentucky,
  1987

Achievements in Areas of Concentration
Successful Negotiation of Hundreds of Millions
  of Dollars in Economic Incentives; Acquisition,
  Rezoning, Financing, Development, Leasing
  and Sale of Industrial, Commercial, Recreational
  and Residential Properties and Air Rights;
  Negotiation and Preparation of Construction
  Contracts; Numerous appearances before
  Planning Commissions and other Government
  Agencies and Authorities.

Achievements
Leadership Kentucky, 1998
Bingham Fellowship in Economic Development,
  1997-98
Recipient, Forty Under 40 Business Leaders of
  Louisville, 1997
Leadership Louisville, 1994
Chairman, Business Section, Louisville Bar
  Association, 1995
Louisville Central Area - Downtown Planning
  Committee
International Academy of Trial Lawyers Award,
  1986
Chief Justice, University of Cincinnati Student
  Court, 1985-86
Fellowship, University of Cincinnati Center for
  Studies in Professional Skills, 1984-85

Professional Memberships
American Institute of Architects, Professional
  Affiliate
American Planning Association
Louisville Bar Association
Kentucky State Bar Association
Ohio State Bar Association (Section of Business
  Law)
American Bar Association (Member, Business
  Law Section, Real Property, Probate and Trust
  Law Section and Forum on the Construction
  Industry)

Associations
Chairman, Board of Directors, E.P. Tom Sawyer
  State Park
Commissioner, Central State Recovery Authority
Board of Directors, Bellewood Home for
  Children
Home Builders' Association of Louisville
Home Builders' Association of Kentucky
Urban Land Institute
National Council for Urban Economic
  Development
Louisville Third Century
Louisville Forum
Louisville Chamber of Commerce-Cornerstone
  2020 Funding Committee, 1996
Mayor's Citation for Service to the City of
  Louisville, 1991

HOLLAND NIMMONS MCTYEIRE V
Member, Louisville

Areas of Concentration
Litigation; Administrative Law, Public Sector,
  Condemnation, Antitrust, and Securities,

Education
Vanderbilt University, B.A., Economics and
  Business Administration (summa cum laude),
  1981
Vanderbilt University School of Law, J.D., 1984

Admitted to Practice
Kentucky, 1984
U.S. District Court, Western District of
  Kentucky, 1984
U.S. District Court, Eastern District of Kentucky,
  1985
U.S. Court of Appeals, Sixth Circuit, 1988
U.S. Supreme Court, 1993

Publications and Seminars
"Extraordinary Appellate Remedies" November
  1990, University of Kentucky CLE
"Recent Developments In Federal Antitrust Law"
  May 1996, Fayette County Bar Association
"Issues In Potential Cyberlitigation" September
  2000, Louisville Bar Association

Achievements
Administrative Law: Extensive practice before the
  Public Service Commission primarily on behalf
  of utilities in the telecommunications industry.
Extensive experience in matters brought pursuant
  to the Telecommunications Act of 1996 for a
  variety of telecommunications companies.
Additional experience before other state
  administrative bodies.
Public Sector: Experience representing clients in
  the public sector in actions involving civil rights
  and state law claims in both federal and state
  courts, including extensive experience
  defending constitutional and 42 U.S.C. § 1983
  claims.
Condemnation: Extensive experience in actions
  brought pursuant to the Eminent Domain Act
  of Kentucky, including damages permissible in
  such actions.
Antitrust: Advice and counseling to clients
  regarding various antitrust concerns including
  manufacturer/dealer relationship, price

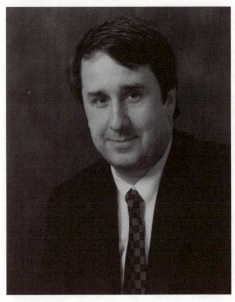

discrimination and monopolization.
Securities: Experienced in complex class action
  shareholder litigation involving federal and state
  securities laws. Experienced in litigation in
  state and federal courts on behalf of broker and
  brokerage house in actions brought by former
    clients. Represented brokerage house in
  federal courts and before the New York Stock
  Exchange in actions against former brokers to
  enforce non-solicitation agreements.

Professional Memberships
Louisville Bar Association
Kentucky Bar Association
American Bar Association

Associations
Louisville Backgammon Club, Board of Directors
Stage One, Board of Directors
June of 1998 to present, currently Vice President
  of the Board

MARGARET A. MILLER
Member, Lexington

Areas of Concentration
General Litigation

Education
Western Kentucky University, B.A., Library
  Science, 1978
University of Kentucky, M.S., Library Science,
  1979
Salmon P. Chase College of Law, J.D., 1984

Admitted to Practice
U.S. Court of Appeals for the Sixth Circuit
  Kentucky, 1984
U.S. District Court, Eastern District of Kentucky,
  1986
U.S. District Court, Western District of
  Kentucky, 1995

Achievements
Law Clerk to Honorable John W. Peck, Senior
  Judge, United States Court of Appeals for the
  Sixth Circuit, 1984-86
Order of the Curia
Graduated ranked 2 out of 54, Chase College of
  Law, 1984
Executive Editor, Northern Kentucky Law
  Review, 1983-84

Publications and Presentations
"Insanity Defense - Jury Instruction on
  Consequences of Acquittal", 9 N. Ky. L. Rev.
  583 (1982)
"Intentional Killing of Viable Fetus Not Murder",
  11 N. Ky. L. Rev. 213 (1984)
"Legal Research - Developments in Current
  Summaries of Kentucky Published Opinions",
  Fayette County Bar Association *Bar News* (Jan.-
  Feb. 1995)

Professional Memberships
Fayette County Bar Association
Kentucky Bar Association
American Bar Association

WILLIAM L. MONTAGUE
Member, Cincinnati and Covington
Trusts and Estates Practice Group
Family Business Group

Areas of Concentration
Estate Planning and Estate Administration
Business and Succession Planning
Charitable Giving

Education
University of Cincinnati College of Law, J.D.,
1982
Wittenberg University, B.A. magna cum laude,
1979

Admitted to Practice
Kentucky, 1982
U.S. Tax Court, 1983
Ohio, 1986

Activities in Areas of Concentration
Member, Cincinnati Estate Planning Council
Member, Northern Kentucky Estate Planning
Council
Board of Trustees, Greater Cincinnati Planned
Giving Council
Board of Trustees, Cincinnati Chapter,
International Association for Financial Planning
American Bar Association, Real Property, Probate
and Trust Law Section, Committee on Estate
Planning and Drafting: Life Insurance; special
projects committees on modified endowment
contracts and standardizing ownership changes
to irrevocable life insurance trusts, published in
the January 1992 *Journal of the American Society
of CLU and ChFC*

Publications & Presentations
Speaker on estate planning and administration
topics:
Louisville Bar Association seminars, January
1983, June 1985; Northern Kentucky
University seminar, April 1983; Cincinnati Bar
Association seminars, April 1987, August
1987, November 1990; National Business
Institute seminars, November 1987, June 1988,
November 1988, May 1989; Chairman 1991,
1992, 1993, and 1994 Cincinnati Bar
Association Basic Estate Planning and Probate
Institutes; Chairman, 1992 Northern Kentucky
Bar Association Estate Planning Institute;

Speaker, 1992, 1996 and 2003 Cincinnati
Estate Planning Institutes; Chairman, 1997
Cincinnati Estate Planning Institute.
Co-author of the following articles: "A Practical
Approach to Death Tax Savings for the
Kentucky Horseman," *Thoroughbred Times*,
Vol. 1, No. 12 (December 6, 1985); "Asset
Freeze Cools Off Death Tax on Bank Stocks,"
Business First, March 31, 1986

Professional Memberships
Cincinnati Bar Association (Chairman, Probate
and Estate Planning Committee, 1999-2000)
Northern Kentucky Bar Association
Ohio Bar Association
Kentucky Bar Association
American Bar Association (Sections of Taxation
and Real Property, Probate and Trust Law)

Associations
Board of Trustees, Cincinnati Opera Association
(1994-present)
Fine Arts Fund Planned Giving Advisory Council
(2001-present)
Advisory Committee, Northern Kentucky Fund
of the Greater Cincinnati Foundation (2002-
present)
Planned Giving Committee, Cincinnati Art
Museum (1995-present)
Planned Giving Committee, University of
Cincinnati Foundation (1998-present)

C. CHRISTOPHER MUTH
Member, Cincinnati

Areas of Concentration
Mergers and Acquisitions
Corporate Law
Tax Law and Litigation
State and Local Taxation

Education
Chicago-Kent College of Law, J.D. *with high honors*, 1980
University of Cincinnati, B.B.A. Accounting, *magna cum laude*, Beta Gamma Sigma, 1977

Admitted to Practice
Ohio, 1980
U.S.D.C. for the Southern District of Ohio
The United States Tax Court

Publications & Presentations
"Environmental Cleanup Costs; Capital Expenditure or Current Deduction," *The Environmental Corporate Counsel Report*, December 1997, Volume 5, Number 8.

"Corporate Taxation," *Kentucky Tax Law*, University of Kentucky College of Law, Chapter 4, 1990 and 1994-1995 Rev. Edition.

"LLC's Lure Investors Seeking Liability Protection with Partnership Tax Advantages," *State Income Tax Alert*, Volume 2, Number 17, October, 1993 and *Ohio Tax Alert*, Volume 2, Number 11, October, 1993.

"VALUATION - The '302 Computation' and the '902 Claim' and Appeals Procedure," *Interstate Tax Report*

"Business/Non-Business Income Distinction in Ohio," *Interstate Tax Report*, Volume 8, Number 6, 1990.

Hi-Tech, Tennessee

Hi-Tech, Ohio

Ohio Sales and Use Tax Seminar sponsored by Lorman Education Services, annually 1993 - 2000.

"S Corporation Tax Law Changes," presented at the *Small Business Job Protection Act* of 1996 Seminar sponsored by the Ohio Society of CPAs, January 1997.

"Corporate Tax Update," presented at the State and Federal Tax Forum sponsored by the Ohio Society of CPAs, December 1996.

"Federal Tax Update," presented at *Akron/Canton Annual CPA;* Day sponsored by The Ohio Society of Certified Public Accountants, October, 1996.

"State and Local Taxation," presented at *The Ohio Accounting Show* Seminar sponsored by the Ohio Society of CPAs, May 1996.

"Recent Developments Update," presented by the *10th Annual Estate Planning Institute* Seminar sponsored by the Cincinnati Bar Association, February 1993.

"Kentucky Corporate Income Taxation," presented at the *Kentucky Taxation* Seminar sponsored by the University of Kentucky College of Law, December 1990.

Frequent lecturer on various estate planning and tax topics for several financial institutions.

Professional Memberships
Cincinnati Bar Association
Ohio State Bar Association
American Bar Association

Associations
Cincinnati/Munich Sister Cities Organization

PETER K. NEWMAN
Member, Cincinnati
Labor & Employment Practice Group

Areas of Concentration
Peter focuses his practice on representing
management in all areas of labor and
employment law with an emphasis on
preventive counseling and litigation.

Education
Georgetown University Law Center, JD, 1980
Miami University, BA, economics and political
science, *cum laude*, 1977

Admitted to Practice
Ohio, 1980
Illinois, 1984
Kentucky, 1999
U.S. District Court, Southern District of Ohio,
1980
U.S. District Court, Northern District of Ohio,
1990
U.S. District Court, Western District of
Kentucky, 1998
U.S. Court of Appeals Sixth Circuit, 1988
U.S. Court of Appeals, Ninth Circuit, 1990

Professional Associations
American Bar Association, Labor & Employment
Law Section, Committee on Equal Employment
Opportunity Law
Ohio State Bar Association, Labor &
Employment Law Section, Board of Governors
(1998 to present), NLRB Region 9 Committee
Kentucky Bar Association
Cincinnati Bar Association

Achievements
Certified by the Ohio State Bar Association as a
specialist in the field of Labor and Employment
Law In Ohio (effective January 1, 2002 to
December 31, 2005)
Member, Editorial Board of Review, The Ohio
Labor Letter (1997-2000)
Associate Editor, American Criminal Law Review
(1979-1986)

Publications and Presentations
The Association for Manufacturing Technology's
2002 Financial Issues and Human Resources
Symposium: Employment Law Update,

Practical Advice on How to Avoid Employee
Claims
Lorman Education Services, "Ohio Wage and
Hour Update" (2002, 2001, 2000, 1999, 1998)
Lorman Education Services, "The Family and
Medical Leave Act in Ohio" (2002, 2001, 1999,
1998, 1995)
Doing Business in and with the United States,
Chapter Twelve - Labor and Employment
(2000 and 2001)
OSBA/CLE "Post-Employment Litigation:
Covenants Not To Compete, Trade Secrets And
Interference With Contract And Prospective
Economic Advantage" (1999 and 2001)
The Ohio Labor Letter, "Stopping Competitors
From Stealing Your Employees And Your Trade
Secrets" (July 2000)
Managing A Work Force In 2000, "The Litigation
of Employment Cases - Are You Prepared?" (2000)
Valley Educational Institute, "Ohio Employment
and Labor Law - 'Hot Topics for the New
Millennium'" (2000)
The Ohio Labor Letter, "Preventing Workplace
Violence - Tips For Ohio Employers" (Nov 1999)
The Ohio Labor Letter, "Supervisor Training - A
Smart Investment For Any Employer (May 1999)
Managing A Work Force In 1999, "Cutting-Edge
ADA Issues: Covered Disabilities and
Reasonable Accommodations" (1999)
E-Commerce Seminar: Searching For Security In
A Digital World" (1999)

PATRICK R. NORTHAM
Member, Louisville
Corporate and Securities Practice Group

Formerly Managing Attorney for Mergers &
Acquisitions and Business Development with
LG&E Energy Corp., Louisville, Kentucky
(1992-1998)

Areas of Concentration
Corporate, Mergers & Acquisitions, Energy Law
and Commercial Transactions

Education
Indiana University, B.A., 1984
Brandeis Law School (University of Louisville),
J.D., 1987
Harvard Law School - Program of Instruction for
Lawyers (Corporate Tax, Securities Regulation,
Corporate Law and Business Planning), June,
1991

Admitted to Practice
Kentucky, 1987

Achievements
Phi Beta Kappa
Louis Dembitz Brandeis Scholar
Executive Editor, Journal of Family Law, 1986-87
Phi Kappa Phi
Pi Sigma Alpha National Political Science Honor
Society
Pleiades Honorary, Alpha Chapter, Indiana
University
Delegate, National Conference of Law Reviews
President, University of Louisville International
Law Society

Achievements in Areas of Concentration
Principal Legal Advisor to a National Energy
Services Company with primary responsibility
for numerous domestic and international
mergers, acquisitions, divestitures, power
project developments and strategic alliances,
including an approx. $1 billion hostile takeover
of a bankrupt rural cooperative in one of the
largest and most complicated bankruptcies in
U.S. history.
Represented numerous public and privately-
owned industrial, commercial and service
businesses in connection with mergers,
divestitures, acquisitions, partnerships and joint

ventures, intellectual property licenses, recourse
and non-recourse financings, executive
employment and compensation plans, and
general corporate and commercial matters,
including in the areas of fossil fuel and
renewable energy services, natural gas, coal,
distilled spirits, telecommunications, paints and
coatings, aluminum smelting, newspapers,
employee benefit and actuarial consulting, real
estate brokerage, franchised restaurants and
commercial graphics.

Professional Memberships
Kentucky Bar Association
Louisville Bar Association
American Bar Association

MARK H. OPPENHEIMER
Member, Louisville

Areas of Concentration
Estate Planning and Administration
Charitable Planning; Elder Law
Member, Family Business Group

Education
University of Florida, B.S.B.A., 1986 (Honors)
University of Louisville, J.D., 1989 (Dean's List)

Admitted to Practice
Kentucky, 1989

Publications & Presentations
Successful Succession Planning and the Closely-
Held Business; American Car Care Centers,
Chicago, Illinois, September 2002
Business Planning Through Succession or Sale;
Indiana University Southeast School of
Business; January 2002
Integrating Retirement Plans into the Estate
Planning Process in Kentucky; Lorman
Education Services, August 2001
Leveraging Techniques in Estate Planning and the
Role of Insurance. 2+2=3; National Insurance
Agents Million Dollar Roundtable Study
Group, September 2000
Basics of Estate Planning; Fifth Third Bank, July
1999
How to Keep the IRS Out of Your Estate Plan;
Home Builders Association of Louisville,
Women's Counsel, April 1998
Keeping Uncle Sam Out of Your Estate Plan;
Christ United Methodist Church, April 1998
Estate Planning; GD&M Law Letter, December
1997
Estate Planning & Personal Trusts; Charles
Schwab & Co., November 1997
The Estate Planning Course -Nuts and Bolts of
Estate Planning; PESI, Inc., December 1996,
November 1997, August 1999, May 2001
Changes by Congress in Estate Planning Laws
Provide Good News for Taxpayers!, Business
First, October 1997
Estate Planning Bar News, Estate Planning
Checklist; Fayette County Bar Association,
January 1996
The Family Limited Partnership-Let Them Eat
Cake!, Owensboro Bar Association, November
1995

FLPs Ease Death-Tax Blow for Family Businesses;
Business First, August 1, 1994
Responsible Parties, Living Wills, Health Care
Surrogates and Death Taxes; Seminar for the
Elderly, March 1994
Where is the Value in Charitable Remainder
Trusts?, Louisville Bar Association, April 1993
Supplement; UKCLE Manual on Estate
Planning, 1992
Charitable Planning - Charitable Remainder
Trusts; Boy Scouts of America, December 1991

Professional Memberships
American Bar Association
Louisville Bar Association
Kentucky Bar Association
National Council on Planned Giving

Associations
1999 Leadership Louisville, Bingham Fellows;
Hearing the Alarm: Raising Healthy Kids
Board of Directors - Hillel - University of
Louisville
Focus of Louisville
Leadership Louisville Alumni
Board of Directors/USA Harvest
Chairman - Professional Advisory Committee
Jewish Federation Permanent Endowment
Committee
Board of Directors - The Temple
Life Member, National Registry of Who's Who

DAVID A. OWEN
Member, Lexington
Chair, Lexington Litigation and Dispute
Resolution Practice Group

Areas of Concentration
Commercial and Environmental Litigation;
Environmental Law and Construction Law

Education
Clemson University, B.S., Chemical Engineering,
1984
Salmon P. Chase College of Law, J.D., (cum
laude) 1987

Admitted to Practice
Kentucky, 1987
U.S. District Court, Western District of
Kentucky, 1987
U.S. District Court, Eastern District of Kentucky,
1987
U.S. Court of Appeals, Sixth Circuit, 1987

Academic Achievements
Order of the Curia
Northern Kentucky Law Review, 1985-87
Associate Editor, 1986-87
Salmon P. Chase Moot Court Board, 1985-87

Professional Memberships
Kentucky Bar Association
Fayette County Bar Association

Publications & Presentations
"The Relationship Between Federal and State
Environmental Agencies," *Kentucky Chamber of
Commerce, 3rd Annual Environmental Permitting
Course*, Lexington, Kentucky, August 10-11,
2000
"Kentucky Division of Water Implements
Watershed Management Framework,"
Kentucky Chamber of Commerce, *Business
Bulletin*,May 1999, Volume 13, Number 14
"Preparing/Cross Examining Expert Witnesses,"
American Institute of Professional Geologists,
*The Use of Expert Witnesses inEnvironmental
Disputes,* Lexington, Kentucky, November 14,
1998
What's Ethics Got to Do with It?" American Bar
Association, SONREEL, *Key Environmental
Issues in U.S. EPA Region IV*, Atlanta, Georgia,
November 6, 1998

"Permitting Fundamentals - Water," Kentucky
Chamber of Commerce,
Environmental Permitting Course, Lexington,
Kentucky, July, 1998
"DEP's Regulatory Agenda," Kentucky Chamber
of Commerce,   *Environmental Newsline*,
Volume VIII, Issue 4, April, 1998
"Kentucky Environmental Initiatives &
Remediation," *Annual Business
&Industry's Environmental Symposium*,
Cincinnati, Ohio, March,   1998
"Update on Waste Issues," *Environmental
Legislative and Regulatory   Breakfast*,
Covington, Kentucky, January, 1998

Associations
Greater Lexington Chamber of Commerce
Board of Directors, 2001-present
Chairman, Public Policy Council, 2001-2002
Chairman, Legislative Affairs Committee, 1999-
2000
Chairman, Local Government Committee, 1998
Prevent Child Abuse Kentucky
Board of Directors, 1998 to present
President, 2001-present
Kentucky World Trade Center, Inc.
Board of Directors, 1999-present
Secretary, 2001-present
United Way of the Bluegrass
Chairman, Professional Division, 2001

TANDY C. PATRICK
Member, Louisville
Finance and Development Practice Group

Areas of Concentration
Acquisition and Dispositions of Property;
Business and Commercial Law (including
Intellectual Property); Business Reorganizations,
Workouts and Creditors' Rights; Commercial,
Retail, Shopping Center, and Residential
Development; Corporate Finance and Loan
Transactions; Equine Law; Retail, Office and
Commercial Leasing

Education
University of Kentucky, B. Mus., 1974
University of Louisville, Louis D. Brandeis
School of Law, J.D., 1978
Bellarmine College, M.B.A. program, 1985

Admitted to Practice
Kentucky, 1979
U.S. District Court, 1980

Publications & Presentations
"Legal Issues in Commercial Real Estate," ICSC
Tennessee/Kentucky Idea Exchange, July 2002
"The Essentials of Office and Retail Leases in
Kentucky," National Business Institute Seminar,
June 2002
"Internet Sites for the Equine Law Practitioner,"
University of Kentucky National Equine Law
Conference, May 2002
"Financing Real Estate," ICSC Tennessee Kentucky
Idea Exchange, July 2001
"Current Issues Affecting Retail Leasing Today,"
ICSC Tennessee/Kentucky Idea Exchange,
August 2000, and Kentucky CCIM Chapter,
December 2000
"Understanding Ground Leases," ICSC
Tennessee/Kentucky Idea Exchange, July 1999
"The Essentials of Office and Retail Leases in
Kentucky," National Business Institute Seminar,
December 1998
"Internet Sites for the Equine Law Practitioner,"
"Financing for Growth," Conference for
Kentucky CPAs in Industry and Government,
June 1989
Speaker at Stable Management Forum, United
Professional Horsemen's Annual Convention,
January 1984

Achievements
Race Chair, Komen Louisville Race for the
Cure®, 2000-2001
1990 Recipient of the YMCA Gil Clark Award
Listed in: Who's Who of Practicing Attorneys;
Law & Business; Directory of Bankruptcy
Attorneys; Who's Who of American Women;
Who's Who in American Law; The World's
Who's Who of Women; 2000 Notable American
Women; Who's Who of Emerging Leaders in
America; Who's Who Among Rising Young
Americans; Who's Who Among Young
American Professionals; Personalities of
America; selected honored member of National
Directory of Who's Who for 1994
USA Track & Field certified track official
Legislative intern for U.S. Congressman William
H. Natcher, 1975
Former instructor, Sullivan College Paralegal
Program

Professional Memberships
Jefferson County Women Lawyer's Association
Louisville Bar Association
Kentucky Bar Association

Associations
International Council of Shopping Centers
Louisville Chapter, CCIM
Member, Cherokee Triangle Association
Victory Athletic Club (President, Editor)

302

TOM POWELL
Member Louisville

Areas of Concentration
Commercial Litigation
Occupational Safety and Health Law

Education
Western Kentucky University, B.A., 1985
  University of Nebraska, J.D. (highest distinc-
  tion), 1994

Admitted to Practice
Kentucky Supreme Court, 1996
U. S. District Court for Eastern and Western
  Districts of Kentucky, 1996
Nebraska Supreme Court, 1994
U. S. District Court for District of Nebraska,
  1994

Publications & Presentations
Kentucky OSHA Newsletter, monthly columnist
  July, 1997 to present
"OSHA & KOSHA Compliance—The Latest
  Developments" Seminar October 1997 and
  1998 "The Truth Will Not Set You Free...in
  Nebraska", 72 Neb. L. Rev.
"Optional Safety Equipment - Who Knows
  More", 73 Neb. L. Rev.
Co-reporter "50 State Defamation and Privacy
  Law Survey in Nebraska", Libel Defense
  Resource Center

Achievements
Nebraska Law Review, Editor-in-Chief
Order of the Coif

Associations
Nebraska Bar Association
Kentucky Bar Association
Louisville Bar Association

GLENN A. PRICE, JR.
Member, Louisville

Areas of Concentration
Land Use Planning
Zoning
Subdivision Law

Education
University of Louisville, B.A., 1973
University of Louisville, J.D., 1976

Admitted to Practice
Kentucky, 1976

Professional Memberships
American Bar Association
Kentucky Bar Association
Louisville Bar Association

Associations
Congress for the New Urbanism
Urban Land Institute, Associate Member
American Planning Association (Kentucky
   Chapter, Charter Member)
Board Member, Learning Disabilities Association
   of Kentucky, Inc., 1995
Home Builders Association of Kentucky
Home Builders Association of Louisville

Achievements in Areas of Concentration
Member, Planning Committee of Governor's Task
   Force on Smart Growth, 2001-present
Chair, Planning and Development Committee,
   Greater Louisville, Inc., 2000-present
Chair, Smart Growth Committee, Home Builders
   Association of Louisville, 2000-present
Chair, Policies & Procedures Committee of the
   Louisville and Jefferson County Planning
   Commission, 1998-present
Instructor, Land Use Law, University of
   Louisville, Brandeis School of Law, 1987, 1995
Chair, Real Estate Section, Louisville Bar
   Association, 1991, 1994
Member, Louisville and Jefferson County
   Planning Commission, 1978-1980
Chair, Louisville and Jefferson County Planning
   Commission, 1979-1980
Co-Chair, Legislative Committee, American
   Planning Association, Kentucky Chapter, 1984-
   2000

Member, Initial Review Advisory Committee,
   Cornerstone 2020, 1998-1999
Member, Community Form Committee,
   Cornerstone 2020 Plan, 1995
Executive Committee Member, Ohio River
   Corridor Master Plan Advisory Committee,
   1995
Chair, Legislative Liaison Committee, Planning
   and Law Division, American Planning
   Association, 1995
Frequent Lecturer and Presenter to Legal and
   Planning Professionals Regarding Land Use
   Issues

Publications
Richard V. Murphy and Glenn A. Price, Jr.,
   Kentucky Land Use and Zoning Law, University
   of Kentucky (1st ed. 1989, 2nd ed. 1991, 3rd ed.
   1998)
Glenn A. Price, Jr., Paul B. Whitty and Andrew
   M. Fleischman, Financing Capital Improvements
   Through Impact Fees: An Option for Local
   Governments in Kentucky? 14 *State Tax Notes*
   1111, April 6, 1998
Glenn A. Price, Jr., The Metes and Bounds of
   Planning and Zoning, *The Louisville Lawyer,*
   VOL.2, NO. 3 (1980)

HARRY D. RANKIN
Member, Cincinnati/Covington
Chair, Covington/Cincinnati Litigation and
 Dispute Resolution Practice Group

Areas of Concentration
Civil Litigation; Personal Injury; Medical
 Malpractice; Product Liability; Commercial &
 Business; Criminal Law (White Collar Crime);
 Domestic Relations

Education
Transylvania University A.B. with Honors, 1975
University of Kentucky College of Law, 1978

Admitted to Practice
Kentucky, 1978
Ohio, 1996
United States District Court,
 Eastern District of Kentucky, 1979
 Western District of Kentucky, 1997
 Southern District of Ohio, 1999
United States Court of Appeals,
 Sixth Circuit, 1990
U.S. Supreme Court, 1992

Achievements in Areas of Concentration
Kenton County Commonwealth Attorney, 1983-84
Salmon P. Chase College of Law, Northern
 Kentucky University, Adjunct Professor,
 Litigation Skills, 1983-1990
International Association of Defense Counsel, Trial
 Institute Participant, Boulder, Colorado, 1983

Publications & Presentations
"Punitive Damages Under K.R.S. §§ 411.184
 and 411.186: A View From The Defense Bar,"
 Bench and Bar, Winter Edition 1992
Co-author, "Independent Medical Exams From a
 Defense Perspective: Trust But Verify," Bench
 and Bar, November 1999

Achievements
Intern and Staff Member in the Office of U.S.
 Senator Wendell Ford, Washington, D.C.,
 1975-1977
University of Kentucky Law School, Alumni
 Board, 1987-89
Northern Kentucky Chamber of Commerce,
 Leadership Northern Kentucky, Class President,
 1981
Northern Kentucky Bar Assn., President, 1988

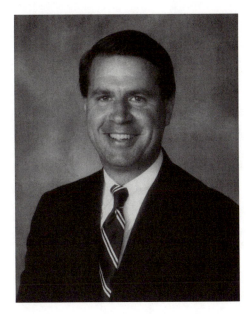

Kentucky Bar Association, House of Delegates,
 1984-1990
Leadership Cincinnati, 1992-1993

Professional Memberships
Kentucky Bar Association
Northern Kentucky Bar Association

Associations
Immanuel United Methodist Church, Lakeside
 Park, Kentucky
Fort Mitchell Country Club
Northern Kentucky Chamber of Commerce
Kentucky Bar Foundation, Board of Directors
University of Kentucky, Law School
 Development Board
Traditions Golf Club
Metropolitan Club

HENRY C.T. (TIP) RICHMOND III
Member, Lexington
Trusts and Estates Practice Group

Areas of Concentration
Estate Planning and Administration
Business Planning
Family Business Group

Education
Wake Forest University, B.A. Political Science,
1973
University of Louisville School of Law, J.D., 1980
University of Miami School of Law, LL.M. (Tax),
1981

Admitted to Practice
Kentucky, 1980
Florida, 1981

Military Service
Active Duty (U.S. Army) - 1973 to 1977
U.S. Army Reserve (JA, LTC) - 1977 to 1997

Achievements in Area of Concentration
Current Member, Legislative Committee, Probate
and Trust Law Section, Kentucky Bar
Association
President, Bluegrass Estate Planning Council,
1990
Vice President and Trust Officer, PNC Bank
Central Kentucky Trust Operations, 1985-
1988
Program Chairperson, 1990 Annual Conference
of National Association of Estate Planning
Councils

Publications & Presentations
"Federal Gift, Estate and GST Tax Aspects of
EGTRA 2001, Qualified Plan Distribution
Rules, Asset Protection and LLCs, and Business
Succession Planning" Seminar presented to
Merrill Lynch, Hilliard Lyons, National City
Bank and Traditional Bank, 2001
"Business Succession Planning" Seminar
presented to Bluegrass Estate Planning Council,
April 3, 2001
"Estate Planning for the Realtor" presented to
Lexington-Bluegrass Association of Realtors,
March 31, 1999
"The Estate Planning Course" sponsored by PESI,
1996, 1997, 1998, 1999, 2000, 2001 and 2002

"Estate and Business Planning" presented to
Home Builders Association of Lexington,
February 26, 1997
"Use of Charitable Remainder Trusts in Estate
Planning" presented to Lexington Clinic,
February 21, 1995
"Advanced Directives" presented to KAHCF, May
3, 1995

Academic Achievements
Research Editor, *Journal of Family Law,* University
of Louisville School of Law, 1979
Dean's List, University of Louisville School of
Law, 1977-1979

Professional Memberships
Fayette County Bar Association
Kentucky Bar Association
Florida Bar Association

Associations
Participant, Leadership Kentucky 2002
Board of Directors, Kentucky Historical Society
Foundation, Inc.
Vice Chair, First Presbyterian Church
Endowment Fund
Past President and Board Directors, Lexington
Hearing and Speech Center
Board of Directors, Breckinridge Health Care, Inc.
Member, Lexington Estate Planning Council and
Bluegrass Estate Planning Council

MARK S. RIDDLE
Member, Louisville
Chair, Louisville Litigation and Dispute
   Resolution Practice Group

Areas of Concentration
Business and Commercial Litigation

Education
University of Kentucky, B.A., Business
   Administration (with honors), 1980
University of Kentucky College of Law, J.D. 1983

Admitted to Practice
Kentucky, 1983
U.S. District Court, Western District of
   Kentucky, 1984
U.S. District Court, Eastern District of Kentucky,
   1984
U.S. Court of Appeals, Sixth Circuit, 1988

Publications & Presentations
Class Action Litigation Challenging NSF and
   Late Fees," 22nd Annual Conference on Legal
   Issues for Financial Institutions, University of
   Kentucky College of Law, April, 2002
"An Overview of Buyer's Rights and Remedies
   Under the Uniform Commercial Code,"
   Purchasing Management Association of
   Louisville, March, 1992
"Control Paper Flow During Business Disputes,"
   Business First, October, 1990

Academic Achievements
Moot Court Board
University of Kentucky Judicial Board
President, Societas Pro Legibus Honorary Society

Professional Memberships
USLAW Network, member of Steering Committee
   for Commercial Litigation Practice Group
Defense Research Institute, member of Business
   Litigation Committee
Louisville Bar Association
Kentucky Bar Association, Member of Task Force
   on CLE and Technology, Litigation Section and
   founding member of Construction and Public
   Contract Law Section
American Bar Association, member of Section of
   Litigation Federal Bar Association

Achievements in Area of Concentration
Obtained defense jury verdict in favor of
   engineering firm in connection with natural gas
   pipeline explosion.
Obtained dismissal of class action lawsuit filed
   against a national bank.
Successful prosecution, defense and resolution of
   a wide variety of business disputes, breach of
   contract, construction and environmental
   litigation matters.
Experienced in litigation in federal and state
   courts in numerous jurisdictions

Associations
Louisville Forum
Jefferson Club

WM. T. (BILL) ROBINSON III
Member-In-Charge, Cincinnati/Northern
  Kentucky
Executive Committee Member

Areas of Concentration
Civil Litigation, Trial & Appellate Practice
Governmental Affairs

Education
Thomas More College, B.A., 1967
University of Kentucky, College of Law, J.D., 1971

Admitted to Practice
Ohio, 1971
Kentucky, 1972
Tennessee, 1999
U.S. District Courts: Southern District of Ohio,
  1971; Eastern District of Kentucky, 1972;
  Western District of Kentucky, 1993;Southern
  District of Indiana, 1996
U.S. Sixth Circuit Court of Appeals, 1972
U.S. Supreme Court, 1978

Achievements in Areas of Concentration
American Academy of Appellate Lawyers, Fellow,
  1998-
American Law Institute, Sustaining Member, 1995-
International Society of Barristers, Fellow, 1988-
Sixth Circuit Judicial Conference, Life Member,
  1988- ;Life Members Committee, Member, 1999-
International Association of Defense Counsel
Chase College of Law, NKU, Adjunct Professor,
  1977-89
Salmon P. Chase American Inn of Court, Co-
  Founder and President 1993-94, Master 1993-
Product Liability Advisory Council (PLAC),
  Sustaining Attorney Member, 1997-
Lead Trial Counsel with Mark Hayden achieving
  in 2001 a plaintiff's Federal jury verdict
  awarding $40 million in a commercial claim -
  one of the top five jury verdicts in history of KY
  (settled 2002 - $27.5 million)

Professional Memberships
ABA, KBA, N. Ky. Bar, Louisville Bar, Ohio State
  Bar, Cincinnati Bar, Kentucky Defense Counsel,
  Inc., Federal Bar Association

Professional Achievements
American Bar Assn., State Delegate, 1989-98; Ky.
  Bar Delegate, 1986-89, 1998- 2000; ABA

Board of Governors, 2000-03; Chair, Finance
  Committee, 2002-03; Member, Executive
  Committee, 2002-03
American Bar Foundation, Life Fellow, 1985-;
  Fellows Chair for Kentucky, 2000-
National Caucus of State Bar Associations,
  President, 1995-96
Nat'l Conference of Bar Presidents, Exec.
  Council, 1987-90
Southern Conference of Bar Presidents, Member,
  1985-
Kentucky Bar Assn., 50th President, 1985-86;
  Chair, House of Delegates 1981-82

Awards and Recognitions
Best Lawyers in America, 1999-2000, 2001-
  2002, 2003-2004 Editions
Covington Award, Friends of Covington, 1998
Judge Learned Hand Human Relations Award,
  American Jewish Committee, 1998
Governor's Economic Development Leadership
  Award, Kentucky, 1997
Volunteer of the Year, Southern Industrial
  Development Council (SIDC), 1995
Volunteer of the Year, Kentucky Industrial
  Development Council (KIDC), 1995
The Lincoln Award, Northern Kentucky
  University, 1994
Knight of Malta, The Sovereign Military and
  Hospitaller Order of Malta, 1992-
Outstanding Lawyer Award, KBA, 1989

DAVID B. SANDLER
Member, Louisville

Areas of Concentration
Labor and Employment Law

Education
University of Louisville School of Law, J.D., 1980
University of Pennsylvania, Wharton School of
Finance, B.S. Economics, 1974

Admitted to Practice
Kentucky, 1981
U.S. District Court, Western District of
Kentucky, 1981
U.S. District Court, Eastern District of Kentucky,
1982
U.S. Court of Appeals, Sixth Circuit, 1981
U.S. District Court, Southern District of Indiana,
1984

Publications & Presentations
"Recent Developments in Kentucky Case and
Legislative Labor and Employment Law," Carl
A. Warns, Jr., Labor and Employment Law
Institute (May 1998)
"Review of Kentucky Decisions Affecting
Employment," Carl A. Warns, Jr., Labor &
Employment Law Institute (June 1997)
"Avoiding Wrongful Discharge and the New
Generation of Torts," Council on Education in
Management (April 1996)
"Review of Kentucky Labor and Employment
Law Decisions," Carl A. Warns, Jr., Labor &
Employment Law Institute   (June 1995)
"Kentucky's Wrongful Termination Update,"
Council on Education in Management (July
1994)
"Avoiding Liability With Sexual Harassment
Prevention Training," Council on Education in
Management (March 1994)
"Defending Against Wrongful Termination
Claims - Legal Issues Surrounding Employee
Discipline and Termination," Louisville Bar
Association (February 1994)
"Controlling Employee Off-Duty Conduct:
Business Necessity or Violation of Privacy?"
Council on Education in Management (March
1993)
"Kentucky Statutes Affecting Labor and
Employment," University of Kentucky
Employment Law Manual (1992)

"Review of Recent Kentucky Cases," University
of Louisville Labor and Employment Law
Institute (June 1992)
"Rightful or Wrongful Termination?," Council on
Education in Management (April 1992)
"Avoiding Lawsuits for Employment Discrimination"
National Business Institute (1991)
"Recent Developments in Kentucky Employment
Law," University of Louisville Labor and
Employment Law Institute (June 1991)
"The Aging Workforce, Demographic Changes in
the 1990s, and Related Legal Issues," University
of Louisville Labor and Employment Law
Institute (June 1990)
"Strategic Disciplinary Actions, Discharge and
Other Separations," National Business Institute
(1988)
"Civil Rights Laws in Employment: They're
Broader Than You Think," National Business
Institute (1988)

Academic Achievements
Dean's List, University of Louisville School of
Law (1977-80)

Professional Memberships
Kentucky Bar Association (Labor and
Employment Law Section)
Louisville Bar Association (Labor and
Employment Law Section)

JEFFREY A. SAVARISE
Member, Louisville

Areas of Concentration
Labor and Employment Law

Education
John Carroll University, Cleveland, Ohio, B.A.,
    Political Science (*magna cum laude*), 1982
The University of Akron School of Law, Akron,
    Ohio, J.D., 1985

Admitted to Practice
Kentucky, 1990
Ohio, 1986
Pennsylvania, 1988
United States Supreme Court, 1995
Third Circuit Court of Appeals, 1988
Sixth Circuit Court of Appeals, 1987
U.S. District Court for the Western District of
    Kentucky, 1990
U.S. District Court for the Eastern District of
    Kentucky, 1997
U.S. District Court for the Northern District of
    Ohio, 1986
U.S. District Court for the Western District of
    Pennsylvania, 1988

Publications & Presentations
Supreme Court Employment Update, Executive
    SupplierConference, Sarasota, Florida, May 2,
    2002
Supreme Court Employment Update, Team
    Member Relations Forum, Erlanger, Kentucky,
    March 26, 2002
*Supreme Court Limits ADA Disability Definition,
    Toyota Motor Manufacturing, Kentucky v.
    Williams,* Louisville Society for Human
    Resource Management (LSHRM), Louisville,
    Kentucky, March 25, 2002
*Toyota Motor Manufacturing, Kentucky v.
    Williams,* Human Resources Supplier Forum,
    Louisville, Kentucky, March 14, 2002
*What's Left of the ADA after Toyota? The Impact of
    Toyota Motor Company v. Williams on the
    Americans with Disabilities Act,* ABA
    Teleconference Panelist, March 5, 2002
*The Aftermath of Circuit City – Arbitrating
    Employment Claims,* Presidents' Conference,
    Palm Beach, Florida, May 28, 2001
How Arbitration Works, BNA, Topic Editor, 1990
    - present

Significant Reported Decisions
Toyota Motor Mfg., Ky., Inc. v. Williams, 534 U.S.
    ____, 122 S.Ct. 681 (2002) (United States
    Supreme Court case defining "disability" under
    the Americans with Disabilities Act as it relates
    to an individual performing manual tasks).
McKay v. Toyota Motor Mfg., U.S.A., Inc., 110
    F.3d 369 (6th Cir. 1997) (Americans with
    Disabilities Act case establishing what is
    necessary to show a substantial limitation in the
    major life activity of working).
Bauer v. Varity Dayton-Walther Corp., 118 F.3d
    1109 (6th Cir. 1997) (Family and Medical
    Leave Act case addressing the medical evidence
    necessary for showing a "serious health
    condition" under the Act).

Professional Memberships
Kentucky, Louisville, Ohio, Pennsylvania and
    American Bar   Associations (Labor and
    Employment Sections); American   Bar
    Association Committee on Alternative Dispute
    Resolution.

GREGORY S. SCHAAF
Member, Lexington

Areas of Concentration
Corporate Reorganization
Bankruptcy/Workouts
Real Estate/Commercial Transactions

Education
Western Illinois University - B.B. Accounting;
B.S. Law Enforcement Administration, 1984
University of Kentucky College of Law, J.D., 1991

Admitted to Practice
Kentucky, 1991

Achievements
Solicitor of the Supreme Court (England and
  Wales) 1999
Certified Public Accountant, Illinois, 1984
Order of the Coif, University of Kentucky
  College of Law
Kentucky National Moot Court Team, 1990-
  1991
Kentucky Moot Court Board, 1989-1991
President, Student Bar Association, 1989 – 1990
Journal of Mineral Law and Policy, 1989 – 1991

Publications & Presentations
Comment, Freede v. Commissioner: Closing a
  Loophole that Closed a Loophole, 6 Journal of
  Mineral Law and Policy 129, 1990 – 1991
Seminar, Property Tax Law in Kentucky, Business
  Law Institute, Lexington, Kentucky, August
  1997
Presentation, Bankruptcy Law Update: What
  Congress Is Doing for You, Louisville Bar
  Association and Brandies School of Law,
  September 24, 1999
Seminar, Representing Creditors in Chapter 7
  Proceedings, UK/CLE Consumer Bankruptcy
  Update 2000, University of Kentucky College of
  Law, Lexington, Kentucky, December 8, 2000
Seminar, Kentucky Foreclosure and Related
  Bankruptcy and Title Issues, National Business
  Institute, February 15, 2001
Presentation, Basic Legal Issues Affecting E-
  Commerce Businesses, Lexington Area Small
  Business Development Center, Spring 2002
Presentation, Bankruptcy and Real Estate
  Transfers, Kentucky Land Title Association,
  February 21, 2002

Seminar, Kentucky Foreclosure and Related
Bankruptcy and Title Issues, National Business
Institute, May 15, 2002

Professional Memberships
American Bankruptcy Institute
The Law Society of England and Wales
American Bar Association
Kentucky Bar Association
Fayette County Bar Association

Associations
Lexington Humane Society 2000-Present
Greater Lexington Chamber of Commerce
Council on Smaller Enterprises Steering
  Committee 1999-2002
Prevent Child Abuse Kentucky President 1995 -
  96, 1996 – 97 Treasurer 1993 - 94, 1994 – 95

PHILIP J. SCHWORER
Member, Cincinnati

Areas of Concentration
Environmental Law (Litigation and Compliance)
OSHA Defense
Toxic Tort Defense

Education
Salmon P. Chase College of Law, Northern
 Kentucky University, J.D., 1986
Environmental Engineering/Science, University
 of Cincinnati, M.S., 1980
Biology, University of Cincinnati, B.S., 1977
Chemical Engineering, University of Cincinnati,
 Course work, 1977/78

Admitted to Practice
Ohio, 1986
Kentucky, 1987
U.S. District Court, Southern District of Ohio,
 1986
U.S. Court of Appeals, Sixth Circuit, 1997
U.S. Supreme Court, 2002

Achievements in Areas of Concentration
Certified Professional Environmental Auditor,
 Environmental Compliance by Board of
 Environmental Auditor Certification
Conduct environmental compliance audits for
 manufacturing operations arising from self-
 assessment and transactional due diligence
Defended toxic tort class action litigation
 involving soil and groundwater contamination.
 Coordinated screening, retention and
 preparation of expert witnesses who testified on
 issues of contaminant mobility in soil and
 groundwater, risk assessment and property
 valuation.
Negotiated interaction between RCRA and DOE
 regulations for a client producing mixed waste.
Obtained summary judgment that each entity
 involved in a regulated
  emission need not obtain individual permits.
Represented clients in negotiating and then
 overseeing environmental remediation and
 restoration projects involving facility shut
 downs and site contamination.
Negotiated environmental permit terms and
 conditions for all environmental media
 including air, water, and waste.

Appealed air emission (including Title V) permits
to state agencies including Kentucky and Ohio.

Publications
"Problems Arising from the Creation of a
 Computer-Based Litigation Support System,"
 Northern Kentucky Law Review, 14, pg. 263
"Environmental Problems and Their Effect on
 Lending Institutions," Northern Kentucky Law
 Review, Vol. 18, pg. 175

Professional Memberships
Cincinnati Bar Association; Member, Board of
 Trustees; Cincinnati Academy of Leadership for
 Lawyers; Former Chairman Environmental Law
 Committee; Former Member, Committee on
 Committees and CLE Committee
Ohio State Bar Association
Environmental Auditing Roundtable, Member,
 Lecturer
Northern Kentucky Bar Association
Kentucky Bar Association
American Bar Association
Bureau of Environmental Auditors Certification

Associations
Leadership Cincinnati Class XXIII
Leadership Northern Kentucky Alumni Assn
Leadership Kentucky Board of Directors
Cincinnati Bar Association Board of Trustees
Cincinnati Academy of Leadership for Lawyers

PHILLIP D. SCOTT
Member, Lexington

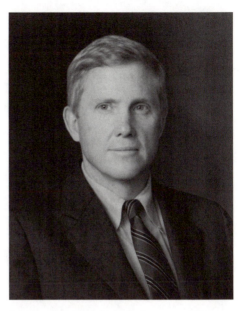

Areas of Concentration
Equine Law, Healthcare Law

Education
Hanover College, A.B., 1964
University of Kentucky College of Law, J.D., 1967

Military Service
U.S. Marine Corps (Captain 1967-1970)

Admitted to Practice
Kentucky, 1967
U.S. District Court, Western District of
Kentucky, 1975
U.S. District Court, Eastern District of Kentucky,
1967
U.S. Supreme Court, 1974
U.S. Court of Military Appeals, 1968

Achievements in Area of Concentration
Represented and acted on behalf of foreign
interest in developing thoroughbred breeding
and racing operations in the United States.
Represented clients in the acquisition of real
estate for equine businesses. Acted as lead
counsel in significant disputes involving equine
interest including bankruptcies.
Assisted in the drafting of Healthcare legislation.
Acted as lead counsel in Healthcare law
litigation and dispute resolution.
Advised administrators and Boards of Directors of
Healthcare institutions regarding legal matters.

Publications and Presentations
"Authority of Local Governments to Protect the
Public from Secondhand Smoke," Lexington-
Fayette County Health Department Tobacco
Control Conference, 2001
"A Roadmap for Engaging in International
Thoroughbred Racing and Breeding" University
of Kentucky Equine Law conference, 1993
"American Equine Property Acquisition by
Foreign Interest," University of Kentucky
Equine Law Seminar, 1989
"A Ride on the Magic Carpet," Doing Business in
the Arabian Gulf, Lexington Rotary Club, 1989
"Injunctive Relief in Kentucky," Kentucky Bar
Association Annual Meeting, Louisville, 1989

"Ability to Control the Risk-Contractual Waivers
of Liability," University of Kentucky Equine
Law Seminar, 1987
"Current Legal Topics For High School Principals,
Administrators & Coaches," Kentucky High
School Directors Annual Meeting, 1982
"Recent Legal Developments," Kentucky
Hospital Administrators Association, Annual
Meeting, 1979

Associations
American Bar Association
Kentucky Bar Association
Fayette County Bar Association (Past Director
Elder, First Presbyterian Church
American Trial Lawyers Association
National Health Lawyers Association

Professional Memberships
Director and President, Gainsborough Farm, Inc.
Trustee, Hanover College
Chairman, Board of Trustees, Presbytery of
Transylvania
Chamber of Commerce
Thoroughbred Club of America
Keeneland Club
Idle Hour County Club

MICHAEL G. SHAIKUN
Member, Louisville

Areas of Concentration
Real Estate; Finance; Secured Transactions;
 Bankruptcy and Corporate Reorganization

Education
University of Pennsylvania, Wharton School of
 Finance and Economics, B.S. (highest honors),
 1963
Harvard Law School, J.D., 1966
Beta Gamma Sigma, National Business
 Administration Honorary Society
Pi Gamma Mu, National Social Science
 Honorary Society

Admitted to Practice
Kentucky, 1966
U.S. District Court, Western District of
 Kentucky, 1966

Achievements in Areas of Concentration
Listed in "The Best Lawyers in America," Real
 Estate Law, Woodward/White, since 1983
Listed in "Who's Who in American Law,"
 Seventh Edition, Marquis Who's Who, since
 1992

Publications & Presentations
"Problems in Professional Responsibility
 Engendered by the Effects of Technology,"
 University of Kentucky College of Law 6th
 Biennial Real Estate Law and Practice Institute,
 Lecturer, 1998
"Opinions of Counsel in Real Estate
 Transactions," Office of Continuing Legal
 Education, University of Kentucky College of
 Law Seminar on Real Estate Law and Practice,
 Lecturer, 1996
Co-Author, *Kentucky Real Estate Law and Practice,*
 Second Edition, Chapter 10 "Opinion Letters"
 (UK/CLE 1996)
"Procuring and Insuring Free and Clear Title,"
 National Business Institute, Inc., Seminar on
 Advanced Real Estate Law in Kentucky,
 Lecturer, 1991
Co-Author, *Real Estate Practice Handbook,*
 Chapter 9 "Opinion Letters," (UK/CLE 1990)

Boards and Honors
Director and Secretary, Venture Club of Louisville
Member, Business Solutions Center Advisory
 Committee, Louisville Chamber of Commerce
Director, Jewish Community Federation of
 Louisville, Inc.
Director and Chair of Financial Development
 Committee, YMCA Safe Place Services
Director and Legal Advisor, Kentucky Indiana
 Personal Computer Users Group, Inc.
Leadership Kentucky, 1996 Graduate
Focus Louisville, 1994 Graduate
Past President, Jewish Community Federation of
 Louisville, Inc.
Past Chairman, Foundation For Planned Giving,
 Jewish Community Federation of Louisville, Inc.
Past President, Louisville Hebrew Home, Inc.
Past President, Louisville Lodge No. 14 B'nai B'rith
Recipient, B'nai B'rith "Person of the Year"
 Award, 1988
Recipient, Louis G. Cole Young Leadership
 Award, 1981

Professional Memberships
Louisville Bar Association
Kentucky Bar Association
American Bar Association (Section of Real Estate
 Property Probate and Trust Law, Business Law
 and Law Practice Management)
American Bankruptcy Institute

GREGORY S. SHUMATE
Member, Covington/Cincinnati
Member, Family Business Group

Areas of Concentration
Corporate Law; Business Succession Planning;
    Commercial Law; Administrative Law

Education
University of Kentucky, B.A., (with Distinction)
    1984
University of Kentucky College of Law, J.D.,
    1987

Admitted to Practice
Kentucky, 1987
Ohio, 1988
United States District Court, Eastern District of
    Kentucky, 1988
United States Court of Appeals, Sixth Circuit,
    1988
United States Tax Court, 1988

Publications & Presentations
"Nuts & Bolts of Non-Testamentary Documents,"
    "Death of the New Death Tax," "Planning for
    Qualified Retirement Plan Beneficiary
    Designations & Tax Consequences", Kentucky
    Bar Association Annual Convention
    (Moderator), 2002
"Federal Tax Update '99," Ohio Society of
    Certified Public Accountants, Cincinnati Tax
    Committee (Author), 1999
"Kentucky Partnership Law Handbook, Second
    Edition - Special Purpose Partnerships,"
    University of Kentucky CLE (Author), 1996
"Preparing Agreements in the Sale of a Business -
    Drafting Techniques and Suggestions,"
    Kentucky Bar Association - Kentucky Law
    Update - '96 (Speaker), 1996
"Corporate Succession Planning - The Use of
    Buy-Sell Agreements," Northern Kentucky Bar
    Association (Speaker, Author), 1995

Professional Memberships
Northern Kentucky Bar Association
Kentucky Bar Association
Cincinnati Bar Association
Ohio State Bar Association
American Bar Association

Associations
Northern Kentucky University Foundation Board
    of Directors, 2002
Kenton County Transportation Task Force,
    Member, 2001-2002
Greater Cincinnati Fine Arts Fund, Chairman,
    Kentucky Division, 1999-2000
Northern Kentucky Area Development District -
    Board of Directors, 1997 - 2001
Covington Business Council, 1997 - Present:
    Government Affairs Committee – Chairman;
    Executive Committee; Board of Directors
Forward Quest - Member, Mass Transit Loop
    Task Force, 1999 - Present
The Carnegie Visual & Performing Arts Center,
    Inc.: Board of Directors, 2000 – Present; Vice
    President, 2001
Lawyers for Bush/Cheney - Chairman, Kentucky,
    2000
Kenton County Republican Party - Chairman,
    1997 - Present
Republican Party of Kentucky - Member, State
    Central Committee, 1997 - Present
Covington Rotary, Member, 1999 - Present
Spartan Youth Football, Board of Directors, 2002
St. Joseph Parish, Crescent Springs, Kentucky,
    1989 - Present
Estate Planning Council of Northern Kentucky -
    Member, 1995 - Present
Northern Kentucky Bar Association - Chairman,
    Business and Tax Section, 1994 - 1996

CRAIG P. SIEGENTHALER
Member, Louisville

Areas of Concentration
Labor and Employment Law

Education
University of Virginia, B.A., English, 1987
University of Georgia School of Law - J.D., 1990
 (cum laude)

Admitted to Practice
Georgia, 1990
Virginia, 1993
Kentucky, 1997
Kentucky Supreme Court
Georgia Supreme Court
U.S. District Court, Eastern and Western
 Districts of Kentucky
U.S. District Court, Northern and Middle
 Districts of Georgia
U.S. District Court, District of Nebraska
U.S. Court of Appeals, Sixth Circuit, Tenth
 Circuit, Eleventh
  Circuit

Publications & Presentations
Kentucky Employment Law Letter, M. Lee
 Publishers & Printers, Contributing Editor
 1998 - present
How Arbitration Works, BNA, Topic Editor, 1999
 Supplement
"Investigation of Harassment in the Workplace" –
 Valley Educational Institute, Ltd., Oct. 1999
"Sophisticated Issues and Recent Significant Case
 Law Interpreting the Family and Medical Leave
 Act of 1993" – Kentucky Association of Health
 Underwriters, March 2000
"Ethical and Practical Considerations for
 Settlement Agreements" – Louisville Bar
 Association, June 2000
"Privacy in the Workplace" – GDM Annual
 Seminar, June 2001
"Leaves of Absence" – Lorman Education
 Services, March 2002
"Overview of Family and Medical Leave Act of
 1993" – Lorman Education Services, May 2002
"Legal and Practical Procedures for Investigating
 Internal Complaints of Harassment" – Paducah
 Area Employee Relations Association, May
 2002

Professional Memberships and Associations
Louisville Bar Association
Georgia Bar Association
Virginia Bar Association
American Bar Association

Associations
Leukemia and Lymphoma Society, Kentucky
 Chapter, Board Member 2000-present
Historic Homes Foundation, Louisville, KY
University of Virginia Alumni Association
University of Georgia Alumni Association

Reported Cases
Smith v. Midland Brake, Inc., 1998 WL 110011
 (10th Cir. 1998); 98 A.D. Cases 1560
Smith v. Midland Brake, Inc., 911 F.Supp. 1351, 5
 A.D. Cases 386 (D.Kan., 1995)
Smith v. Midland Brake, Inc., 162 F.R.D. 683, 33
 Fed.R.Serv.3d 718 (D.Kan., 1995)
*Biggers on Behalf of Key v. Southern Ry. Co. and
 City of Duluth, Georgia*, 820 F. Supp. 1409
 (N.D.Ga., 1993)
Girone v. City of Winder, 467 S.E.2d 612 (Ga.
 App. 1996)
City of Winder v. Girone, 462 S.E.2d 704 (Ga.
 1995)
Girone v. City of Winder, 452 S.E.2d 794 (Ga.
 App. 1994)
Food Lion, Inc. v. Johnson, 448 S.E.2d 59 (Ga.
 App. 1994)

JENNIFER S. SMART
Member, Lexington

Areas of Concentration
State and Local Taxation
Governmental Affairs

Education
Louisiana State University, B.A., Journalism,1981
Tulane University School of Law, 1985

Admitted to Practice
Louisiana, 1985
Kentucky, 1991
United States Supreme Court, 1995
United States Courts of Appeal, 4th Circuit and
6th Circuit

Achievements in Areas of Concentration
Assistant General Counsel and Staff Attorney,
Kentucky Revenue Cabinet (1993-1998)
Handled the representation in the following
published Kentucky tax cases:
City of Lebanon Junction v. Cellco Partnership,
2001 WL 427583 (Ky. App. 2001)
Revenue Cabinet v. Wyatt, 963 S.W. 2d 635 (Ky.
App. 1998)
Revenue Cabinet v. St. Ledger, 912 S.W. 2d 34
(Ky. 1995) & 942 S.W. 2d 893 (Ky. 1997)
Revenue Cabinet v. Gaba, 885 S.W. 2d 706 (Ky.
App. 1994)
Handled amicus curiae representation for the
Commonwealth of Kentucky, Revenue Cabinet,
in the landmark United States Supreme Court
decision in *Fulton Corp. v. Faulkner*, 516 U.S.
325, 116 S. Ct. 848, 1996 WL 71109 (1996)
Successfully handled numerous state and local tax
controversies, both before the Kentucky
Revenue Cabinet and in litigation before the
Kentucky Board of Tax Appeals, Kentucky
circuit courts, the Kentucky Court of Appeals,
and the Kentucky Supreme Court
Represented numerous clients in lobbying efforts
before the Kentucky General Assembly
Prepared legislation for the Kentucky General
Assembly on behalf of numerous clients
Obtained tax exempt status for several large
educational, religious and charitable institutions

Publications & Presentations
"Kentucky State Tax Developments", COST
Audit Conference, Committee on State
Taxation, 1998, 1999, 2000, 2001,2002
"Property Tax in Kentucky," Lorman Education
Services, 1998, 1999, 2000
"Kentucky State Tax Issues Update," Professional
Education Systems, Inc. 1998, 1999, 2000,
2002

Professional Memberships
American Bar Association
Kentucky Bar Association
Louisiana Bar Association
Fayette County Bar Association

MARK F. SOMMER
Member, Louisville

Areas of Concentration
State, Local and Federal Taxation, Civil and
 Criminal Tax Controversy/Litigation and
 Business
Law Economic Development/Incentives,
 Governmental Affairs, Bankruptcy Taxation

Education
Xavier University, Williams College of Business,
 B.S.B.A. Finance, 1985
University of Cincinnati College of Law, J.D., 1988

Admitted to Practice
Supreme Court of Kentucky, 1988
U.S. District Court, Western District of
 Kentucky, 1988
U.S. Tax Court, 1988
U.S. District Court, Eastern District of Kentucky,
 1989
U.S. Court of Federal Claims, 1989
U.S. Court of Appeals for the Sixth Circuit, 1989
U.S. District Court, Northern District of Illinois,
 1990
Supreme Court of the United States, 1995
U.S. District Court, Southern District

Professional Memberships
Advisory Board, *Journal of State Taxation* (Panel
 Publishers)
Advisory Board, Multistate Tax Institute/Deloitte
 & Touche National Tax Conference at the
 University of Wisconsin-Milwaukee
Advisory Board, Paul J. Hartman/Vanderbilt
 University School of Law, State and Local Tax
 Forum
Kentucky Bar Association (Section of Tax,
 including past service as Liaison to the
 Kentucky Society of CPAs)
American Bar Association (Section of Tax,
 Committees on State and Local Taxation and
 Environmental Taxes)
Federal Bar Association (Section of Tax)
Louisville Bar Association (Section of Tax)
Louisville Bar Association Board of Directors,
 including service as Tax Counsel (1997-2000)
Louisville Bar Center, Inc., Tax Counsel (1997-
 2000)

Achievements in Areas of Concentration
Successfully counseled and advocated in hundreds
 of federal, state and local tax controversy and
 planning matters, both administratively and in
 litigation, involving multiple types of
 businesses, trusts and individual taxpayers
 wherein collectively hundreds of millions of
 dollars were at risk
Actively involved in the following landmark
 Kentucky tax cases:
GTE and Subsidiaries v. Revenue Cabinet, Ky., 889
 S.W.2d 788 (1995) (lead case affirming use of
 unitary method of corporate filing)
Joy Technologies Inc. v. Kentucky Revenue Cabinet,
 Ky.App., 838 S.W.2d 406 (1992) (nationwide
 first impression case on application of sales tax
 to labor in component exchange program)
Herschel St. Ledger, et al., v. Revenue Cabinet, Ky.,
 912 S.W.2d 34 (1995) & 942 S.W.2d 893
 (1997) (constitutionality of ad valorem
 intangibles tax exemption on corporate stock)
*Inland Container Corporation v. Mason County
 Board of Education*, Ky., 6 S.W.3d 374(1999)
 (lead case on ability to recover tax overpayment
 from local taxing authorities)
Louisville Bar Association Tax Section, Chair
 (1995)
Kentucky Bar Association Tax Section, Chair
 (1996-97), Chair-Elect (1995-96), Vice-Chair
 (1994-95)

RAYMOND J. STEWART
Member, Covington/Cincinnati

Areas of Concentration
Corporate
International
Taxation Capital Formation
Business Transactions

Education
Thomas More College - BA Accounting (1975)
University of Kentucky College of Law - JD
 (1978)
Georgetown University College of Law - LLM
 Tax (1985)

Admitted to Practice
Kentucky (1978)
Texas (1979)
District of Columbia (1989)

Professional Memberships
American Bar Association
District of Columbia Bar Association
Kentucky Bar Association
Texas Bar Association
United States Tax Court
American Institute of Certified Public Accoun-
 tants

Achievements in Areas of Concentration
Served as Partner in the Washington D.C. office
 of an International law firm heading its
 International Practice Group.
Served as an Adjunct Professor in the Georgetown
 University Masters of Tax Program, teaching
 U.S. Taxation of International Operations.
Served as a partner with Deloitte & Touche,
 responsible for providing federal, state and
 international consulting and compliance
 services for numerous clients.
As a certified public accountant, combines a
 strong legal background with a solid understanding of the financial consequences of
 business transactions.
Assists in the development of business plans and
 the financial structuring of start-up and middle-
 market companies.
Assists U.S. companies in doing business in
 emerging markets, as well as emerging markets-
 based companies that wish to access U.S. capital
 markets.

Assists U. S. corporate employers develop and
 maintain expatriate compensation packages that
 attract and retain employees while holding costs
 to a comparative level.
Served as legal counsel to a group of senior
 technologists (Sun Microsystems, BEA Systems
 and PWC) to form a web-based e-business
 solutions start-up company, including
 structuring and formation, papering three
 rounds of private equity, intellectual property
 protection, employment agreements, stock
 option plans, content contracts, leases and
 strategic relationship agreements.
On behalf of a $20 million IT Government
 Contractor, in addition to handling all routine
 legal matters, renegotiated a senior debt facility
 with an international bank, negotiated and sold
 a $10 million division, negotiated all employ-
 ment agreements, launched an equity-raise
 effort, negotiated three acquisition transactions
 and settled a $6.5 million claim against the
 U.S. Navy.
On behalf of a provider of wireless telecom
 services (voice, data and Internet) to international markets, negotiated the sale of $10
 million of international termination facilities to
 a public company, created a stock option plan,
 negotiated all strategic relationships in all the
 foreign markets, and reviewed and revised all
 business plans and confidentiality agreements.

JOHN H. STITES III
Member, Louisville

Areas of Concentration
Real Estate and Corporate; Coal and Mineral
  Law; Bank Secured Lending

Education
Phillips Exeter Academy, 1967
Yale University, B.A. History, (cum laude), 1971
University of Kentucky College of Law, J.D.,
  1974

Admitted to Practice
Kentucky, 1974
U.S. Supreme Court, 1978
U.S. District Court, Western District of
  Kentucky, 1974

Achievements in Areas of Concentration
Order of the Coif

Professional Memberships
Louisville Bar Association
Kentucky Bar Association
American Bar Association
Eastern Mineral Law Foundation
Rocky Mountain Mineral Law Foundation

STEPHEN W. SWITZER
Member, Lexington

Areas of Concentration
Commercial Finance, Secured Transactions, Real
  Estate

Education
University of Kentucky, B.A., 1982
University of Kentucky College of Law, J.D.,
  1986

Admitted to Practice
Kentucky, 1986

Achievements in Areas of Concentration
Kentucky Law Journal, Staff Member, 1984-85
Kentucky Law Journal, Comments Editor, 1985-86

Publications & Presentations
"Considerations for Documenting and Holding
  Assets to Maximize Financing Value," Eastern
  Mineral Law Foundation Ninth Annual
  Institute, co-author, 1988
"Real Estate Financing," National Business
  Institute's Law Review Series on Basic Real
  Estate Law in Kentucky, Lecturer, October 1989

Professional Memberships
Fayette County Bar Association
Kentucky Bar Association
American Bankers Association (Attorney
  Division)
Kentucky Bankers Association (Bank Counsel
  Division)

Associations
Lexington Arts and Cultural Counsel, Board of
  Directors 1996 - present
Lexington Arts and Cultural Counsel, Campaign
  Chair for Annual Fund Drive, 1996 - 1997
Lexington Arts and Cultural Counsel, Co-Chair
  ofProfessional Division for Annual Fund Drive,
  1993-94 and 1994-95, and 1995-96

JOB D. TURNER III
Member-In-Charge, Lexington

Areas of Concentration
Corporate; Real Estate; Estate Planning

Education
Woodberry Forest School, 1963-66
University of Kentucky, BBA, 1970
University of Kentucky College of Law, J.D.,
1973

Admitted to Practice
Kentucky, 1973
U.S. District Court, Eastern District of Kentucky,
1973
U.S. Court of Appeals, Sixth Circuit, 1982
U.S. Supreme Court, 1985

Achievements in Areas of Concentration
Fayette County Bar Association; Board of
Governors, 1980-86; Treasurer, 1980-82;
President, 1985-86
President, Lexington Estate Planning Council,
1985-86
Kentucky Bar Association, Convention CLE
Chairman, 1988
Kentucky Bar Association, Convention CLE
Committee, 1990

Publications & Presentations
"Methods of Construction - Design Build,
Construction Management and Fast Tract,"
Construction Law Seminar, University of
Kentucky, 1985
"Taxes and the Small Business Owner," Federated
Insurance Co., Seminar, 1987
"Land Use and Zoning Law Development,"
Kentucky Bar Association Convention, 1988,
Kentucky District Bar Meetings, 1988, in 7
Locations throughout Kentucky
"Conflicts and Other Ethical Dilemmas in Estate
Planning," 16th Annual Estate Planning
Seminar, University of Kentucky, 1989
"Powers of Attorney - Guardianship -
Conservatorship," Lexington/Bluegrass Chapter
of Alzheimer's Association, 1989
"Legal Potpourri in Public Housing,"
Southeastern Regional Council of the National
Association of Housing Development Officials,
1992

"Overview of Compelling Need, Competition
and Civil Rights as Issues in Kentucky Zoning
Law," Land Use Law Seminar, 1994
"The Law of Nonconforming Uses," Land Use
Law Update in Kentucky, National Business
Institute Seminar, 1995

Professional Memberships
Lexington Estate Planning Council
Fayette County Bar Association
Kentucky Bar Association

Associations
Lexington Rotary Club, President 1986-87;
Board of Directors, 1984-86; Secretary, 1984-85;
Christ the King Church, Parish Council, 1983-
86; Council President, 1985-86
Opportunity Workshop of Lexington, Board of
Directors, 1980-83, President, 1983
Catholic Social Service Bureau, President, 1993-
1995
Children's Advocacy Center, President, 1994-95
United Way, Chairman 2000-2001; Chair of
Major Gifts Cabinet, Chaired Attorneys'
Campaign, 1983-84; Allocations Panel
Member, 1982-84; Chaired Panel, 1984
Greater Lexington Chamber of Commerce,
Chairman-Elect 2002; General Counsel 2000-
2001

PATRICK JOSEPH WELSH
Member, Louisville

Areas of Concentration
Corporate Law; Mergers and Acquisitions; Contracts; Distribution; Leases; General Corporate; Securities and Banking; Health Related Law; Limited Partnerships; Limited Liability Companies

Education
Bellarmine College, B.A., Business Administration, 1977
University of Louisville School of Law, J.D. (magna cum laude), 1984
Harvard Law School, Program of Instruction for Lawyers -
International Law, Corporate Taxation, Banking Law, July 1986

Admitted to Practice
Kentucky, 1984

Military Service
Captain, U.S. Army, Helicopter Pilot; Active, 1968-72; Active Reserve, 1972-79

Achievements in Areas of Concentration
Former V.P. and General Counsel, Abrasive Industries Inc.
Acquisitions in both North America and Europe of manufacturing, distribution and service companies in a variety of industries, including abrasives, coatings, industrial equipment, engineering, retail and restaurant
"Advising Closely-Held Corporations," University of Louisville School of Law, Office of Continuing Legal Education, September, 1985
"Successful Loan Documentation and Procedures - Legal Lending Limits of Banks," Professional Bank Services, Inc., March, 1985
"Compliance Series - Legal Lending of Banks, Loans to Insiders," Professional Bank Services, Inc., Fall, 1986
"Distribution of Goods-Drafting the Distribution Agreement," Louisville Bar Association, March, 1993
"Business Entities and Partnerships-Starting One and Saving One," Moderator and Panelist, WUOL Peoples' Law Radio Program, March, 1993

Achievements
Editor-in-Chief, University of Louisville *Journal of Family Law*, 1983-84
Louis D. Brandeis Scholar
Bernard Flexner Scholar

Professional Memberships
American Bar Association (Section of Corporation, Banking and Business Law, Health Law Section)
Kentucky Bar Association
Louisville Bar Association

Associations
Former Director, Bridgehaven, Inc.
Leadership Kentucky
Focus Louisville

Publications & Presentations
"Recent Developments In Corporate Law," Louisville Bar Foundation, Annual Update Series, November, 1985

JOHN A. WEST
Member, Covington/Cincinnati

Areas of Concentration

Civil Litigation (emphasis on Employment Law,
Intellectual Property Law; Environmental Law
and federal litigation);

Criminal Litigation - Former Assistant United
States Attorney; current emphasis on white
collar crime defense and grand jury
representation;

Alternate Dispute Resolution - Certified
Mediator, Mediation Center of Kentucky.

Education

University of Kentucky – Bachelor of Arts Degree
from the Patterson School of Diplomacy and
International Commerce;

University of Cincinnati College of Law – J.D,
1967; Board of Editors, University of
Cincinnati Law Review 1965-67; Dean's Honor
Roll 1965; William Worthington Prize for
editorial note 1967; American Jurisprudence
Prize for excellence in Civil Procedure 1966.

Admitted to Practice

Kentucky, Ohio

Supreme Court of the United States

U.S. District Courts,
    Western District of Kentucky
    Eastern District of Kentucky
    Southern District of Ohio

U.S. Court of Appeals for the Sixth Circuit

U.S. Court of Appeals for the Federal Circuit

Teaching and Publications

Member, Kentucky Evidence Rules Review
Commission - 2000

Instructor - Alternate Dispute Resolution - Chase
Law School (Northern Kentucky University),
Spring 2000

Instructor - National Institute of Trial Advocacy -
University of Cincinnati College of Law,
Summer 1998, Summer 2000

Author, *Negligent Violations of Environmental
Laws: What Standard for Criminal Prosecution?*
KY. Law Review, 1993;

*Claims Against the State of Ohio; The Need for
Reform,* 36 Cin. L. Rev. 523 (1966)

Speaker, Federal Law Update, Kentucky Bar
Association District Bar Meetings: 1986, 1987,
1989, 1991 and 1992

Speaker, Mineral Law Seminar, Criminal
Enforcement of the Environmental Laws, 1992

Speaker, Environmental Law Seminar, Criminal
Enforcement of the Environmental Laws,
Salmon P. Chase College of Law, Fall 1991

Speaker, Seminar on Federal Practice, Lexington,
Spring 1986

Speaker, Trial Advocacy Course, University of
Kentucky, Summer 1986

Speaker, Seminar on Evidence Law, Chase Law
School (Northern Kentucky University),
Highland Heights, Kentucky, 1983

Program Moderator, Advance Civil Trial
Advocacy, Chase Law School (Northern
Kentucky University), Highland Heights,
Kentucky, 1982

Speaker, ALI-ABA Legal Issues of the Eastern
Coal Industry, 1980

Adjunct Instructor for Legal Writing, University
of Kentucky College of Law, 1978-1980

Member, Committee of Kentucky Bar
Association to Recommend Joint Local Rules of
Practice for the U.S. District Courts for the
Eastern and Western Districts of Kentucky,
Summer 1986

Professional Memberships

American Bar Association, Section of Dispute
Resolution, Section of Litigation; Section of
Criminal Law; Life Member, Sixth Circuit
Judicial Conference

JOHN V. WHARTON
Member, Covington

Areas of Concentration
Commercial Real Estate Law; Commercial and
Construction Lending Law; Equine Law; and
Business Planning Law; Stateand Local
Incentives

Education
Vanderbilt University, B.A., 1976
University of Kentucky College of Law, J.D., 1978

Admitted to Practice
Supreme Court of Kentucky, 1979
U.S. District Court, Eastern District of Kentucky,
1979

Publications & Presentations
"Uniform Commercial Code Update," Corporate
and Securities Law Institute of the Cincinnati
Bar Association, October 25,1996
"Advalorem Taxes on Minerals in Kentucky,"
Eastern Mineral Law Foundation Special
Institute on Abstracting Mineral Titles in the
Appalachian Basin, December 3, 1992
"Basic Real Estate Law in Kentucky," National
Business Institute Law Review Series, October
5, 1989
"American Equine Property Acquisition By
Foreign Interests," 4th Annual Equine Law
Seminar, University of Kentucky College of
Law, May 4 and 5, 1989
"The Royalty Clause and the Use and Effect of
Division Orders," Eastern Mineral Law
Foundation Special Institute on Oil and
Gas Lease Payments and Administration,
September 18 and 19, 1986
"Commercial Leases," Midway College
Department of Paralegal Studies, Property Law
Seminar, May 9, 1986

Professional Memberships
Kentucky Law Journal, 1977-1978; Comments
Editor 1978
Fayette County Bar Association
Kentucky Bar

Associations
Board of Trustees, Greater Cincinnati United
Way & Community Chest Member, 2001 -
Present

Board of Trustees, Japan America Society of
Greater Cincinnati, 1998 - Present; President,
2001-Present
Board of Directors, Northern Kentucky
Symphony, 1998 - 2001
Board of Directors, Northern Kentucky Action
Council of United Way & Community Chest,
Member, 2000 – Present; Vice Chair, 2002 –
Present
Board of Trustees, Cincinnati Playhouse in the
Park, 1998 - Present; Member, Executive
Committee, 2002 - Present
Board of Directors, People Working
Cooperatively, 1997-Present
Co-Chair, Major Firms Division (Kentucky),
Greater Cincinnati Fine Arts Fund, 1999
Leadership Cincinnati, 1997 Graduate
Board of Directors, Lexington Philharmonic
Society, Inc., 1992-
1996; President Elect, 1993-94; President,
1994-95
Board of Directors, Lexington Arts and Cultural
Council, Inc., 1989-1996; Secretary, 1989-90;
Chair Elect, 1990-91; Chair, 1991-92
Board of Directors, Lexington Council of the
Arts, Inc., 1987-89
Member, Lexington Comprehensive Plan Update
Review Committee, 1993-94
Past President and Treasurer, Lexington
Vanderbilt Club
Leadership Lexington, 1985 Graduate

PAUL B. WHITTY
Member, Louisville

Areas of Concentration
Real Estate, Zoning and Land Use Regulation

Education
University of Louisville School of Law, J.D., 1983
University of Southern California, School of
 Library Science, Los Angeles, California,
 M.L.S. 1978
Edinburgh University, Scotland, British History,
 Certificate, Summer 1973
Spalding University, Louisville, Kentucky, B.A.
 History, 1974

Admitted to Practice
1983

Achievements in Areas of Concentration
Advised Planning Commission on goals and
 objectives regarding Cornerstone 2020
 amendments to Comprehensive Plan
Presented ethics seminars for County
 Commissioners
Mediated disputes between developers and
 neighborhood groups
Director of legal research for County Attorney's
 office
Advised Planning Commission in the creation of
 cellular tower regulations
Moderated community meetings regarding
 enforcement of flood plain regulations
Member, Land Development Code Update
 Committee

Academic Achievements
Caritas Medal, Spalding University Distinguished
 Alumnus (1996)
Dean's List, University of Louisville School of
 Law, 3 semesters

Education Alumni Award (U.S.C.) (1978)
Who's Who in American Colleges and
 Universities (Spalding University 1974)

Professional Memberships
International Council of Shopping Centers,
 Kentucky Government Relations Chairman
 (1999 -)
Chairman, Real Estate/Planning & Zoning
 Section, Louisville Bar Association (1987, 1988)

American Planning Association
KAPA (American Planning Association —
 Kentucky Chapter; Legislation Committee)
Louisville Area Law Librarians (Founder;
 President 1981-82)

Associations
Scenic Kentucky, Inc., Director (1989-90);
 (2000-)
Board of Overseers, Spalding University (Vice
 Chairman 1988-89)
English-Speaking Union, Kentucky Branch
 (President 2001)
Ancient Order of Hibernians in America, Ryan
 Division (President 1993)
Sigma Delta Kappa (U.L.) (law fraternity)
 (President 1980-81)
Beta Phi Mu (U.S.C.) (library fraternity)

Prior Professional Experience
General Counsel, Louisville and Jefferson County
 Planning Commission (1991-1997)

WILLIAM PLUMER WISEMAN, JR.
Member, Louisville
Chair, Real Estate & Finance Practice Group

Areas of Concentration
Real Property; Titles; Commercial Lending;
Zoning and Land Use

Education
Washington & Lee University, B.A., English
(cum laude), 1970
University of Virginia School of Law, J.D., 1973

Admitted to Practice
Kentucky, 1973
U.S. District Court, Western District of
Kentucky, 1974

Publications & Presentations
Lecturer on Law of Property, University of
Louisville School of Law, 1975-76
"Lending Aspects of Mineral Financing,"
Kentucky Mineral Law Manual Banks-Baldwin
Law
"Acquisitions of Mining Concerns," *Coal Law
and Regulation*, Matthew Bender & Co., 1983
"Authorizations and Special Entity Conveyancing,"
Chapter 13, *Real Estate Practice Handbook*,
College of Law of University of Kentucky, 1990
"Representing the Buyer or Owner of Leasehold
Real Property in Difficult Financial Times,"
University of Kentucky Continuing Legal
Education, 1992
"The Real Estate Title," National Business
Institute, 1994

Professional Memberships
Louisville Bar Association
Kentucky Bar Association
American Bar Association

Associations
St. James' Episcopal Church (Sr. Warden, 1979-
81, 1988, 1991; Vestryman, 1979-81, 1984-
1987, 1988-1991.
Preservation Alliance
Filson Club
National Beagle Club (Director, 1981-1991)
Mid-America Foxhound Club (President, 1985-
1990)
Loudoun Agricultural and Chemical Institute
Foundation (President, 1986-1991)

Clear Creek Beagles (Joint Master 1987-)
Trout Unlimited
Kentucky Nature Council
American Friends of the Game Conservancy
Ruffed Grouse Society
Long Run Hunt
Countryside Alliance
British Association for Shooting and
Conservation

R. VAN YOUNG
Member, Louisville

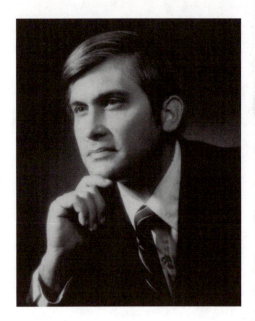

Areas of Concentration
Commercial Litigation; Administrative Law;
Product Liability; Securities; Domestic
Relations; Broker/Dealer Litigation;
Construction Law

Education
Centre College of Kentucky, B.A., 1967
University of Louisville School of Law, J.D., 1970

Admitted to Practice
Kentucky, 1970
U.S. District Court, Western District of
Kentucky, 1979
U.S. District Court, Eastern District of Kentucky,
1973
Fourth Circuit Court of Appeals, 1967-1976
U.S. Supreme Court and Sixth Circuit Court of
Appeals, 1985

Achievements
Associate Editor, *Journal of Family Law*, 1970
Phi Alpha Theta (national organization for
recognition in field of history), 1967
Who's Who in American Colleges and
Universities, 1967
Omicron Delta Kappa, 1967

Professional Memberships
Louisville Bar Association
Lexington Bar Association
Kentucky Bar Association
American Bar Association

Associations
Former Member of Board of Directors, Kentucky
Mountain Laurel Festival
Former Counsel to Board of Directors, Second
Presbyterian Weekday School
Second Presbyterian Church